The Ice King

Frederic Tudor and His Circle

To *Nancy Light and Faith Paterson*

The Ice King

Frederic Tudor and His Circle

BY *Carl Seaburg and Stanley Paterson*
EDITED BY *Alan Seaburg*

Published by the MASSACHUSETTS HISTORICAL SOCIETY, *Boston*
and MYSTIC SEAPORT®, MYSTIC, CONNECTICUT, 2003

Published at the Charge of the Publication Fund.
Editing of this book was made possible in part by the proceeds of an endowment fund created with the assistance of a Challenge Grant from the National Endowment for the Humanities, a federal agency that supports research, education, and public programming in the humanities.

Seaburg, Carl, 1922–
The ice king : Frederic Tudor and his circle / by Carl Seaburg and Stanley Paterson ; edited by Alan Seaburg.
p. cm.
Includes Bibliographical references and index.
ISBN 0-939510-80-4
1. Tudor, Frederic, 1783–1864. 2. Industrialists—United States—Biography. 3. Ice industry—United States. I. Paterson, Stanley. II. Seaburg, Alan, 1932– III. Title.

HD9481.U4T837 2003
338.7'66402852—dc21
[B] 2003046427

Designed by Dede Cummings

Massachusetts Historical Society
1154 Boylston St.,
Boston, MA 02215

Mystic Seaport
75 Greenmanville Ave., P.O. Box 6000
Mystic, CT 06355-0990

Contents

Illustrations

ACKNOWLEDGEMENTS

DURING THE PREPARATION of this work we received much assistance from the descendants of Frederic Tudor and the Tudor family. We would particularly like to thank Mrs. Dolores Daniels, James Garland, Elizabeth D. Gardiner, Margaret T. Gardiner, Mrs. Katherine Gilbert and Miss Katherine Gilbert, Mrs. Hope Ingersoll, S. Tudor Leland, the late James Peabody, John D. Peabody, Mrs. Mary Peabody, Daniel H. Tudor, Dr. Frederic Tudor of Milton, Mrs. Frederic Tudor of Boston, Seth Tudor, and Tasha Tudor.

Friends and acquaintances were of great help and we want to thank Timothy Chasson, Alan Crist, Mrs. Helen Cutter, Eric Makris, Mary Morgan, Mavis Ross, the late Jean Seaburg, and the Rev. Theodore A. Webb.

The following institutions and the people named proved immensely useful and without their aid this work could not have been completed: Baker Library (Robert Lovett), Old Sturbridge Village (Etta Faulkner), New Jersey Historical Society (Robert C. Morris), Oregon Historical Society (Steven Tanassea), Pierpont Morgan Library (Herbert Cahoon), Yale University Library (Judith A. Schiff), Andover-Harvard Theological Library (Gloria Korsman), Guernsey Memorial Library of Norwich, N.Y. (C. Spicer), Alice M. Ryne, Houghton Library, Library of Congress, National Archives, Nahant Public Library (Daniel A. deStefano), Boston Public Library, Massachusetts Historical Society, Historical Society of Pennsylvania, New-York Historical Society,

Bordentown Public Library, Boston Athenaeum, American Antiquarian Society, Mystic Seaport (Andrew German), Maine Historical Society, and Lynn Public Library.

We also wish to thank the several institutions that permitted us to quote briefly from the manuscripts under their care and control: the Houghton Library of Harvard University; the Baker Library of the Harvard Business School; the Historical Society of Pennsylvania; the New England Historic Genealogical Society; the Library of Congress; Baring Brothers of London; and, of course, the Massachusetts Historical Society. We could not have illustrated this book so beautifully without making use of the collections of many institutions and the generous assistance of their staff. For this, we would like to thank the Baker Library, Harvard Business School (and Nicole M. Hayes); the Boston Athenæum (Lina Coffey and Catharina Slautterback); the Lynn Museum (Diane Shephard); the Massachusetts Historical Society (Seth Vose and Jennifer Smith); the Metropolitan Museum of Art; the Museum of Fine Arts, Boston; the Nahant Public Library (Daniel A. deStefano) and the Nahant Historical Society; the Northwest Room, Spokane Public Library, Spokane, Wash. (Nancy Compau); the Peabody Essex Museum (Christine Michelini); and the U.S. Naval Academy Museum (Scott Harmon and Dolly Pantelides).

Finally, we deeply appreciate the editorial work of Dr. Conrad E. Wright, Ford Editor of Publications, and Ondine E. Le Blanc, Associate Editor of Publications, as well as that of the other members of the staff of the Massachusetts Historical Society, who carefully and thoughtfully guided this biographical study of Frederic Tudor, his family, and his associates into print.

CARL SEABURG
STANLEY PATERSON
ALAN SEABURG

The Ice King

Frederic Tudor and His Circle

Frederic Tudor, about 1830
Francis Alexander, American (1800–1880)
Oil on canvas; 29 1/8 x 25 1/4 in. (74 x 64.1 cm)
Gift of Dolores de P. Danniels, Katharine de P. Gilbert and S. Tudor Leland, heirs of Elsa Tudor de Pierrefeu, 67.1160

CHAPTER 1

A Pride of Tudors

TUDOR: IT'S NOT YOUR EVERYDAY NAME! Most people will think first of a famous trio, that English threesome: the much-bedded Henry, the much-dreaded Mary, and the much-unwedded Elizabeth. Frederic Tudor was none of these. But some might call him the greatest little Tudor of them all—for he introduced the world to refrigeration and thus transformed forever the way we all eat and drink and live. In his own eyes he was no less regal than the English Tudors, and it pleased him to be styled the "Ice King." Not that he invented ice—he graciously allowed that to God—but he had the wit to turn it into a commodity and make it pay handsomely.

New England from the first was poor in natural resources: what it had was wood and fish, and what the adventurers wanted was gold and precious stones. New England's necessity forced it to mother some good ideas, and this nurturing had to be done over again in each generation. Exporting ice was Frederic Tudor's idea and from it he eventually made a fortune, becoming one of America's first millionaires. At the same time he extended New England's mercantile activities another generation, but not immediately, not easily, not without harassment and trouble and despair, and not without thinking more than once that he had bet on a dead horse.

These New England Tudors began lowly. Deacon John Tudor, Frederic's grandfather, arrived in Boston from England in 1715 at the age of six with his thirty-six-year-old widowed mother. She—Frederic's great-grandmother—promptly sought and got herself another husband, Capt. John Langdon. This put food on the table for young John and herself. The captain was a good provider in more ways than one. As prompt as she, the captain shortly had her with child, and by May 1716, young John had a half-sister, Elizabeth, to play with.

Nothing about John's childhood is known. One suspects the usual brief schooling (since he wrote a fair hand, which he learned somewhere) and early apprenticeship to some trade (because he had to earn a living). But when he was twenty-three two interesting things happened: he began to jot down brief notes, or, as he called them, "Memorandoms," of events, and he got married. His entry of this latter event startles the modern eye. It reads: "I was married to Ms Jane Varney."[1] The only entry for 1736, when he was twenty-seven years old, records that he went into the "Bakeing Business."[2] Over the next seventeen years they made a family of three boys and three girls, a nicely balanced group. Our concern is the youngest, William, born in 1750 in the eighteenth year of the marriage and the thirty-sixth year of his mother.

Deacon John Tudor, about 1750 Oil on canvas, attributed to Joseph Steward (1753–1822). Collection of the Massachusetts Historical Society.

So, slowly, the Deacon began to rise. In 1739 he was elected a constable of Boston for a year, and in 1745 he was elected treasurer of his church, a post he held for eight years. He was now, in his early forties, a man of some small position in the community. Beginning in 1751 he was regularly elected as one of Boston's Overseers of the Poor. By that time the Deacon had left off baking and had become a general trader and merchant, dabbling in real estate on the side. He dabbled so shrewdly and successfully that he began to amass what is called "a competence"—that is, sufficient means for a comfortable existence.

On January 18, 1782, in company with Capt. Henry Atkins, the Deacon took a short sleigh ride that gave a glimpse of his family's future. For Atkins was a grandfather of Delia Jarvis, whom son William would marry. The two went out to watch men cutting ice on frozen Boston Harbor "to open the Channel way for Vessels to go oute. The ice was 9 Inches thick, But they cut with Saws &c from as low as the Castle up to Clark's Wharfe in 9 or ten Days & finish'd Jany 21st. The next Day a Number of Vessells Sail'd."[3] So wrote the Deacon. There would be many a winter that grandson Frederic would have exulted at ice nine inches thick and called that a fortunate day.

The year 1765 is remembered in history for the Stamp Act riots in Boston, the first public demonstration against the imposition of British taxes that were to lead to the separation between England and the colonies. The Deacon, who had been silent when two of his sons died in 1756, now let his pen run on for pages when it came to the hanging of the effigies of the stamp collector and Lord Bute, and the destruction by a mob of the dwelling house of the lieutenant governor of Massachusetts, Thomas Hutchinson.

Four days before the destruction of Hutchinson's house, the Deacon's son William had passed his examinations for college and entered Harvard, across the river in Cambridge. He was fifteen years, four months, and eleven days old. The Deacon was a patriot, but active participation in the coming revolution would depend on son William. A child of the midcentury, William had been born on April 8, 1750 (New Style). He had the daring required for that revolutionary generation. Once, as a lad on a visit to an English warship in Boston harbor, he proposed jumping from the very high taffrail at the stern of the ship into the water, if anybody else would. A sailor accepted the challenge. The boy jumped but the sailor was afraid to follow.[4]

At Harvard it was a time of rising student unrest that paralleled the adult political unrest. William was soon in the thick of it. In his junior year, student resentment surged in response to a faculty decision to tighten discipline by refusing to let unprepared students escape recitations as easily as they formerly had. These students were, on average, older than their predecessors of two generations earlier, and they felt that such recitations were more appropriate to schoolboys than scholars. The juniors, including nearly eighteen-year-old Tudor, held a meeting and resolved to "take no notice" of the change and to expel any fellow pupil who did. Through March 1768, tension between the angry students and the stiff-necked tutors snowballed. A bit more and it would avalanche.

The bit more came on an icy Saturday, April 12, when word spread that a young freshman, Thurston Whiting, had been locked up in Tutor Samuel Willard's room all that cold day without food, drink, or heat. Willard, it was said, hoped to force Whiting to tell him who had been throwing brickbats through his windows at night and ransacking his things. Incensed, the students muttered of mobbing Willard that night. Later, sixty students appeared and some started throwing brickbats and rocks. Waiting for them were Willard and two fellow tutors. They raced out and caught one of the perpetrators, who promptly blabbed the names of many of the others.

Tudor, along with some friends, acted more responsibly. He was now in the thick of the rebellion, his room practically a headquarters. They went to Willard's rooms to try and determine the truth of Whiting's charges. Were the rumors of his lock-up true? The qualities that were to make William a judge were thus early evident.

Sunday, the faculty decided to expel the students who had attacked Willard's chamber. Monday morning, in an almost empty Chapel—most of the students, but not the seniors, remained outside in protest—President Holyoke announced the sentence of expulsion. William Tudor, Stephen Peabody, Jonathan Austin, and James Varnum were cited as the principal agitators. After the morning breakfast, with persuasion from the ringleaders, more than two-thirds of the lower classes vacated their rooms and went home. Only the seniors, who were soon to graduate and therefore were immune to the new recitations rules, remained along with about forty undergraduates. Although they had taken little part in the rebellion up to this point, they now entered the controversy by asking the faculty to investigate the matter. But it was too late for them to have any influence.

With the ringleaders gone from campus, Holyoke moved speedily to discredit them by taking depositions from the students who remained. From these sworn statements it was easy to create the appearance of a pattern of vindictive intrigue against the faculty. All the expelled students who would make a public confession in Chapel were to be re-admitted, except the four principals. The real key to breaking the strike, however, proved to have been the decision of more than one hundred students to vacate their chambers and go home.

By mid April the revolution had fizzled out and most of the students were back, either from a desire to get on with their education or because of pressure from families and friends. Tudor, Peabody, and Austin reapplied but were rejected. Yet they were the sons of prominent families. Influence was exerted. Ultimately the Overseers, persuaded as they said by "many who have been great friends and benefactors to the society," allowed them to return after suitable confession. Tudor abjectly apologized for his "imprudence" and "folly" and promised future obedience to all college laws. He thus learned how hard it is to buck the establishment. His college career now proceeded uneventfully to graduation in July 1769.[5]

Deacon Tudor had created his subsistence out of bread and real estate. William Tudor was to create his out of politics and influence. Soon after William's graduation the Deacon went to John Adams seeking a position for his son in Adams's law office. At first Adams hesitated, for he had just taken on another of the Harvard riot ringleaders, Jonathan Austin, for three years. Deacon Tudor persisted, however, and Adams at last consented.

Tudor went to work on August 11, the day after Adams had made his decision. He was to become a lifelong friend and correspondent of his new mentor, an orderly man opposed to the incipient mob rule in Boston suggested by the 1770 Boston Massacre. The two students wrote the writs that had to be filed, made notations in Adams's dockets and accountbooks, copied forms into his pleadings book, learned to enter actions, kept track of the court docket, and collected fees from clients. When the young men had completed their training with Adams and had been admitted as attorneys to practice before the Suffolk Inferior Court in July 1772, Tudor set up his own practice on Queen Street.

It was not, however, the best of times for a young lawyer. The Boston Tea Party episode in December 1773—which John Adams hailed as the turning point in colonial relations with Great Britain—prompted the British Parliament to shut up the port of Boston and send troops to enforce trade restrictions. This put a near stop to commerce and so to most legal business. When Adams learned of the financial problems his former student was facing, he wrote the Deacon beseeching him to help his son now rather than to leave him a good legacy years later: "I know him to have a clear Head and an honest faithful Heart. He is virtuous, Sober, Steady, industrious, and constant to his Office. He is as frugal as he can be, in his Rank and Class of Life, without being mean. It is your peculiar Felicity, to have a Son whose Behavior and Character are thus deserving."[6] The Deacon, who had recently moved to Cambridge, responded by giving William the rental income from his Boston home.

But a different employment awaited the struggling young lawyer. In less than a year, hostilities had begun between the British and the Americans. Again, Adams, now in Philadelphia with the Continental Congress, came to the rescue of his former law clerk by recommending him as secretary for George Washington, new commander of the Continental army gathered outside Boston. The general, however, wanted his own man for that position, but on July 29, 1775, he did appoint Tudor as his judge advocate general (with the rank of lieutenant colonel, but a captain's pay). It was a considerable post for a young man of twenty-five.

Adams had a hidden agenda, however, in placing Tudor with Washington. He wanted to keep an eye on the army that southern gentleman was forming. He asked Tudor to find out the "name, character and behavior of every stranger that shall be put into any place in the army and let me know it."[7]

Besides being an eye for Adams, Tudor had his hands full as judge advocate general. Washington's efforts to discipline his raw New England recruits produced numerous courts martial, and within three months he had a pretty good idea of the efficiency of his new judge advocate general. Soon Tudor sent the general some "observations" of ways to improve the court martial procedure. Strangely, the ways all involved shifting many of Tudor's cases to regimental courts, "where," as Washington commented perceptively in a letter to a friend, "he had nothing to do."[8] Did the general also know that his judge advocate was in communication with a Loyalist?

Several years before the war began, young William had begun a flirtatious correspondence with Miss Delia Jarvis of Boston and Dorchester. Her family had Tory leanings, and Delia is said to have served tea to British troops returning from the battles at Lexington and Concord. William and Delia wrote to each other in the sentimental style of the day, William signing himself as "Crito" and Delia replying as "Felicia."[9] Though three years younger than William, she considered him her best friend.

At the outbreak of the fighting Tudor had been caught in Boston, but he quickly made his way to the American camp before Gen. Thomas Gage imposed restrictions on departures from the town. Delia, along with some other young ladies, was sent by her parents to Noddles Island (now East Boston) to stay with the Henry Williams family. It was thought they might be safer there if the rebels bombarded Boston. Fortunately for the lovers, Tudor could swim. If he had visited the island in a boat he would probably have been detected and captured by the British. Tying his clothes in a bundle and carrying them on his head, he would swim to the island from Chelsea, woo his beloved, and then much later return to the patriot lines, safe, wet, and happy.[10]

By the end of May the war spread to Noddles Island and Delia had to return to Boston. William wrote Delia that he had obtained a pass for her to leave Boston with her mother and some friends. He sent it to her by Henry Williams. Tudor arranged to meet Delia at the ferry in Charlestown on a Saturday morning, June 17. When William arrived he found that the war had beaten them both there. The peninsula swarmed with American soldiers erecting an entrenchment on Breed's Hill, just below Bunker Hill. Tudor realized there would be no ferry that morning bringing his beloved to him. He went up to the entrenchment and saw that "our People had nearly got the Breast Work finished." Within an hour the British battery on Copps Hill began firing at the entrenchment. Tudor promptly and prudently left the bombs to the soldiers, "being unarm'd and only a Spectator." Once again war pushed romance into the background.

When, in March 1776, the British abandoned Boston, Washington shifted his army to New York and Tudor went with them. The letters back to his "amiable Loyalist" were as full of military news as of a lover's endearments. In May 1776, Crito told Felicia he was going to Philadelphia to pick up a new military code. Felicia wrote that she hoped to see Crito in Boston soon. Crito replied that that was not likely and then—as soldiers in all wars have written to their sweethearts—wrote that if he fell in battle, his dying prayer would be for his country and Felicia.

By November, having relinquished New York to the superior British forces, Washington had retreated to New Jersey. "Our situation very bad," Tudor wrote Delia. Then Washington's stunning surprise attack on the British at Trenton and Princeton over Christmas gave the Americans a victory to cherish. William's father could crow in his diary by mid February that his son had written that "The British Army are Ensurkel'd in Brunswrick & are so short of provision that they are Dayly Deserting to Gen: Washingtons Army."[11] In late March 1777, after refusing an offer from Gen. Henry Knox of a position in the artillery, Tudor resigned his service and returned to Boston. A year later, on March 5, 1778, he married his Delia.

Tudor's wedding coincided with the annual oration in memory of the dead of the Boston Massacre. That year the speaker was his fellow Harvard rioter and law student, Jonathan Austin. The next year's orator was another Harvard troublemaker, Tudor himself. By then he was the father of a young son, also named William, born the previous January. One of the most pleased auditors who heard his noon speech in the Old Brick Meeting House was his father, the Deacon. He confided to his diary that "the

Councle, and a great number of all ranks of people assembled, when the oration was deliver'd, which tooke near 40 minutes: when finished there was a general clapping of hands to show their Approbation."[12]

As well as siring a family, the former judge advocate devoted himself to establishing his law practice, but he was not too busy to celebrate Lord Cornwallis's defeat at Yorktown on October 19, 1781. The following June he was celebrating his parent's fiftieth wedding anniversary. "We kept," wrote the Deacon in his diary, "a Day of jublee and made an Entertainment for our Children & their Children (all that was Living). And a Lovely sight & day we had of it, to see so many of a family to gather on such an acation."[13] William and Delia would have been there with young William and baby John Henry, born that April. Another child, Delia, born in 1780, had lived only a day.

Within a year there was another jubilee that had a wider audience of celebrants. On April 23, 1783, a cessation of hostilities between Britain and America was proclaimed from the balcony of the Town House. The town of Boston, where it all began, rejoiced. A very special celebration took place on July 4 that year, as the inhabitants looked ahead to their existence as an acknowledged independent nation. The treaty of peace was signed September 3, 1783, in Paris, and on the next day in Boston, Delia Jarvis Tudor was delivered of a baby boy. Finally Frederic! He came in with the peace.

CHAPTER 2

Days of Great Felicity

FREDERIC WAS BORN NEAR THE COURT HOUSE ON COURT STREET, then, as now, a short street connecting the center of government with the center of commerce. Imagine a Boston with scarcely sixteen thousand inhabitants confined to a small peninsula; a Boston whose Back Bay was still a bay flooded by tides twice a day—where snipe could be shot, where eels slithered through the marsh grass, and where the town lads bathed on hot summer days. It was a Boston that wanted to be more, that wanted to reach out to the surrounding mainland and make contact. Frederic was not quite three years old when the first bridge from Boston was completed and dedicated on the eleventh anniversary of the Battle of Bunker Hill, June 17, 1786.

His grandfather, the Deacon, walked over the new wooden bridge to Charlestown, climbed Breed's Hill where the battle had been fought, sat down at one of the two long tables with eight hundred other distinguished people, and fed the inner man. Never before had the Deacon seen so many folks and carriages in one place.

Nor had he or Boston seen such a bridge. It was over 1,500 feet long, was 42 feet wide, and had been built in exactly a year and three days. It was ornamented with forty lamps, "which," the Deacon marveled, "make a Sparkling Show in the Night." He added that "the town & Contrey soon found the Advantage of this Bridge."[1] Forty years later his grandson would also find this bridge advantageous.

In 1791, William Tudor had been elected a representative to the Massachusetts legislature, which called itself the Great and General Court. So Frederic was not just anybody's son, he was a somebody's son. When of age, he was sent to Boston Latin School two streets away from his home. All the Judge's children weathered the severe smallpox epidemic of 1792. The next fall, when his brother William entered Harvard, Frederic witnessed the passing of one of the heroes of the Revolutionary period—the death of John Hancock. Although he died October 5, his burial was delayed until October 14. "The Bells," wrote the Deacon in the last memorandum in his diary, "began to Toll at SunRise for 1/2 an hower. A great parade &c this P.m. of Guns &c &c." It was an extraordinarily hot October, and the Deacon noted that "Flys very Busey at Noon."[2]

Within a year and a half the Deacon had followed the governor. He was buried in Tomb No. 13 (still extant), near the back fence in the King's Chapel burying ground. The body was carried from his son's house on Court Street at four o'clock on Monday, March 23, 1795. Young Frederic would have been left with an eleven-year-old's memory of his grandfather, who had laid the foundation of the family prosperity. The next day the will was entered into probate. After a suitable provision for his wife and some minor bequests to other descendants, the remainder of the estate went to son William. It amounted to some forty thousand dollars, in those days an extremely large sum, making the Judge at age forty-five a wealthy man.[3] He promptly retired from his law practice and began to live the life of a gentleman of leisure.

William Tudor, Sr.
Heliotype Printing Company, Boston, 1874.
Collection of the Massachusetts Historical Society.

But he would not have been too unbusy to miss the big celebration on July 4, 1795, when the cornerstone of the new State House on the top of nearby Beacon Hill was laid. After all, it had been his committee two years before that had worked out the compromise whereby the state government had given the town of Boston the old State House and the Province House in return for the town providing the state with a new capitol building. His committee had helped to choose the site in painter John Singleton Copley's pasture on the eminence of Beacon Hill, a location that would dominate the town and harbor until the age of high-rise Boston.

Despite such satisfactions there were other things the Judge wanted to do with his life. Now that wealth had finally come his way the Judge decided to make use of it. In 1796 he settled his affairs in Boston, sent his wife and children down to live on his farm in Saugus, called "Rockwood," and took off for a long-desired trip to Europe. The main part of the Rockwood estate had been purchased by the Deacon in May 1788 from Edward Weld for three hundred dollars. It consisted of ninety-nine acres, a house, a barn, and other outbuildings on the road from Chelsea to Reading (now Route 1 north of Boston). The farmhouse burned that November, and the Deacon had to have a new one built. He added some stone walls and fences and bought eighteen additional acres by 1794. Then he died and it all went to the Judge.

Rockwood! That name was to be as important to the Tudors as was that of Boston. The two words that combined to make its name also indicated what the farm was composed of—stone and trees.[4] It made a convenient place for Delia and the children, who at this time included William, John, Frederic, Emma, James, and Henry. James, seven years old, would die in 1797. Living with them at Rockwood were Mrs. Tudor's mother and her second husband, Capt. John Young.

In November 1796, young Frederic wrote to his father in Europe from Boston, not Rockwood. In an excellent hand for a thirteen-year-old, he told his father "of the new situation I am in": "Mr. Ducator & Marshall have opened a Store in state Street. . . . I am with them & at present the youngest Apprentice but they have so much Business that they are going to take an other."[5] He was quite happy there, pleased with both partners and treated with "great kindness" by all. "I hope you will not be displeased with my going so young." This meant he had had to give up school, but he assured his father he was attending an evening school "& shall learn faster there than if I was not in a Store." The box of tools his father had given him was being neglected since he had little time to use them. "We all hope you will return in the Spring Mama lives at Rockwood & I board with Anna now Mrs. Laidain."[6]

Regardless of how the Judge viewed Frederic's decision to become an apprentice at such an early age, brother William felt that Frederic's rejection of college for a business career was a blot on the family name. Frederic did not continue his apprenticeship for the standard three-to-five-year period. No reason is given for this abrupt change. Soon the slender lad was back at Rockwood playing farmer with his grandfather Young, though more often he was hunting in the woods accompanied by Sambo, a black servant on the estate.

Judge Tudor finally returned from Europe in 1798. He moved from his house on Court Street into quarters in the stylish new Tontine Crescent at 1 Franklin Place, then the most elegant address in town. After his graduation from Harvard in 1797, brother William took his turn visiting Europe. Frederic, back on the farm, wrote William that he had been in Boston yesterday but missed the "Pompous" funeral of the governor: Governor Sumner had died while holding office and been given an elaborate burial. While in Boston, Frederick had met a certain Casneau, an acquaintance of William's "who was pursuing the general chace & who said. Bill was a damn'd clever fellow & wished him success with his smattering of french."[7]

Their father was again playing at being a gentleman farmer and alternating days in Boston with days at Rockwood. However, he gave little proper attention to that business, nor was the soil of Rockwood good. Although much money was laid out on the farm, it yielded little. A relative commented later that "neither the Judge nor Mrs. Tudor had the least notion of economy. He had spent freely abroad and she freely at home, and a large sum advanced to William, which was sunk in an unfortunate voyage to Italy, made large inroads upon his property." John Stocker was hired as a tenant farmer to manage the farm, but the Judge was, as Frederic later observed, "too impatient" for results and laid out on the estate "probably $1000 a year more than it produced." Frederic termed this period of his life as "days of great felicity."[8]

Having received an appointment as commissioner of bankruptcies in Boston, the Judge gratefully turned his attention away from agriculture and to other concerns. One of these was the need to help his son John recover his health. Because John had injured his knee in 1801, it was decided that he should be sent on a trip to recuperate. The family chose Havana, Cuba, as a destination and appointed Frederic to accompany his older brother as nurse, companion, and correspondent. Havana had not been chosen haphazardly nor because of a reputation for curing injured knees. John and Frederic already had engaged in business speculations there from Boston. They had purchased some mahogany furniture, which they sold in Havana at a profit. John was then almost nineteen and Frederic seventeen.

John was something of a prig, judging from a letter he had written to his friend Moody Noyes in Newburyport shortly before. The young men were both temporarily unemployed, but John was

> looking out every day for a store, and will enter any one where I can have plenty of work and be treated like a gentleman. I will do any thing which requires clean hands, but on the last point am rather *squeamish*. I do not conceive how one is taught trade by sweeping a store, or making a dirty fire, & I do not like the idea of of [*sic*] putting myself under 3 or 4 uneducated young men—for any body who can read and write may be a merchant, and our rich Tradesman would never dream of bringing up their sons to their own employment.[9]

Their education was going to be of great help to them in their careers, he told Moody, because they could spend less time learning "the tricks of trade." But he felt that merchants generally "are a contemptible set of beings. They are afraid to receive a young man from College, lest they should expose their meanness and ignorance."[10]

For Frederic it was good-bye to Boston and to Rockwood and a venture out into a much larger world. The Judge gave John a thousand dollars for the trip. The brothers sailed from Boston in the *Patty* on February 26, 1801. In the journal John kept of the trip he wrote that they were "much in the dumps" when they inspected the ship and their cabin, which was "dark, damp, crowded & dismal."[11]

The first week out they were mostly sea-sick but had also quickly tired of the ship's diet of beef and soup. About all they could keep down were roast apples. But the sickness passed after six days, and the young men were soon eating heartily from the stores they had brought with them—all wise sea travelers in those days carried their own food supplies. Soon the Boston winter was far behind them and the southern sun began to beat down. Their noses got sunburnt, then peeled. The ship sailed smartly along and at the end of a week they were halfway to Cuba.

The sun was so hot on deck John developed a headache. Frederic had no such problems, and this annoyed his brother. Frederic spent the principal part of the day sleeping. Then the wind dropped, and the voyage dragged on nearly three more weeks. By the end of March, however, they were comfortably settled in Havana in the house of a Mr. Morton. How could the new world of Havana, this Paradise, possibly be described? It was "a contrast to everything which a New Englander has been used to & never till I visit the other world can I be so stupefied with wonder & admiration."[12]

John, whose knee continued to give him pain most of the day, decided to study Spanish and work with a local merchant who was acting as a commission agent for New Englanders in this prime southern market. Given just a few years, John thought he might make himself a fortune. The Tudors were always chasing after a fortune slightly out of their reach. From the Morton house the brothers moved to new quarters that were not as pleasant, but perhaps less expensive. They hired a servant named Francisco, who along with their landlady strictly limited John's diet, which was most annoying to him as he saw Frederic stuffing himself on "oranges & sapotillas, guaver jelly & green figgs." John was not allowed to touch fruit, but he was determined to eat some even "if I have to fight Francisco, kick the old woman & tell the doctor he's a quack."[13]

Mostly, John was alone in his room except for a daily ride. Frederic did nothing. Sometimes he declared he would get up every morning "& leave off smoking for a walk but the next morning and the next dinner totally changed his resolution." Yet Frederic did not spend all his time in idleness, for John reported that he had entered "Hernando's Compting room."[14] Since John could not find a Spanish master there was no employment for him.

Frederic might have seemed lazy to his brother, but his brain was busy hatching ideas. One was the invention of a new kind of water pump. Apparently the original idea had come to him before he went to Havana. He needed to raise water from a spring to supply an aqueduct, most likely at Rockwood. After his voyage to Havana he saw how beneficial it might be to mariners. Vessels fitted with one of his pumps would never sink. Or so he wrote the Royal Society of London when he described the virtues of his invention to them. Thousands would owe their lives to this invention, he immodestly told the Society. On land it would save immense labor, supply aqueducts, and power mills. "No machine which the last century has produced can be of such universal utility," he boasted.[15] But nothing came of this idea.

About this time, the brothers got involved in some speculative ventures that quickly lost them $150. The rest of their money was melting away on the pleasant living. They were aware of the impositions practiced on strangers, "but we never suffer them without a quarrel, and make use of all the hard names we are master of in Spanish."[16] "Paradise" had another difficult side, too: mosquitoes, scorpions, and the fierce heat, and John's knee did not get any better. In fact, by the end of May it was worse. Yet the doctor—who knew a good thing when he saw it—was urging his patient to linger the whole summer. Wiser Americans were already fleeing the stifling city, and John himself was anxious to get home. So quickly do the charms of paradise fade.

June 1 found them on a brig loaded with "stinking molasses," lumbering slowly along to Charleston, South Carolina. Since they had a good captain and plenty of supplies, they were content, particularly since every league they sailed put Havana further behind them. "Our joy at having left the Havana is unspeakable."[17] They had laid in 16 dozen eggs for four persons in a week's passage. That amounted to 192 eggs in all or 48 eggs per person or nearly 7 eggs for each person to eat every day. They ought to have been crowing when they landed. Whether it was the eggs or not, the effect on Frederic was noticeable to John. "As for Frederic he sleeps longer, eats more, & gets *fuddled* easier than the rest of the company."[18]

The ship was almost swamped in Charleston Harbor when a violent gale sprang up suddenly. After some dangerous hours, they landed in the city, where they were impressed by the wide unpaved streets lined with trees. John went looking for old college friends and found all but one. Washington Allston, the artist from Boston, whom he had expected to meet, had already sailed for Europe. Charleston was as hot as Havana. How long they could bear it was questionable. Some Boston friends, Mr. and Mrs. Josiah Sturgis, who were living and working there, brightened their stay. "The Yankees," John burst out patriotically in his journal, "are the best people after all, and the advantage is infinitely on their side if manners & information are compared."[19]

His knee was no better. If only he could straighten it out he would fear nothing. His complexion was yellow, and he hoped that the Charleston air would brace him up. Perhaps it was Frederic's behavior that gave John jaundice, for Frederic to his brother was most infernally lazy! "It is with the greatest difficulty I can get him to do anything. I hope there will be a time when I shall be able to rouse him."[20] John now decided that he should try some mineral springs to heal his knee. Drawing on their father for a few more hundred dollars, they embarked for Virginia and shortly were becalmed in Chesapeake Bay. "Our tongues roll out of our mouths with the heat."[21]

John did not like any of his fellow travelers except a Frenchman. He was the only one who was not stupid. Once their ship was moving again, they could enjoy the scenery along the "Patowmack," as he spelled it. Mount Vernon, he thought, was one of the most handsome estates on the river. By July 3 they had arrived in Alexandria. John had decided that the river scenery was the best on the globe, even though he had seen little of the globe.

After discussing with his brother a number of plans of how to get home, John elected to try the mineral waters at Bath, Pennsylvania. Two days of hard riding over rocks and mountains nearly shook them to pieces, and John, blaming his knee, decided that he would never want to travel again. But there were more dangerous signs—he had developed two lumps on his side. Furthermore, since the journey had inflamed his knee he had resumed using his crutch. He drank two gallons of mineral water each day. But he was no fool. There were three hundred people at the spring taking the waters "& hardly an instance of an invalid receiving a benefit."[22]

By mid August, when John had become extremely despondent, they suddenly learned that brother William and mother Delia were only a few miles away. They were soon together and most happy to be with one another. By the end of the month the four Tudors fled Bath and headed for Philadelphia. After the rough roads they had traveled over, the turnpike to the city of "brotherly love" evoked their ardent admiration. Constructed of pounded pieces of marble and limestone at great expense, it was, declared John, "one of the greatest works ever executed in our country."[23]

There in Philadelphia, in the middle of September, Frederic and John parted company. William and Frederic took the stage for Boston, while John and his mother stayed on. When four months later news of John's death on January 28, 1802, arrived in Boston, the entire family was greatly affected. Later, his mother told a friend that "Frederic tries to drive painful thoughts from his mind by constant occupation in the country."[24] His mother had come home from a trip to "comfort my distressed family and also to prevent William's going to Europe if possible—if not, to take his farewell embrace."[25]

A farewell embrace it turned out to be, and young William sailed for Europe. The Judge now cast around for some gainful employment for son Frederic, who was getting along toward nineteen. Frederic had not had much schooling and but a few years apprenticing. Yet he wrote an excellent hand and from his family had acquired a good cultural background. There was still much to learn, however, in the business field.

The Judge wanted Frederic to find a position where he might acquire it. He applied to an old friend, Maj. William Sullivan, to take Frederic under his wing. Sullivan responded with an ambiguous proposal. First, he talked the matter over with his brother. Then he replied that their friendship for Frederic would prompt them to do all they could to help "his acquirement of mercantile knowledge." But there was a "but." Their business at present was "very confined"—hardly enough to give him employment. Still, if the little they had could be of use to him, or what he could learn from their books, or from forming the habit of "every day resorting to a particular place," then Frederic would be welcome in their compting room "as a friend"—and those words were underlined—until "you, and he can find another more suitable to your purpose."[26]

It seems then that Frederic began his business career as an unpaid employee of the Sullivan brothers. He stayed there two years and made small ventures on his own in the odd lot shipment: some pimento, nutmeg, flour, sugar, tea, and the like. Work was not foremost in his mind, and he was very much a young man around town, fond of the gaiety that delights the young. At the end of that period, his father set him up in a joint business venture, Frederic providing the day-to-day supervision and his father providing "his assistance & a competant capital!" On the occasion of leaving the Sullivans, Frederic wrote them that his intention was "with prudence to advance by slow degrees to some importance in the commercial world." The "advancing" proved far slower than he anticipated.[27]

View of Boston and the South Boston Bridge
Tinted lithograph [1828]; Henry Gaugain, Publisher: Paris, 1828
A/B64B6/V.g.1828.a
Boston Athenæum.

CHAPTER 3

Bridge or No Bridge

ONE THING GENTLEMEN IN BOSTON DID was make money. They did not dirty their hands for it, but they made it nevertheless. Some made it by sitting in their compting rooms and importing tea or exporting lumber and fish. Some made it by insuring other merchants. Some made it by speculations in coffee, umbrellas, mahogany, horses, or slaves. Some made it by investments in hotels and banks, bridges and real estate. However they made it, it was done genteelly and over good Madeira and while puffing on an aromatic "segar."

Now the Judge was a gentleman who needed a great deal of money, and he was anxious to be like other gentlemen and make money the easy way. So he speculated. He was an original subscriber to the Charles River Bridge project in 1784. He liked the idea that people passing in or out of Boston would have to pay him a toll for the privilege. He acted as agent for some New Yorkers who wanted to take a flyer on Maine lands in 1791. He bought stock in the Middlesex Canal, developed in 1793. He joined a select group of citizens who intended to build a hotel in Boston in 1795. Unfortunately, nearly all of these were losing ventures.

Like other Bostonians, he had enviously watched the successful sale of lands around the new State House on top of Beacon Hill by the group of gentlemen who styled themselves the Mount Vernon Proprietors. One of these was Joseph Woodward of Tewksbury, Massachusetts. Delighted by his profits from that venture, Woodward looked around Boston for other possible areas to develop and exploit. Confined as it was to its little peninsula, the town was tightly populated by 1800. Yet, standing down on Windmill or Wheeler's Point in the southern part of town, Woodward could look across a long backwater to a large piece of undeveloped land temptingly close to the heart of town called Dorchester Neck, now South Boston. Land was extremely cheap on the Neck even though it was so close to Boston. This was because the only non-water route to it was a long drive out along Boston Neck and then back in across Dorchester Neck, a distance of three miles each way. Yet, thought Woodward, if a bridge were to be built across from Windmill Point, easy and fast access would be assured, for then the Neck would be virtually in downtown Boston.

To develop that area, Woodward would need people in the right places. This was particularly important, since he was known to be a difficult character with a fiery, impulsive temper. What better partners than his associates in the Beacon Hill speculation? Most prominent among them was Harrison Gray Otis, Boston's leading gentleman, lawyer, and politician.

In the late fall of 1803, Woodward and his associates quietly purchased ten parcels of land on the Neck, 126 acres in all. Then they started talk around town about the virtues of annexing Dorchester to Boston and building a convenient bridge to it. Nearly a decade earlier, in 1794, Judge Tudor had also admired the position of Dorchester Neck. Enough so, in fact, that he bought the piece of land opposite Wheeler's Point, the obvious terminus of any proposed bridge. So Tudor became necessary to Woodward's plan and was invited to join the speculators.

One obstacle interfered with the easy accomplishment of Woodward's idea, however. All along the Boston shore front opposite Dorchester Neck were wharfs. A bridge at Wheeler's Point would cut off the South Bay, as this area was called, from access to Boston Harbor. The wharf owners were outraged with Woodward's proposal of a bridge and said so, out loud and in print. The newspapers leaped into the fray, debating the pros and cons of the proposed bridge, when two bills were filed in the 1804 session of the state legislature. One, on behalf of the Town of Boston, called for the annexation of Dorchester Neck; the other, submitted by Judge Tudor, asked for a corporation to erect a bridge to the Neck. The "bridge" game was now in play! Frederic followed it avidly. He termed the conflict "Bridge or no Bridge."[1]

The proponents of the bridge, now publicly led by Judge Tudor and Otis, called a special town meeting in Boston to discuss annexation. Interest was so keen that it had to be moved to a larger hall. At the gathering Judge Tudor moved his proposal, seconded by Otis. "Lengthy and animated discussion then ensued," reported the *Independent Chronicle* of January 19, 1804. Frederic, writing in a more partisan spirit to his cousin James Savage, put it that "noise was opposed to our arguments. We *proved* that the Town would be benefited but they said that 'The southend will be injured.'"[2]

Not sure of winning, the bridge proponents threatened during the meeting that they would leave Boston, settle on the Neck, pay their taxes to Dorchester, and become "forever citizens of Dorchester." Not only that, but in three years, when they should have three hundred houses on the peninsula, the legislature would grant them a bridge without paying anything. They pointed out that Boston could not grow in size except by annexation and that now was the time it must add the six hundred acres of Dorchester Neck to Boston proper. The addition would also bring in four or five thousand dollars of new tax revenue.

That appeal to size and wealth prompted one gentleman to rise and pontificate upon the corruptions of larger cities. "Wealth and liberty," he declaimed, were "incompatible." The town of Boston was quite large enough, thank you, he said smugly, and reminded them of the bounds of their ancient commonwealth. He concluded with the popular warning that "The southend will be injured."[3] The moderator, whom Frederic thought had been against them, now put the question to a vote and the bridge proponents carried the question.

The *Independent Chronicle* for January 19, 1804, saw the matter quite another way than Frederic did. The South Enders were not gentlemen "in the habit of delivering themselves in public" and thus were not able to make the best arguments. "Four or five lawyers," said the *Independent Chronicle*, thought to have a particular interest in the matter, should be considered "an overbearing body" when united against men who lacked "mechanical volubility."

It was now the turn of the South End wharf owners. They realized they needed a counterproposal or they would soon have a bridge where they did not want one. They met and decided to build a new street on filled land along the South Bay shore. It would cross the wharfs and extend nearly half a mile. At the end of it they would erect a bridge to Dorchester Neck. This would give the people in Dorchester a bridge but put it in a place that would not damage their shipping trade. As a small bonus they would gain nine acres of new land for themselves, not an inconsiderable financial windfall. They petitioned the legislature for this new plan.

Meanwhile the bridge advocates were running into opposition from the citizens of Dorchester, whom they thought would welcome the annexation of their town by Boston. At the Dorchester town meeting, a month after Boston's, a committee reported that they had sent a protest to the legislature against annexation. One of the committee reported that Otis had approached him offering a six thousand dollar gift to the town of Dorchester as compensation if Dorchester would not oppose annexation. It looked like the gift would have its desired effect until John Howe, an influential Dorchester citizen, rose and spoke feelingly against the action. Otis increased the offer to twenty thousand dollars but to no avail. Now the people of Dorchester were lined up against the bridge advocates. They would not be bribed.

The offer of the South End wharf owners to build a new street and relocate the proposed bridge half a mile out of town was accepted. They won that much. But the Dorchester residents did not win and did not even get any compensation. Dorchester Neck was annexed to Boston on March 6, 1804. The settlement was in effect a compromise. Although it was not where they wanted it, the proponents accepted the alternative bridge location. The permit for construction of the bridge was granted to Judge Tudor, Otis, and the others. They were allowed the tolls for seventy years to compensate them for their expenses.

That May, caught up in the enthusiasm prevailing in his family for the bridge and for the development of South Boston, as the newly annexed area was now being called, Frederic and brother William decided to speculate too. The certainty of a bridge caused land values to soar. Where the buyers of 1803 had paid only an average of $30 per acre, Frederic and William heard quotes of more than ten times as much. On May 19, the brothers bought eleven acres of land for $3,790, and ten days later another parcel for $3,850. In short order they had invested $7,640 in the new development. By this sale, the original speculators had earned all their investment back with 100 percent profit.

Another kind of bridge under construction in this period was of equal interest to the Tudor family and to the fortunes of Frederic in particular. Marriage brought in a new family member—Robert Hallowell Gardiner, then twenty-three, who was considered by many to be Boston's most eligible bachelor because he was both handsome and rich. The bachelor's father, Robert Hallowell, had been customs collector of the Port of Boston for King George III before the Revolution. As an officer of the Crown, he found it expedient to flee the country with his family when the town was evacuated in 1776. Back in England they lived in Bristol on a small pension and there Robert had been born in 1782.

Robert's mother came from the Gardiner family. Old Dr. Silvester Gardiner owned thousands of acres along the Kennebec River in Maine. They were scattered through forty-five townships, including what later became the city of Gardiner. When he died in 1786 he left it all to his son William, who succumbed a year later to a violent attack of colic. A dose of laudanum, taken to ease the pain, proved an overdose. Dying childless, William bequeathed the estate to his nephew Robert when he reached twenty-one, provided he would change his name to Gardiner. Robert was delighted to fall to the temptation.

In 1792 the family moved back to Battery March Street in Boston and into the old family mansion, which had escaped confiscation by the Revolutionary government after the war. Then it was school for young Robert until he graduated from Harvard in 1801. He spent summer vacations in Maine with his father, who managed the estate he would ultimately inherit.

After Harvard he became a law student of Judge John Lowell, but it was thought he might have consumption, a disease that had killed his mother and sister, so a trip to Europe was prescribed. By 1803, when he was twenty-one, he had returned to Boston, added Gardiner to his name, and received his bequest. He moved to Maine to manage his estates. Although his health was much improved, his friends advised him to spend the winters in Boston. So, in December 1804, he was at his father's house on Battery March Street, dining out almost every day and attending one or two parties nearly every evening, "till I became wearied and disgusted with the nothingness of such social intercourse."[4]

During that winter of "nothingness" he met a young woman of twenty: Frederic's elder sister Emma Jane Tudor. She was thought to be one of the most beautiful girls in town, and her father was thought to be wealthy and influential. The "acquaintance produced an earnest desire" in Gardiner "of gaining her affection and of inducing her to share with me the joys and sorrows of this checkered life." A natural shyness kept him from declaring himself, but with the help of an older woman who "made it the chief pleasure of her life to promote matrimonial unions," he received permission to visit Emma and declare his affection and interest. Soon, he was spending every evening at the Tudors. Mrs. Tudor disliked long courtships, though she had certainly strung out her own long enough, and the Judge was impatient of delay in "anything to which he had once assented," so the wedding was speedily announced.[5]

At 8 A.M. on June 25, 1805, at Trinity Church on Summer Street, the young couple were united. Dr. John Silvester John Gardiner, the groom's cousin and rector of Trinity, performed the Episcopal service. The newlyweds then went to the Tudor home for a wedding breakfast, after which they climbed into carriages and headed for the Tudor country estate of Rockwood to spend the rest of the day in rural delights. The party was in high spirits, and the Judge amused them with his wry descriptions of his prowess as a "farmer." He had built large barns, warm poultry houses, and a convenient dairy, but his hay, his chickens, his eggs, and his butter all had to be bought in the market.

In the afternoon, the guests dispersed, leaving the couple to spend the first part of their honeymoon on the farm. But not alone, for Mrs. Tudor stayed with them! Later, they went by chaise to the groom's estates in Maine, leaving "Mother Tudor" behind.

This new and rich brother-in-law would prove useful to Frederic in the years to come. At one of the parties that summer at Rockwood, perhaps even at the wedding celebration, while they were downing drinks cooled with ice from the farm's icehouse, brother William offhandedly remarked how much residents of the West Indies would give to have such a luxury available to them. The guests laughed. Ship ice to the Indies? It would melt long before the ship could reach there. Frederic, however, saw the possibilities. Maybe it could be done. Already the prospect fired him up. He would make it happen!

Since Frederic's health was not good he decided on a pleasure trip to Ballston Springs in New York. Maybe the waters of that famous spa could cure his condition. His cousin James Savage was to go with him, and the two young men decided that they would also visit the spectacular falls at Niagara.

James Savage was the same age as Frederic. His mother had died when he was only four, and his father soon afterwards became insane. Young Savage, one of eleven children, was moved from foster home to foster home during his youth, yet somehow he managed to acquire a Harvard education. He studied law with Isaac Parker in Portland and then with Samuel Dexter in Boston. Law was not his passion, but he had no wealthy family to support him so he had to make a living. Although he was only a poor cousin to the Tudors, he looked upon the Judge as a substitute father, and the lad spent so much time either at Court Street or at Rockwood that he and Frederic were almost like brothers.

On August 12, Frederic and James shut up Frederic's store and set out for Ballston in a rented horse and chaise that cost Frederic $100. He took along $278 to pay for their expenses on the journey, and he had put $100 in his mother's hands to use during his absence. It took them about four days to make their way across Massachusetts to Ballston. The spa "disgusted" them when they first arrived. Gradually, however, "the easy nothingness of the place became more engaging as we staid the longer." After a few days indulging in the "easy nothingness," they remembered their goal and set out across the interior of New York for Niagara Falls. On August 23 they reached Utica, where Frederic wrote a hasty line to friends in Boston. They would continue on in the horse and chaise for another 120 miles until they reached Canandaigua. Since the turnpike ended here they planned to switch to horseback for the three- or four-day ride to the falls. "The roads & Taverns are very good as far as we have come."[6]

All during this trip the ice scheme buzzed in Frederic's head, though Savage was not yet fully aware of it. While at Ballston, Tudor had studied Mr. Low's icehouse and found that three of its walls were exposed to the air even though they were two and a half feet thick, while the fourth was banked against the ground. Frederic suspected that this structure did not keep ice very well—it had a moist floor—but he noticed that the ice still lasted for seven or eight months. In the hold of a vessel, he concluded, it would be no more exposed. On a voyage to the West Indies the ice would not have to be preserved for more than a month, and at best not much over two weeks.

Another icehouse that he saw later in his trip encouraged him even more. Here in the middle of September this house was still half full, and the building was at best eight feet deep with only a thatched roof. Back in Boston by the first of October, feeling much better—the Ballston waters had helped and the sight of Niagara Falls had cured him—he plunged eagerly into preparations for his ice speculation.

That same fall the bridge between Boston and Dorchester was completed. It ran east from South Boston at the narrowest part of the channel. Even so, it was 1,551 feet in length, with a draw in the middle to permit the passage of ships, and cost the speculators $56,000. Judge Tudor's share of this amount absorbed most of the remainder of his capital. It opened on Monday, October 1, 1805, with the militia parading on the common in the morning. Although the weather was not the best, quite a few spectators turned out. After refreshments, the militia marched down to the bridge. Its draw was hoisted and the Boston Light Infantry, assisted by pieces of artillery and the men of the Winslow-Blues, "defended" the bridge. After a mock battle the militia, now in control of the bridge, launched an attack upon the heights. It was nearly dark before this sham battle was concluded. The brigade marched back to town and was dismissed. So the first part of the speculation was completed as it had begun—in battle.

After the South Boston bridge was opened, Frederic and his family expected land buyers, not troops in mock battle, to rush across it. They visualized a golden harvest from inflated land prices. But the fall of 1805 came and went and no one stormed Dorchester Heights throwing money at the Tudors and their partners. That lack of ready cash came close to smothering Frederic's ice venture before it even began.

CHAPTER 4

A Slippery Speculation

TWO MONTHS BEFORE THE BRIDGE CELEBRATION, on the first day of August 1805, Frederic opened a leather-bound volume and grandly inscribed it as his "Ice Diary." He headed the first page "Plan etc. of transporting Ice to Tropical Climates." On the embossed cover he drew a tombstone-shaped frame and wrote in it these admonitory words to himself: "He who gives back at the first repulse and without striking the second blow, despairs of success, has never been, is not, and never will be, a hero in war, love, or business."[1]

Frederic was never to be a war hero, but he was to succeed in both love and business. "William & myself," he wrote in the diary, "have this day determined to get together what property we have & embark in the undertaking of carrying ice to the West Indies the ensuing winter."[2] For many years New Englanders had been cutting ice out of their frozen ponds and storing it for use in the warmer seasons. What no one had thought of before the Tudors was the possibility of sending this pond ice south some fifteen hundred miles, where it had almost never been seen, and selling it to the residents. It was a daring concept.

One important element in the success of the scheme would be the elimination of competition. Would Congress allow them a monopoly on the business for a few years until they could get established? Otherwise "some enterprising Yankee might be induced to attempt the thing," and they would lose the advantages that ought to go to those who had risked starting the trade.[3] So Frederic went directly to the most influential man he knew, one of his father's associates in the South Boston development project, now a United States senator, Harrison Gray Otis.

Outlining the project to Otis, he admitted that on the face of it the scheme might sound absurd. What if the vessel dropped anchor in Havana Harbor and the hold was full of water instead of ice? This is what people generally believed would happen. He mustered all the examples he could to show that the general opinion was wrong. Not only would the scheme work, but its investors would realize "a profit beyond calculation."[4] He cited various stories of people who had successfully transported ice from Norway to England, of boards shipped from New England in the winter that arrived with ice on them in the West Indies some weeks later. He also said that ice had been successfully kept in the Carolinas. As Frederic saw it, the scheme had advantages that outnumbered the risks. They could enter into contracts with rich planters to supply them with a year's worth of ice for their own private icehouses. The supply would allow the planters to enjoy meat and other produce in the warm weather.

The ice, being a rarity and luxury, would sell for such high prices that several vessels might be profitably loaded with coffee and sugar for the return voyage. The results for the investors would be "fortunes larger than we shall know what to do with." Such was the vision that would drive Tudor. Otis tactfully excused himself from this glittering scheme, though he remarked that he thought the plan plausible. "Whether he really did or no," grumbled Frederic, "he is to [*sic*] much of a politician for me to find out."[5]

Rebuffed by Otis, Frederic abandoned the attempt to secure a monopoly; instead, he reasoned that they could get the same protection from the West Indian governments. Around this time, Frederic's cousin James Savage joined in the effort to promote the project. Frederic had never succeeded, however, in fully winning over his brother. William was too busy dreaming of being a literary gentleman.

In the fall of 1803, with a group of his friends William formed the Anthology Club. A circle of fourteen Boston gentlemen, it included liberal clerics such as the Reverend William Emerson (Ralph Waldo Emerson's father) and the brilliant Reverend Joseph Stevens Buckminister; Boston's leading medical pair, Doctors John Collins Warren and James Jackson; and other young gentlemen. Most of the members were in their twenties. Only the Reverend John Silvester John Gardiner, the rector of Trinity Church, was of mature age at forty. William Tudor was a charter member.

The gentlemen met weekly at each others' houses, where, after they had consumed beefsteak and oysters washed down with wine, the members shared fervid literary conversation in clouds of cigar smoke. They read bookish papers to each other, and to preserve the "excellence" of these papers the group published a magazine, *The Monthly Anthology; or Magazine of Polite Literature.* William became a regular contributor. After his graduation from Harvard College in 1796, he had spent some time in

Europe, first on business, then on pleasure. Failing one and tiring of the other, he returned to Boston to live as a gentleman's son engaged in nonremunerative literary pursuits such as the Anthology Club.

The club may have fascinated William, but Frederic was intent on promoting his ice project. He proposed that William and Savage make a trip to the West Indies to lay the groundwork for their first shipment of ice. Savage had "some business habits & character in him," commented Frederic, and would provide the necessary balance to his head-in-the-clouds brother on the trip.[6] Their assignment was to sail to the French island of Martinique by November 1 and get an agreement for exclusive rights to sell ice to the inhabitants. If they could not achieve this goal, at least they could explore the matter with the most influential men on the island. They were to write him constantly of their progress. Even if they could not obtain a monopoly, perhaps they could secure orders for ice, or they might get permission to build an icehouse on the island to store their commodity. If they could get the right to do this exclusively, it would be almost as good as a monopoly. But even if that concession were not granted, perhaps they could circulate subscription papers among wealthy people to obtain a cash advance in exchange for the promise of future delivery of ice.

William Tudor, Jr., about 1831
Oil on canvas, by Thomas Sully.
U.R. 31.1854
Boston Athenæum.

Since it was now so late in the season, they had to abandon the idea of building a local structure to store their ice. Not only would it save them an immediate cash outlay, it would also avoid tipping off other enterprising Bostonians about their long-range plans. Frederic planned to follow his two advance men with a shipment of ice, and he wanted to be sure that there would be neither difficulties nor duties at the customhouse to delay landing the ice. He could visualize the disaster of the vessel sitting in the harbor, unable to land its cargo, as the ice all melted away. After much persuasion William finally agreed to leave his club and go.

The great speculation was an adventure of young men: Frederic and Savage were both twenty-one and William was only twenty-six years old. So on Saturday, November 2, 1805, Frederic bade good-bye to his brother and cousin. He paid a boatman $1.50 to row them out to their vessel, the brig *Jane*, and saw them set sail for Martinique. The first step of the venture was launched, and much was to depend on how well these two laid the groundwork for the enterprise. Although Frederic remained behind, his heart and thoughts were very much with the two men now sailing down Boston Harbor.

On board the *Jane*, James began a journal of the voyage.[7] The weather was brisk and the vessel raced along, cutting sweetly through the water. A week and a half out, the *Jane* encountered a vessel from Liverpool almost out of provisions and gave it a few supplies. William also sent letters home by this vessel, while James reflected on the differences between the two ships, "on the abundance of delicacies we every day enjoy," while even with what the British crew had received from the *Jane*, "their hopes of reaching port without further assistance are almost presumptuous."[8] Sunday they had an encounter with a French privateer that ended without incident. As a neutral country during the Napoleonic Wars between France and Britain, America engaged in trade with both. American merchants and their ships benefited by carrying on such open trade but were frequently subject to search and sometimes seizure by privateers and warships of the two warring nations. On Tuesday, December 3, a British warship inspected the *Jane* and permitted it to sail on towards Martinique, now clearly visible on the horizon. Drifting toward land at night they were fired on by shore batteries until they hung a lantern in the shrouds. The next day they dropped anchor in the harbor.

William and James thought St. Pierre, with its thirty thousand inhabitants, the finest city in the West Indies. "Through every street runs a stream of water, which conveys all the filth from the houses to the sea, and at the same time produced a constant agitation of the air."[9] Perhaps because of such "agitation" Savage came down with a fever. Tudor had two interviews with the prefect and conversed with several of the "first in the island concerning our project. They seem to favor it strongly."[10] By the end of the week they had presented their petition asking for an exclusive privilege to sell ice there. Now it was William's turn to come down with the fever, and James conducted the interviews. On December 24, 1805, the prefect told them that their petition had been granted in the name of the Emperor Napoleon and that James should call for it the next day. However, the next day there were difficulties. The government granted no monopolies without the payment of a large sum. "I think he mentioned four hundred Dollars."[11] Further, Tudor and Savage had to detail their modus operandi.

This obstacle was more than they had bargained for. They held a war council and

St. Pierre, Martinique
Harper's New Monthly Magazine, *Jan. 1874.*
Collection of the Massachusetts Historical Society.

then went directly to the prefect's secretary. He was hard to locate until they left a letter with some gold coins at his home. He appeared the next morning, assuring them he had conversed with the prefect and that all obstacles had been removed. There was to be no fee and they would have the grant before dinner. Writing the good news to Frederic in Boston on December 26, William and James left the next day for a holiday in Trois Islets with a Mr. D'Aubifret; they intended to stay for two or three days. D'Aubifret had spent his boyhood in Boston and was an old acquaintance.

They left St. Pierre early and arrived about half past eight. That same night James was attacked by a fever so severe that a doctor was summoned from town. For four weeks he was confined to bed; the fifth week he had to be supported by two slaves everywhere he went, resting during the day in a hammock swing in the salon. Not until the sixth week could he walk without support. At the end of seven weeks of this enforced vacation he returned to St. Pierre, full of praise and gratitude for the care and concern shown him by his friends.

In the second week of his fever, James had persuaded William to leave him and return to their mission. William went north to the French island of Guadeloupe, continued up to the British island of Antigua, came back by way of British Montserrat, and finally sailed to St. Croix in the Danish Virgin Islands, near Puerto Rico, where he was to meet James. When James rejoined him, they sailed for Jamaica on February 25, 1806, on a vexing voyage. The captain was drunk for several days, then was sick the rest of the passage and never left his cabin. The mate did not know how to manage the vessel and was more than happy to take orders from the passengers. On March 3 they docked in Santo Domingo, which was then under French rule. Here, to their surprise, they were told that their vessel would return to St. Thomas in the Virgin Islands and not go on to Jamaica. James was distressed because it was difficult to book passage to Jamaica from that port.

Since they were in Santo Domingo, however unintentionally, they applied to the government for permission to sell ice, which was quickly granted. Now they had a chance to stroll around this ancient city, the first one built by the Spaniards in "the Western world." They viewed the ruined "palace" that Columbus had started to build and which was the pretext used by the Spaniards to send the great Admiral of the Ocean Sea back to Spain in chains like a felon. Wandering through the college started by the Jesuits and then taken over by "their enemies, the Dominicans," the young men were startled to see that it had become a public warehouse. "The knee-worn stones are covered by barrels of flour and pipes of wine, piled even against the altars."[12]

Friday, March 28, the pair boarded a Danish schooner bound for Jamaica. After a week-long stop en route to take on some mahogany, and another week's sail, just in sight of Port Royal the schooner was stopped by a privateer. William was relieved of his elegant pistols, but they were permitted to proceed to port. Having finally reached Kingston, they stayed there several weeks. At last, on the evening of Sunday, May 4, they boarded the schooner *Huntress*, bound for Boston. Twenty-seven days later, after a wandering voyage during which they were uncertain of their latitude most of the way, they reached Boston convinced that "a seaman's life is a dog's life."[13]

Frederic was at quarantine to meet them. Since he had received no letters since they left Santo Domingo, he was amazed at their early return. He had been to the islands and back while they had been on their long leisurely expedition and was bursting with good news to share with them.

Once his brother and cousin left to prepare the way for the ice cargo, Frederic busied himself with what needed to be done to ensure that there would be such a cargo and that it could be shipped to the West Indian ports. First he pulled together some venture capital; after considerable difficulties he had about five thousand dollars, part of which came from a mortgage on some of his South Boston land. Then he had to locate a good vessel. "I have got my eye upon a Brig which is a fine fast sailing vessel & remarkably fitted for the voyage. She is called the *Favorite* 134 tons."[14] He thought it likely he would buy her.

Frederic had a lecture from his father every morning urging him to abandon the voyage, which the Judge deemed as dangerous with little chance of success. Nevertheless, Frederic purchased the *Favorite* for $4,750. By January 10 he had heard of the arrival and good reception William and James received in St. Pierre. So things looked hopeful at the southern end. In the North things were promising too. "It has now begun to freeze for the first time this winter!"—so the prospect of a cargo was encouraging. The brig was ready, a captain had been engaged, "& the sky looks bright for the success of the scheme!"[15] Ten days later, however, he would write in his diary that everything but the weather was favoring their enterprise. For his purposes, it turned out to be a remarkably bad winter. "Nothing but storm frost & snow."[16] There were other problems. When he was about to cut the ice Boston Harbor froze over. When the harbor thawed, there was no ice. Then storms prevented him from cutting ice. When the storms ceased the ponds were covered with snow. By the beginning of February, finally, he was accumulating a cargo of ice.

He had two worries beside the weather: that he might get to the West Indies too soon, before his partners had completed all the necessary arrangements, and the contrary one that it would take so long to obtain sufficient ice that it would be too late in the season to make a successful voyage. By now his closely kept secret was out. He had involved too many people in the preparations to keep it quiet. It was known that he intended to do the unbelievable—to ship ice to the West Indies. Some people only laughed at him; others did not believe him and thought it was a cover for some other kind of venture. "Let those laugh who win," he boasted in his diary.[17]

Frederic was pioneering in a new enterprise, and he had much yet to learn. How to preserve the ice, for example. He included a page in his ice diary with a cross-section of a stone icehouse and various methods for insulating it against outside heat. Wood shavings or sugarcane straw five feet thick in every direction became his main prescription. He noted that at the bottom of the icehouse heat leaked in and melted the ice. To avoid this problem, he decided that the drainage pipe itself should always be partly full of water to keep heat from getting into the house that way. The entrance to the house was through a four-foot opening in the top so that the ice had to be put in and removed that way too. He would spend many years experimenting with different materials to use for insulating the ice before he hit upon sawdust.

Oddly enough, Frederic assumed that no particular care needed to be taken to preserve the ice once it was put on board the vessel. However, he did have a carpenter build a compartment of wooden planks inside the ship to keep it from contact with the deck above the hold, which would be baked by the sun. Eventually he learned that insulating the ice aboard ship was as important as while it was stored in icehouses prior to delivery. In this initial period, too, he did not know how to cut ice out of the frozen ponds efficiently. His men simply hacked it out in chunks of varying shapes. This wasted space and allowed large pockets of air between the chunks. It would be many years before a farmer-inventor developed a satisfactory method of plowing ice into neat cubes that stacked well and allowed the most possible tonnage in a ship's hold.

Once the news of his speculation was public, just what Frederic had anticipated happened: another trader sent a shipload of ice to Cuba. Although Frederic felt that the Cuban market was too important to overlook, he knew his roving ambassadors would not be able to get to Cuba. One of James Savage's brothers, twenty-seven-year-old William Savage, had gone to Havana as a merchant to make his fortune. Frederic wrote William asking him to attempt to get an exclusive privilege for them for that island. Finally, with his ice cut, the brig packed and the tide favorable, the *Favorite* cleared the Boston customhouse and, with the inventor of the idea aboard, set sail for Martinique. The *Boston Gazette* headlined the event "No Joke" and added archly, "We hope this will not prove a slippery speculation."[18]

Frederic left on February 13, 1806, and after twenty days anchored at St. Pierre on March 5. His brother and cousin had just arrived in Santo Domingo. So far he was confident of the success of his venture because he had arrived with his ice intact, but William had left letters for him that were discouraging in tone: he did not anticipate much sale of ice there and advised his brother to leave immediately. They had made almost no preparation for his arrival. Nonetheless, since Frederic could not afford to leave, he had to see what could be done. It was a disadvantage not to have an icehouse, but he was not worried because the ice in his vessel was keeping so well.

The government granted permission to sell on board the vessel, and Frederic began as soon as possible, charging sixteen and a half cents a pound for the ice. He sold fifty dollars worth of ice from the ship in the first two days. Then he had a handbill printed in French advertising the sale of "Glace" for the next three days only, before the ship left for another island. For the islanders' information, the handbill recommended that those purchasing ice carry it away covered either by a blanket or by a linen cloth to keep it from melting.

Frederic's disappointment and chagrin at having to shift for himself were great. His partners had not even secured the subscription papers he had requested, which he regarded as of utmost importance. There he was, without money and without friends, with only a cargo of ice in the torrid climate to depend upon for a supply of both. Had they secured an icehouse, he could have stored his cargo and slowly sold it off. He estimated that he should have realized $10,000 for it. A local merchant offered him $4,000 for the whole cargo. He refused, preferring to take the chance of getting more by selling it for himself.

Although the brig had preserved the ice perfectly, once customers took it away problems developed. Being unacquainted with this new product, they did not realize that ice would melt if they did not take steps to preserve it. One man brought his ice home through the hot noonday sun and left it in front of his door on a plate. Shortly, he came complaining to Tudor that "il fond" [it melts]! A second customer put his ice in a tub of water; a third put his in salt to preserve it and complained about the taste it gave his drinks. It was obviously necessary to educate the public. Frederic recorded one of his efforts to do so this way:

> The man who keeps the Tivoli garden insisted ice creams could not be made in this country & that the ice itself would all thaw before he could get it home! I told him I had made them here—he said to his wife in French supposing however I did not understand him I was a charlatin.—but I did— & so putting my fist pretty hard upon the table I called for a pen & ink. I wrote an order for 60 lbs. of ice & in a pretty warm tone directed the man to have his cream ready & that I would come & freeze it for him in the morning which I did accordingly being determined to spare no pains to convince these people that they can not only have ice but all the luxuries arising as well here as elsewhere. The Tivoli man recd. for these creams the first night $300—after this he was as humble as a mushroom & shrugging up his shoulders said he knew nothing hoped monsieur would take some coffee—some liqueurs. "Devil take your coffee." said I & came home.[19]

Frederic continued to sell small quantities of the ice—from $20 to $40 worth each day—and was just ready to try a new port when a local merchant offered him an advance of $3,000 worth of sugar for the vessel to take back to Boston and agreed to take the ice off his hands and sell it for him on commission. This was the best offer Frederic had received, so he took it. A place was now prepared to receive the ice and on March 26, 1806, Frederic reported that the *Favorite* was almost unloaded.

While waiting for some repairs to the vessel, Frederic sailed off to the British island of Barbados to see if he could get a privilege from that government. Meeting with no success, he soon returned to St. Pierre to find his vessel loaded with sugar and ready for sea. But his ice lasted only until April 10, and the whole amount sold did not much exceed $1,000. When Frederic computed the results of his first speculation in ice, it had indeed proved a slippery venture, as predicted. On the credit side he had proved to his own satisfaction that the plan of transporting ice to the tropics for sale was perfectly sound. But on the debit side, he had to admit that the first year it had produced a loss of from $3,000 to $4,000.

He was even less satisfied with the exertions of his brother and his cousin. Their part of the venture had not been equal to the expense of it, which came to about $2,000. Tudor decided that they had not announced the project with the confidence that defies all ridicule and opposition. However, he blamed them only for not understanding how to conduct a new enterprise. He felt himself unfortunate in having connected himself with relatives who had not made sincere efforts to aid him. Having reached that conclusion, he promptly acted against it by sending his brother to England to see if he could secure an exclusive right to sell ice to the British colonies in the Caribbean. It seemed to him, after personal experience in dealing with the island bureaucracies, that he could move faster by securing licenses directly from the Board of Trade in London. Apparently it also made sense to him to send as emissary a person who had shown that he neither understood the project nor had the initiative to make it a success.

Meanwhile, Frederic went to work improving the construction of his icehouses. As he told a prospective investor in the scheme, icehouses on the old European style of construction had become obsolete. They were expensive and kept ice poorly. Underground icehouses, a common American design, kept ice longer while costing only a tenth as much as European ones. But he was making improvements on these, too. Frederic's icehouses were built so all the moist air would be vented from the top.

Needed also, after their losses that first season, was a partner with money. Frederic drafted a proposal giving the history of the first season in extensive detail, leaving out any mention of the money they had lost so far. He sent this to a gentleman he thought might invest with them, assuring him that he had been completely honest in his statement. He must have had his fingers crossed when he wrote that. In his proposal he talked cheerfully of shipping seven or eight cargoes the next season to the islands, including two to Havana and one to New Orleans. How could they possibly lose? In such an optimistic mood he began his preparations for his second season.

View of the City of Havana
Gleason's Pictorial Drawing-Room Companion, *Mar. 11, 1854.*
Collection of the Massachusetts Historical Society.

CHAPTER 5

A Man without Money

WILLIAM TUDOR SAILED THE MIDDLE OF AUGUST 1806 from New York to beard the Board of Trade in its London lair. Embarking at the same time from Boston for France were Judge Tudor, his wife, and young daughter Delia. They were not traveling on business, as was William, but purely for pleasure. The Judge's wife had been urging him for some time to take them abroad. She and daughter Delia had never been to the Continent and both had ambitions for a more fashionable life than Boston could provide. They wanted to try their wings in a wider sphere.

To finance this junket would take a great deal of ready money, a commodity of which the Judge had very little, due to the South Boston speculation. Not only had his share for the construction of the bridge been heavy, but he had laid out additional money to build a block of fine brick rental buildings in South Boston, finished in magnificent style. To pay for these he had borrowed fourteen thousand dollars in December 1805 from Samuel Parkman, a merchant notorious for charging ruinous interest rates. The Judge had put up his Court Street house as collateral for the loan.

When the anticipated flood of prospective South Boston residents did not materialize in 1806, the Judge found himself in a bind. Land sales were few, only one of his houses was rented, and that for a paltry $120 a year. The bridge tolls that were supposed to reimburse him for his assessment toward its construction were not sufficient to keep the structure in repair. Now his wife wanted him to take her to Europe for an extended tour.

So he mortgaged a quarter interest in fifty acres of South Boston land to John Hawes for ten thousand dollars. His fine house on Franklin Place he sold for seven thousand dollars to the ever-obliging Samuel Parkman. And Frederic received the task of selling off the family furniture at auction. Thus having hocked himself to the hilt, the Judge with his wife and daughter happily boarded their ship and sailed to Europe. By the middle of October 1806, James Savage could write to his French friend D'Aubifret that his Uncle Tudor "with Madame and Madamoiselle" had arrived safely in France and that "Delia is a fine, accomplished, beautiful girl, and it is not impossible, that some one of your countrymen may be conquered by her charms."[1] Particularly someone who was exceedingly rich! Such a thought was not far from Mrs. Tudor's mind.

In the fall of 1806, land sales in South Boston picked up, bringing in over ten thousand dollars to the Associates. Prospects looked bright, but then sales dropped off again. Sales were not much more than two thousand dollars in all of 1807. The long ride down to the bridge and over to South Boston apparently discouraged buyers.

While the bridge itself became a fashionable place for people to stroll on a pleasant evening, and young swains found it agreeable for courting and flirtations, that did not put money into the pockets of the South Boston Associates. However, Woodward and the others hoped to bail themselves out by continuing to agitate for the nearer bridge site that had earlier been denied them. So they pressed the issue relentlessly. "Bridges! Bridges!" exclaimed the *Independent Chronicle* testily on February 9, 1807. "Do not," it warned the Associates, "crowd an undertaking so hard as to press it to death." Eventually the Associates succeeded in getting their bridge bill passed in the state senate, only to see it go down to defeat in the house.

Frederic, meanwhile, was trying to strike the second blow for the success of his ice venture. To bring his ice to the West Indies, he decided that he needed agents on each of the islands to promote his product. He quickly began a correspondence with merchants in Jamaica, Barbados, Guadeloupe, and St. Thomas. He also had a new icehouse built in the spring of 1807 on the island of Martinique. James Savage's brother William had reported back to Frederic in December 1806 that he was unable to get the desired monopoly but was interested in the project enough to build an icehouse in Havana. In January 1807 Frederic sent 180 tons of ice on the brig *Trident*.

All this enterprise required money, and Frederic had reached the bottom of his wallet. He certainly could not borrow from his father. He talked to a Mr. Putnam in Newburyport, but the answer there was no. William Savage was only interested in investing for Havana. Frederic made a trip to Kennebec to persuade another prospective investor, but he too declined. Almost all his business correspondents in the islands refused to advance money to build icehouses.

In March 1807, Frederic sent a second cargo of ice to Havana, and a third followed it in April. All arrived safely with the ice in good condition. The Havana icehouse kept the cargo for a couple of weeks, but then the heat got in. Frederic learned that this was due to poor construction. This was the first of a series of accidents that seemed to plague the second year of his enterprise. Savage had managed, nonetheless, to sell six thousand dollars worth of ice in Havana.

Savage then loaded the *Trident* with a return cargo of molasses to sell for a profit back in Boston. This was sold to a customer in Connecticut whose business failed before he could pay for the molasses. In March Frederic heard that the facility had been finished in St. Pierre, but lacking money he could not ship them ice. For fifteen months it stood empty and finally had to be taken down. The only result of its construction was to plunge him further into debt. Thus, the second year ended as poorly as the first.

Meanwhile, to comfort himself, he entertained hopes that William in England was accomplishing something. James Monroe, who had been sent to London by Pres. Thomas Jefferson to negotiate with the British government on the impressment of American seamen and the seizure of their vessels, gave William a letter of recommendation to aid him in his quest for a monopoly. It might help since Lord Auchland, with whom Monroe was negotiating, was also the president of the Board of Trade, with whom William had to deal.

William soon learned that the very originality of the idea of carrying ice to tropical climates was regarded by the British government as nothing more than a subterfuge for smuggling. As a result, they refused to grant the precious monopoly. However, they suggested that a deal might be possible if William could produce a document justifying the need to allow American vessels to deliver ice into these colonies.

This William quickly did by securing from a doctor a letter stating that ice had medicinal value in the West Indies. Thus he obtained licenses, which the British government promised it would not allow any other Americans to have, for the importing of ice into Jamaica, Barbados, and Antigua. Finally, Frederic had his desired monopoly. But he soon discovered that it did him little good to have permission to sell ice in those islands if he had no money to buy and ship his product.

As Frederic began the third year of his venture in the fall of 1807, he decided to go to Havana himself and construct a better icehouse, for Cuba was the one place where he was having some success. He arrived in December 1807 only to find that some other Bostonian had shipped a cargo of ice to that port. So his fear that other people would leap into the trade as soon as he had shown the way seemed about to materialize. Fortunately, this competitor had shipped out his ice in bad order, and Frederic estimated that nearly three-quarters of it had melted in transit. Frederic had nearly completed his new icehouse when the startling news arrived that the American

Congress, at the urging of President Jefferson, had declared an embargo on all shipments from American ports as of December 1807. Jefferson, trying to stop the seizure of neutral American vessels by the warring British and French, as well as the impressment of American sailors into the British Royal Navy, had decided to withhold the American ships that carried so much essential cargo to both nations.

It was not the best way for Frederic to get his struggling business established, however. Now, no matter how much money he might be able to raise, how many fine icehouses he might have waiting, or how cold the winter was in New England, he was not allowed to ship ice. The embargo came as a grand climax to his run of bad luck. With it, his third season was aborted. Frederic packed his bags and returned to Boston. To add to Frederic's frustration, William reported that he had gone to Paris and had obtained for him a monopoly in the French islands of Martinique and Guadeloupe.

Not only did Frederic return to Boston with his tail between his legs, but he was soon followed by his father. The Judge returned to Boston alone—for his wife and daughter preferred the delights of Europe to Boston. They thrived on foreign society, but the Judge did not speak any foreign language and did not share their literary and artistic tastes.

He returned broke and jobless, but through the exertions of some of his political friends he was appointed to the office of secretary of state of Massachusetts. It was a position exactly suited to his talents, although the salary was moderate. His son-in-law Gardiner described why it suited the Judge: "He had a large office handsomely furnished, and supplied with all the newspapers of the day, while the drudgery was performed by clerks long familiar with the duties, and requiring but slight superintendence. His principal duties were to keep the records of the Council when in session, and to carry messages from the Governor to either branch of the Legislature, which he did with some parade, dressed in his velvet coat and preceded by a messenger, with his staff of office, to announce his coming."[2] The position was to last two years; then he was appointed clerk of the Supreme Judicial Court, an office he held for the rest of his life.

The prospects of South Boston still looked bright to some investors in spite of the economic depression caused by the embargo. Frederic reported to his brother-in-law Gardiner in February 1808 that he and his father had talked with Senator Otis, who had assured them that the Judge's South Boston property had a value of $100,000. If that were so, the Judge—in terms of today's dollar—was easily a millionaire. But the reality was far different, for when he had to mortgage this land twenty-two months later all the moneylender John Hawes gave him was $9,000.

The Judge was taken care of by his political appointment, but Frederic, hamstrung by the embargo, had no such sinecure. So he retired to the family estate at Rockwood and, for want of something better to do, became a farmer—not a happy farmer, but one "groaning" over his bad luck. He kept looking forward to the next winter, not knowing how long the embargo might last, as one that would bring him employment, money, and relief. His faith in his ice speculation was still high. "It has cost me a great deal of trouble but I believe it will eventually repay me if I am able to carry it on."[3]

In the meantime he hunkered down at Rockwood and continued to experiment with ways to preserve ice in large casks. He felt this would be an advantage when he could resume trade. During the summer of 1808 he carried out a number of such experiments and carefully described them in his icehouse diary. On June 16, he put one barrel of 160 pounds of ice in a hogshead surrounded by pulverized charcoal. He did the same with another packed in pulverized peat. Both the charcoal and the peat were completely dry. When opened forty days later, the ice in both barrels had melted, but the meltwater insulated by the charcoal was warm, while that protected by the peat was as cold as spring water.

He decided to repeat the experiment but this time open them sooner, before the ice had melted. He left both casks outdoors, fully exposed to the summer sun. Opening them on August 12, he found that in the charcoal barrel the ice was all gone and probably, by the feel of the water, had been melted for at least a week. In the cask insulated by peat some ice remained. It made further sense to use peat rather than charcoal since the type used—a light and spongy peat—made the poorest fuel. Despite such experiments, Frederic was soon bored with Rockwood. His mind searched restlessly for other employments and undertakings. Once again, William gave him an idea.

One day in September 1808, William, now back from Europe, went to Boston to have his watch repaired. The watchmaker told him he had discovered a coal mine but needed capital to exploit it. Upon his return to the farm William mentioned this to Frederic, who took an immediate interest in the idea. Maybe their father—the Judge—would finance it. Since the South Boston speculation had been laid low by the embargo, the Judge found that he had no free cash. They had mortgaged everything else, but why not a mortgage on Rockwood to secure the necessary funds?

When Frederic first proposed the idea of a coal mine to his father he represented it as his personal project. The Judge was interested. But as soon as he heard that others were also to be involved, he began to warn his son about schemers. Frederic felt he did not have to be warned, but he did decide they ought to take a look at the mine first.

There were to be six people in the mining company; a committee of three, Frederic, cousin William Savage, and one of the original discoverers of the mine, set out to examine the property. The sites were a long way from Boston, one hundred miles to be exact, on Cape Cod and on the island of Martha's Vineyard. Suspicious, as always, that everyone in Boston was watching his every movement and ready to steal from him his valuable ideas, he decided to camouflage his trip. Accordingly, they took their guns and put the word around that they were going off on a shooting expedition.

The first leg of the journey went off without incident, and the party arrived at the first mine site on the mainland. Here they filled their trunks with specimens of the coal, then proceeded to the second site on the island in a hired forty-ton schooner.

They arrived at the second site and again loaded themselves down with specimens. It was nearly sundown when the storm that had been gathering all day broke. A strong wind blew directly in their faces, making walking difficult. The drenching rain soon soaked through their heavy coats. This, plus the burden of the coal specimens and their guns, weighed them down. Fearing that they might lose their way in the confusing woods of the upland path, they elected to follow the shore, which lengthened their journey by another mile. Finally, near exhaustion, they came to a house near the tavern where they had put up when they had arrived on the island; many sought shelter from the storm and the old woman who came to the door welcomed them in, thinking that they might have been shipwrecked. There they spent the night.

Leaving their partner on the island to make a bargain for the land, Savage and Frederic set sail the next day in their hired boat for the mainland. Their course took them through Woods Hole, a rocky, twisting passage where the tide ran so rapidly as almost to create a waterfall. The boatman knew nothing of the passage and Savage only knew that it was dangerous. The ignorant boatman steered them directly into the rocks.

The tide pushed their boat on with such speed that for a time they had no control and could only go where it took them. Night came on, and in the darkness they had no idea where they were. Finally, after what seemed like several hours of sailing in the dark, they caught the gleam of a lighthouse and tried to sail for it, but made no headway. Down came the sails and out came the oars. After rowing about eleven miles across Buzzards Bay against the wind and wave, they reached port just after midnight.

The specimens they had brought back seemed to prove the value of the coal deposit, and the plan to develop it seemed feasible. It took two months to obtain a deed to the lot on Martha's Vineyard. The original lot belonged to a Native American tribe, and the best they could obtain was a ten-year lease. Frederic estimated that if all the papers required for this transaction were bound together they would make a small octavo volume.

Meanwhile, the family farm was languishing under the management of the two brothers. Their joint administration for the year 1808 showed that very uncertain hands were on the plow. The estate that year boasted 2 horses, 2 yoke of oxen, 2 cows, 1 heifer, 3 hogs, and 50 fowl. Their cash crops, which consisted of 27 tons of hay, 35 bushels of corn, 90 bushels of potatoes, and 60 bushels of carrots, brought them an income of $384. But to make that much money they had laid out $40 in taxes and $50 for sundries, and they had paid a hired man $395 and a hired woman $104; their total cost amounted to $589. This produced a loss for the year of $207.

Given the financial situation at Rockwood, Frederic's immediate source for ready income remained the coal deposits. But were they really worth anything? To find out required money, and he was a man without money. So, for the time being, the coal mine project languished along with Rockwood.

Mrs. Charles Stewart (Delia Tudor), about 1815
Gilbert Stuart, American (1755–1828)
Oil on panel; 33 1/8 x 26 3/4 in. (84.1 x 67.9 cm)
Gift of Dolores de P. Danniels, Katharine de P. Gilbert and S. Tudor Leland, heirs of Elsa Tudor de Pierrefeu, 67.1159
Courtesy, Museum of Fine Arts, Boston. Reproduced with permission.

CHAPTER 6

"Circumstances" Are at Fault

"CIRCUMSTANCES" ALWAYS SEEMED TO WORK AGAINST the Tudors. So they thought. But the family was also somehow inept, not only the Judge but the children, too. Take, for example, Frederic's attractive sister Delia. In some ways, she was the most troublesome of the brood. She had gone to England with her mother in 1806. While she and her mother doted on the high society of England, which far outshone the little backwater of Boston, apparently the main purpose of the trip was to snare Delia a rich and titled husband.

Delia's philosophy was summed up in a letter she wrote to her father when she was but fourteen:

> what does it signify to be always working after money to leave a few thousand pounds to your children that they may have the benefit of living a little more at their ease and having a few old codgers say that, Bill Tudor was a grand fellow he understood the art of making money I am of opinion that let everyone work for themselves and as for the girls let them see a little of the World and I will be bound they will get their husbands worth thirty thousand pounds a year eh![1]

In this process of seeking a husband Delia proved to be extraordinarily choosey. Her mother could report home that one rich and willing old man turned out to have gout and so was rejected. The goal, of course, was an "old man"—almost any "old man." Probably the hope was that being married to a nubile young woman would encourage him to such connubial extravagances that she would soon be a widow. Delia was said to be desirable and talented, so she had the raw materials for the task. But she was a Tudor, with the typical Tudor competence. Ergo, she botched the job.

Another potential candidate for the position of Delia's husband was Samuel Williams, an American who had made a comfortable fortune for himself as the English agent of other American traders. Williams was what was styled an old bachelor. While he was more than twice Delia's age, he possessed a great practical advantage: Delia was in debt to him for £600, her father owed him £6,000, and brother William had borrowed another £300. Marriage would wipe out all that debt at the same time it set her up in fashionable society.

Samuel had already made an initial proposal to Delia just before he left on a business trip to France. But as Frederic reported to brother-in-law Gardiner in Maine, "She had the very great indiscretion to throw cold water upon his advances, but if he has any *spunk* a first rebuff will only increase his assiduity."[2] Samuel's "assiduity" was not equal to Delia's acidity. He too joined the ranks of the rejected.

Lack of a suitable husband might be the "circumstance" that hindered Delia's progress; lack of money was the "circumstance" that blocked Frederic's advance. Although the embargo ended in the spring of 1809, it was too late for any ice business that season. The next winter should prove profitable for Frederic's plans, but only if he could afford to ship ice to the West Indies. Unfortunately, hard luck still dogged him.

One day near the end of 1809 he was arrested for debt. It happened on State Street, where the merchants gathered at noon to transact business. Usually debtors were immediately taken to jail until their obligation was paid, but the sheriff kindly gave Frederic a week to raise the money. His friends and his father came to his aid in this emergency and loaned him the cash to settle up. This public arrest before the entire Boston mercantile community humiliated and discouraged Frederic. It was "abominable," he later fumed to Gardiner.[3]

Broke, and in despair, he took ship for Havana. William Savage had agreed to send him some ice cargoes. Once in Havana, Frederic succeeded in borrowing enough money to construct an icehouse. In April 1810, he received two cargoes from Boston that sold well. It pleased him to see that his new house preserved the ice as well as he had intended.

In May 1810, another competitor arrived with ice. Happily Frederic discovered that "he made so poor a hand of it that after some days he threw his ice overboard & I encountered no further difficulties in my sales."[4] He did, however, suffer first from a bout with yellow fever and then from the oppressive summer heat; in August he fled back to Boston. By that time, he had sold about $5,600 worth of ice. He then put the business in the hands of another cousin, Arthur Savage, who sold $1,800 more before the end of the season. Together they had grossed $7,400 and kept ice from the middle of April to the first of September. In addition, the authorities in Havana gave Frederic a monopoly on ice sales there. He could return home feeling satisfied that, despite his sickness, he had put his "slippery Speculation" on a firm footing at last. It "must forever remain a monument," he told himself grandiloquently, "of the advantage of steady perseverance in a project that is good in the main."[5]

Frederic's profit from the venture was just under a thousand dollars, and it did not last long. Besides his own expenses and debts, he had his father's necessities to pay for. He still did not have enough money to pursue the development of his coal mine on Martha's Vineyard, and though he remained convinced that there was coal there worth harvesting, he had to set that job aside for the moment. He arranged with Nathan Whiting to manage the operation in Havana, planning himself to stay in Boston and ship ice.

Havana proved a more encouraging endeavor for the 1811 season. Sales improved still more. Nathan Whiting, however, turned out to be unreliable. More than that, he was pocketing a percentage of each day's sales. Frederic soon replaced him with a new manager, David Day. When Frederic assessed his ice operations at the end of the season, the final tally did not look that good. He was disheartened after all the efforts he had given to this project. He spent the next winter organizing ice shipments to Havana and selling shares in the ice sales to any Boston merchants he could interest in the business. As before, he relied heavily on the assistance of his cousin William Savage in Havana.

Then, at his busiest moment in this season, a stunning blow fell. On March 9, 1812, he was arrested for the second time for debt. This time he was imprisoned in a Boston jail. On that memorable occasion he recorded in his diary that he was twenty-eight years, six months, and five days old. After seven years' hard struggle, his affairs had finally begun to look up. Piously he told himself that he would meet this new event head on and that with courage it would strengthen his spirit. Released from jail when he settled his debt, he sent a cargo of ice to Havana in April 1812, rented two cellars in the North End of Boston to store additional ice, and in June sent another load to Havana in the bark *Circle.*

War was brewing with England, which Frederic knew would lead to another embargo. By the end of June the war and trade stoppage became the reality. So once again, just when success appeared to be within Frederic's eager grasp, outrageous fortune tossed it beyond his reach. As to the cellars full of ice, he waited hopefully for six weeks and then had to open up the cellars and let his profit melt away. When he tallied up his gains and losses, Frederic found that his assets, including the South Boston land

and the Court Street and Saugus properties, came by his reckoning to $28,400. But his liabilities amounted to $38,772, owed largely to a variety of people, including his blacksmith and his tailor.

Although Frederic had to suspend his ice shipments for the duration of the war, his busy brain was not still. Why not then design a ship? So he did. Turning around the ship design conventions of the time, Frederic modeled a shallow, rounded hull deepest at the bow, with a pronounced keel at the stern. The *Boston Daily Advertiser* described the goal of Frederic's innovation: "The plan contemplates making a complete distinction between the body and the keel giving to each its separate power in the best position so that the one shall not counteract the effect of the other." The newspaper concluded that "She is built upon certain theoretical principles and must be considered as an experiment. A theory may be beautiful; but it is to be carried into effect before it can be relied upon."[6] Frederic, with his customary confidence in his own genius, reasoned that this must inevitably become the fastest ship afloat.

In December 1812, he started writing to important people in the government, soliciting them to use his invention. The list included Rep. Josiah Quincy, the secretary of the navy, and Thomas Jefferson. None responded. In maritime Boston, however, Frederic's novel concept attracted attention: he had several offers to build the vessel. By the spring of 1813, a new ship in his design had been constructed in Barker's shipyard in Charlestown. It was 66 feet long and 22 feet in breadth, with a volume of about 130 tons. Frederic christened it the *Black Swan*.

May 1, 1813, was selected for the launching. Frederic boarded his *Black Swan* for what he hoped would be a triumphant test sail. Then, as the vessel was heading for the Charles River bridge, a sheriff came aboard with an execution against Frederic for three hundred dollars. Once again the chagrined designer was hauled off to prison. Here he stayed for three days while bail was raised. Years later, he recalled this galling experience this way:

> The jail was an old one & the room in which they put me had no chair in it. It did not smell very sweet: but there was a long bench which I pulled into the middle & laid down upon my back to reflect upon what was to be done next. I smiled to think that any one should believe I was beaten, or in the slightest degree daunted in the steady purpose I had formed of accomplishing the payment of every dollars of debt & lifting myself to lord it over, if I chose, my humble creditor & his instrument. I never doubted I should accomplish, what I have accomplished. I never doubted it less, than when I was laying on the bench.[7]

To add to his disappointments, when the *Black Swan* was tested against another vessel, she failed to live up to his expectations. The rig was changed three times before Frederic felt she was ready for a trial against the brig *Rambler*, considered the fastest sailer in Boston Harbor. In the end the design proved a failure. Despite his mortification, Frederic was soon writing to his brother William, who was in England again on another adventure; Frederic asked William about the possibility of promoting his ship design in London. William replied that he had better not try it there unless he had the protection of a patent. This would cost him four hundred pounds. William also questioned if the design would be stable in heavy seas.

While Frederic was waiting out the war years in Boston, brother William was trying his hand at getting a fortune in England. William had gone to London as an agent of Stephen Higginson, Jr. Stephen was one of twelve children accumulated by Stephen Higginson, Sr., from three wives. The father had been a member of the Continental Congress and a power in Federalist Essex County politics. One of his sons, Thomas Wentworth Higginson, became a Unitarian clergyman, an active abolitionist, and eventually a commander of one the earliest black regiments in the Civil War. Stephen, Jr., was a shadowy, unsuccessful figure who would eventually end his days as a functionary at Harvard College, the kind of job to which many unsuccessful but well-connected Bostonians gravitated.

In 1810, Stephen, Jr., was a merchant helped along by his connections with Boston's mercantile aristocracy. He was thirty-seven and seeking a quick fortune. His kinsman George Cabot, who had been a United States senator from Massachusetts and thus considered himself an authority on foreign affairs, suggested that Napoleon was about to fall—five years before he actually did. Cabot thought this a good time to flood the Dutch and German markets with cheap English goods, believing that whoever had the courage to do this would make a fortune. Despite remonstrances from Stephen, Sr.—who was in London at the time—that the plan was foolhardy and dangerous, Stephen went forward with the scheme, ignoring that Napoleon and Britain were, at the time, still interdicting each other's trade.

In the summer of 1810 William went to England as Higginson's agent to organize this project. When he had been there before, he had developed connections in high places. Besides, there was not much to keep him in Boston. He had acquired some land on which there was a spring; if it were found to contain minerals, it might become a resort, as it was convenient to several towns. Before going abroad William disposed of a half interest in his spring to settle large debts he owed to several Boston gentlemen.

Like everything the Tudors touched in those years, the Higginson speculation ended in failure. The fault belonged largely to Higginson, who was none too shrewd; he had also failed financially at home, which further unbounded the European speculation. With the Higginson project gone, William looked around for something else to do. When he learned that the United States consul in London had died, he applied for the post to Secretary of State James Monroe—without success. Then William involved himself with Samuel Williams and some other Americans in the manufacture of cut nails. Machine-made nails were then something new on the market.

William and his friends opened their factory in Birmingham, England, at the same time that Frederic was designing his ship in Boston. Soon William was writing Frederic: "I am busy here having a great many workmen of different descriptions under my direction—forgers, filers, chippers, turners, model makers at the workshops on the machines—and within my own precincts, engineers, stonecutters, brick-layers, laborers & planting our steam engine."[8] He loved it all until he sent his first shipment of nails to market in the fall. Then he found that the marketplace still wanted hand-wrought nails and not machine-made ones. Clearly the Tudor luck had not changed.

When William came to figure out his finances he discovered that while he had taken in £500 that year he had paid out £250 on his expenses and another £200 toward Delia's support. That left only £50 to go towards his obligation to Samuel Williams. That debt had arisen as a result of loans William had made to his high-living sister when she was being courted by Williams.

At this point William's associates in the nail business wanted him to become a partner in the enterprise. He was tempted, for in England, unlike in America, he had comforts "which many worthy persons would roll their eyes at my giving up."[9] But it would mean a prolonged stay, from three to five years. He put the matter to Frederic: "What shall I do in returning? I suppose you will say I must answer that question myself."[10] Circumstances had always prevented William, like the other Tudors, from success. By late 1814 he was back in Boston, with no money, no job, and no prospects. Frederic was waiting for the end of the war so that he could resume his ice business.

And Delia? All this time, along with his other commitments, Frederic was bankrolling his mother and sister's sojourn in London. Their wants were far from meager. Although they were staying with various aristocratic families, thus saving board and room, they required expensive wardrobes and many other incidentals. Finally Frederic lost patience with his sister and wrote her that it was impossible for him to send the amount of money she needed, so she should pack her petticoats and furbelows and return home forthwith.[11] Still she stalled. She and her mother had been in England five and a half years when war was declared between the United States and Great Britain in June 1812.

Along with other Americans fleeing England they reluctantly returned home to the dismal and contracted rooms of Belknap Street. The trip on the *Galen* must have been an exciting one, as it arrived in Boston on September 8, 1812, "under jury rig," meaning that they had lost some of their spars to the weather. Furthermore, during the voyage, a British frigate had stopped the ship and boarded it but finally released it. Delia, back in Boston and discontented by her reduced situation, made everyone around her miserable. Ultimately, Frederic told her this was intolerable and said she should have to get married. What Delia thought of these efforts to dispose of her like a piece of meat about to go rotten is not recorded.

Fortunately, a new candidate for her hand had just appeared on the scene.

CHAPTER 7

A Hero Might Be Useful

On a Monday evening early in February 1813, five months after Frederic's sister Delia returned to Boston, the United States frigate *Constitution*, carrying forty-four guns and fresh from a cruise of one hundred days, arrived at the navy yard in Charlestown for repairs. The captain of the *Constitution* was thirty-nine-year-old William Bainbridge. He had just been appointed supervisor of the navy yard and the commander of a new seventy-four-gun ship of the line, *Independence*, which was to be built at the yard. This left the *Constitution* without a commander.

President Madison selected an officer who had been of service to him for the job. The new captain was destined to be of service to the Tudors as well. Irish-born and five feet, nine inches of genuine hero, with red hair to top it off, Charles Stewart was his name.[1] He arrived in Boston on June 23, 1813, to take command of the *Constitution*. Stewart quickly saw that the ship needed substantial repairs. The work would keep him in port for some time.

That summer Stewart was introduced to Delia Tudor. He was obviously attracted to her. She was impressed that he was an "able and gallant officer," even though his manners were, in her eyes, unpolished. However, she knew even English naval officers had a salty roughness about them.

To Frederic, Stewart represented a husband for Delia, and he despaired that another good "catch" might escape the net. So he told his sister that as she was now twenty-six and had no other interested beaus, she should not abandon this one. Although Stewart was nine years older than Delia, he was thought to have money, was reputed to be generous, and had as good a position in life as she was likely to find in a husband. In Frederic's opinion—and he was adamant in this—she should invite him back to the house. This amounted to an ultimatum.

Stewart was invited back, but it took Delia and Frederic five months to land him. Delia and Charles were married on November 25, 1813, in Trinity Church. The relatives in Maine only heard of the engagement the day before the wedding took place. Ostensibly, the ceremony was rushed because the captain had to take off to sea after the enemy. However, he remained in port a month longer—which probably did not do his marriage any good. "Never," said Robert H. Gardiner, "was a match more ill assorted." He went on to say that while Stewart was an excellent naval commander he was also "sensual, fond of gaming and of convivial company, retaining the feelings of the forecastle from which he had been elevated." Clearly not really Delia's cup of tea—in Gardiner's words, she "placed her happiness in shining in society, which she was enabled to do by the grace of her manners, her numerous accomplishments, and her acquaintance with the language and literature of the most polished nations in Europe."[2] No wonder they had quarrelled on their wedding night.

Charles Stewart
Watercolor miniature on ivory, n.d., unidentified artist.
Courtesy of the U.S. Naval Academy Museum.

They may not have been compatible, but Stewart obviously did not neglect his marital duties. When on December 31 at three o'clock in the afternoon, Stewart and the *Constitution* departed Boston for the war, he left his bride of five weeks pregnant with her first child.[3]

Stewart sailed south, made a few captures, and ran into a British frigate, which he promptly chased until he lost her in a fog. Then he discovered that the mainmast of the *Constitution* had a serious crack. He was heading back to Boston for repairs when on April 3, 1814, he encountered two large British warships that had been assigned to block Boston Harbor. It seemed likely that the British ships would capture him before he could get to safety. Stewart set all his sails, taking the chance that the mast would hold, and the chase was on. To lighten the ship they threw overboard everything they possibly could—including the rum. His chance worked and they reached Marblehead Harbor in one piece. He anchored above Fort Sewall. The British ships did not follow, fearing the cannon of the fort.

The news spread rapidly. In order to come to the *Constitution*'s aid on this Sunday afternoon, church services were canceled and the city lifted the ban on Sunday travel. Salem sent over a number of heavy cannon, and an express rider went to the navy yard in Charlestown to alert the New England Guards to go to Marblehead. They were not able to muster until 7:00 P.M., but it was discovered they had no ammunition anyway. So Commodore Bainbridge, at the yard, requested they take charge of the heavy artillery. At this point word came that Stewart had moved to Salem. Two weeks later, when the coast was clear enough of British warships, Stewart brought the *Constitution* home to the port of Boston, where spectators on the wharf greeted her with hearty cheers. Stewart, who had been away for just over four months, came home to his very pregnant wife.

With British warships patrolling their harbors, this second war with Great Britain, which had forced Frederic to suspend his ice shipments and had seemed so remote to New Englanders, suddenly was at their very front door. A third British ship arrived on May 22. It was HMS *Ramillies*, a seventy-four-gun ship of the line commanded by Rear Adm. Thomas Hardy, who was with Lord Nelson when he died during the Battle of Trafalgar. Bostonians lived in a state of constant alarm. Every time any of the squadron approached the town the citizens feared invasion.

On June 4, the *Columbian Centinal* reported that Napoleon had been defeated in Europe and banished to Elba. Boston decided to celebrate Europe's victory from tyranny with a religious service at the "Stone Chapel" on June 15—admission, one dollar. The legislature and other dignitaries, such as Judge Tudor, however, were to be admitted free. Two days before the celebration, however, more British vessels were spotted off Boston. The end of the war in Europe did not mean the end of the war in America. These were the ships that had been raiding coasters and other vessels in Massachusetts Bay. The British had sunk several of their targets, sending the prisoners to Halifax. In response to the June 13 sighting, the Charlestown Light Infantry volunteered to stand guard throughout the night.

On June 15, two thousand persons attended the religious services along with the governor and the rest of the state government. If the newspaper estimate was correct, at least fifteen hundred people must have stood outside the church, as it could not possibly accommodate the full throng. In the evening, there was a concert of music in the Colonnade, "Carbonic comets" were discharged from Boston Neck, and the State House was illuminated by 2,600 lamps. Not everyone found it appropriate to be rejoicing while the British were, as the *Independent Chronicle* put it, "illuminating our coast with bonfires of our vessels and our adjacent villages."

Six days later, the *Independent Chronicle*'s foreboding became concrete in its report that, before dawn, a boat from the blockading squadron came within a mile of the navy yard and set fire to a sloop anchored nearby. The British sent a note by a fisherman to the *Boston Patriot* boasting of their action. Perhaps this was done to take the edge off the celebration planned for the launch of the *Independence* the next day. British intelligence was good—nothing happened in Boston without its knowledge.

In July, the war news got worse. A fleet of transports arrived with troops, fresh from the battles against Napoleon. Bostonians wondered what the British were up to. Could their town be threatened? A delegation representing the governor and the Boston Town Council suggested that the *Constitution* and the *Independence* be moved out into the harbor so the town would not be a target. Others recommended sinking hulks to block the harbor. Commodore Bainbridge countered with a plan to fortify the harbor further. Stewart received orders to move the *Constitution*, which by now had been made seaworthy, so that her guns could cover the harbor approaches. At the same time, he was recruiting a new crew of 150 men. Apparently he had been living apart from Delia, for on August 30, 1814, the *Daily Advertiser* noted that "General Cushing has obtained permission for Mrs. Stewart and her family to repair to her husband and on Wednesday last they went on board the flag vessel." Shortly afterwards, Delia delivered her baby; it was a boy.

By December 1814, the British squadron was running low on provisions. The largest vessel went to Halifax to get supplies. This was Stewart's chance to escape. On December 17, in a westerly gale, the *Constitution* slipped out of the harbor unnoticed. When Stewart sailed from Boston he left his wife behind with one babe in her arms and a second on the way. Not even the British could say that the Captain was a man who neglected his opportunities.

Stewart had an exciting cruise in the North Atlantic, where he took two prizes—a brig loaded with wine and brandies and an Indiaman whose cargo brought in seventy-five thousand dollars. On February 20, 1815, he engaged two British warships, the *Cyane* and the *Levant*. The *Constitution* bested them and both ships surrendered. For years afterward the talk in navy circles was of the great skill Stewart showed in that battle.

On the morning of March 10, 1815, Stewart was in his cabin shaving. Outside there was a heavy surface fog. Above the fog bank the topsails of three large warships were reported. It took the Yankee crew of the *Constitution* only ten minutes to get her underway and a chase ensued. His pursuers were three of the ships that had been blockading Boston the summer before. As in his adventure at Marblehead, Stewart proved himself a slippery customer and got clean away. He headed down the Atlantic to the coast of Brazil, where he obtained the supplies he needed and then headed northward. All this racing about the ocean was actually an anticlimax as, unknown to the Captain, the war had been over since the day before Christmas 1814. Stewart did not learn this until April 26. Nevertheless, when he sailed into Boston Harbor eleven days later he received a hero's welcome.

Stewart went from triumph to triumph. On June 10 the Corporation of New York voted him the freedom of the city, and on August 8 Philadelphia showed its thanks with a gold-hilted sword. Delia, not one to miss this excitement, accompanied her husband to both events. Congress authorized the payment of forty thousand dollars to the officers and crew of the *Constitution* as their share of the prize money from the capture of the *Cyane*. Of course, Stewart received more than any of the others. The word was that his share was very handsome—and a rich brother-in-law was exactly what Frederic Tudor required.

With the war over, Frederic was anxious to resume his ice business. As usual, however, he was without funds. Why not approach his new brother-in-law? After all, Stewart had already tried to involve him in a couple of business ventures. In the summer of 1814, for instance, Stewart had suggested that the two of them make a fifty-fifty investment in a herd of 180 merino sheep. Frederic looked into the matter but decided it was a bad proposition and declined. Next Stewart offered him ten thousand dollars if he would transfer his business to Philadelphia, but Frederic replied that the Delaware River was frozen solid at the period his vessels would have to sail.

Now banking on Stewart's previous offers, Frederic wrote him on July 20, 1815, requesting a loan of two thousand dollars for his ice business. Receiving no reply, Frederic, with his usual lack of tact, shot off another letter to Stewart on August 4, explaining that he had only asked for that lesser sum because of the earlier offer of ten thousand dollars. To this letter there was a reply, and in Frederic's eyes, not a friendly one. Not one to give up, Frederic again wrote his brother-in-law, apologizing and saying that even if he would not offer any help, Frederic still thought most highly of him.

CHAPTER 8

Reversals of Fortune

WITH THE WAR ENDED, and no money coming from Stewart, Frederic had to look elsewhere for capital to restart his ice business. He managed to scrape up $2,100 from a variety of sources. On November 1, 1815, he sailed from Boston for Havana. Since there was another warrant out for his arrest for debt, he was pursued to the wharf by the sheriff, but he managed to escape.

His mother sent some sweetmeats and a bundle of shirts to the ship as a going-away present. When he failed to thank her for her gift, his father reprimanded him for this apparent lack of proper affection toward his mother. Frederic's response opened a floodgate of pent-up resentment toward his parents.

The latest in what Frederic perceived as a long line of affronts had occurred the previous year when he thought he could improve his chronic lack of capital for his various ventures by mortgaging the family farm, Rockwood. To make the idea palatable to the family, there had to be something in it for everyone. Father was to get $2,400 to save him from being hounded by one of his creditors; mother, $400 to $500; and younger brother Harry, $1,056. But mother wanted more—a lot more. She valued her interest in the property at $2,000 and insisted on that figure. This reduced Frederic's share of the proceeds far below what he needed. Mother thus killed the deal. Frederic loudly complained that she did not appear to be aware of what she had done to him and laid the blame for her uncooperative behavior on her nerves. He also suggested that she might be insane.

So it was money that ruled the affections of the Tudor family. None of them had any. They all needed lots of it but did not have the inclination to get it for themselves. Frederic felt that they all looked to him to supply it. His sentiments were summed up in a single sentence: "It is in vain that I put water again & again in a sieve, it will forever run through."[1]

When he arrived in Havana on November 27, 1815, he discovered that the hiatus of the war had encouraged others to venture into the Cuban ice market. Frederic's original right to hold the market exclusively, while still technically in place, had fallen by the wayside. Unaware that Frederic already held the monopoly, his Havana partner, Nathaniel Fellows, had petitioned for the right. This had opened the way for the government to pretend that the grant had expired. Other bidders were encouraged, including an ambitious adventurer named Carlos Goberto de Ceta. Goberto, audaciously claiming he could make ice in Havana, had persuaded the government to grant him the monopoly for eight years.[2]

Immediately, Fellows had tried to remedy this. It was all maneuvering and intrigue. Petitions, memorials, and documents fell like hard rain upon the different government departments. Goberto replied with his own fusillade of paper bullets. Finally the governor just threw his hands up in horror. And there the dispute stood when Frederic arrived, planning to build an icehouse.

Frederic declared he had one rule: "never to be beaten."[3] So he had a long document sent to the governing council that had granted Goberto the decree. In response the council demanded that Goberto post a bond for thirty thousand dollars to prove he could actually make ice. This was not what Frederic wanted. Fellows took Frederic to talk with one of the judges of the case, and Frederic noted drily in his diary that "*ex parte* talk with judges is the custom of this virtuous country."[4] He thought that the visit guaranteed that the decree would issue in his favor. Imagine his surprise when it favored Goberto!

When Frederic totaled up his costs, he estimated that the suit alone had cost $350, plus another $2,000 for fees and what he delicately termed "gratifications." Obviously Goberto had "gratified" more people than he had. Frederic now changed his strategy and demanded the right to import ice under the royal order that had declared the ice trade free for two years. Reluctantly, the governor, whom Frederic found was "constantly unfriendly to me although always professing a great deal of regard," granted his petition to build an icehouse and provided him with some government land on which to erect it.[5] Frederic (who was nothing if not vindictive) rejoiced at length on his "victory."

Construction of the new icehouse began on Saturday, January 27, 1816, but within a few days the government ordered the workmen to stop on the pretext that the building was too large. Patiently, Frederic ordered his carpenters to take down the roof and reduce the building size by about three feet, hoping this would satisfy "these people." Since he had instructed his agents in Boston to ship ice as if there were no problems in Havana, he could not afford many such delays. But there were to be more of them.

The three-foot reduction did not satisfy the authorities. Frederic had to take down the half-built icehouse. Then he looked for a new site on which to rebuild. The first lot he applied for the governor rejected. Instead, he offered Frederic a site that was the worst possible place. Back and forth Frederic trudged between the governor and the intendant, finding himself caught between their petty jealousies of one another. The governor then said that if Frederic would reduce the size of his icehouse by half, he could rebuild on the first site. Since that would not have accommodated the ice shipments, Frederic had no alternative but to reject that plan.

Frederic and Fellows explored the whole city. They found several likely sites, settling on a spot in St. Francisco Square. Approaching the governor with this new location, they must have "gratified" him exceedingly, because he immediately gave them permission to build there. But as Frederic discovered, no resolution went further than a "but" from the Spanish authorities.

A new wharf was being built in that area. The man in charge of the work said he wanted to pile lumber right in the spot Frederic had chosen. He made a thousand other objections, but Frederic was confident that he could take care of them. Once again Frederic and Fellows had to apply to the council for permission, which they secured. That still was not the end of the matter. On February 10 a man came to see Frederic about another site the governor now favored. Frederic thought it was excellent except that it was not as near the water as he would like. Ultimately this was where Frederic built his icehouse and the endless objections came to an end.

But what new schemes was Goberto hatching while Frederic danced this icehouse minuet? He had gone to Boston, where he was attacking Tudor's operation at its roots. He sent a letter to John Russell, owner of the brig *George Washington*, whom Frederic had contracted to carry the first ice cargo to Havana. Since they were both family men, said Goberto, he wanted Russell to know that he, Carlos Goberto de Ceta, had the monopoly for selling ice in Havana. He intended no harm, but he warned Russell that he would retaliate instantly if Russell exposed himself "by any indiscreet & imprudent measures." Goberto, the "sole contractor" for the ice business for eight years, was determined to protect his right "to the utmost of my power."[6]

Goberto had a notice to this effect published in two Boston papers; he sent a formal warning to Russell six days later. He informed Russell he had already purchased a brig and a cargo of ice, and he forbade Russell from sending out the vessel that was already loaded and ready to sail. Vessel and cargo would be seized and condemned in Havana, wrote Goberto.

Russell naturally hastened to brother Harry, who was arranging the ice shipments for Frederic. Harry gave Russell assurance that there would be no problems. Brother William, meanwhile, cheerfully informed Frederic of the goings on in Boston, including Goberto's machinations, of which he said in one breath that it could do "no harm" and in another that Harry had mortgaged Rockwood in order to finance the ice shipments. If Frederic failed "Rockwood may be added to your other losses."[7]

This must have been a great comfort to Frederic! Before he had left Boston, Frederic had arranged with John Kettell to supply him with ice. Frederic was not long gone when Kettell went out of business. Fortunately, David Stanwood, another vendor, assumed Kettell's contract. Stanwood sent Frederic his first shipment of ice on the brig *George Washington*, which reached Havana in March 1816.

Over the next five days, workmen transferred ice into the still unfinished icehouse. Soon the drain was gushing a steady stream of melted ice water. Frederic was losing two tons of ice a day. The weather was "uncommonly bad," and sales were small. In desperation, he tried covering the top of the ice with a foot thick layer of shavings. This greatly reduced the wastage.

Now he hatched a new scheme. He designed a water-cooling "jar" and persuaded the owner of a large coffeehouse in the neighborhood that selling cold water could be profitable.[8] For a cost of about two dollars, the coffeehouse would be able to sell fourteen gallons of water, averaging 216 tumblers per jar (about a four-ounce cup), for about a cent a tumbler. Frederic scurried around to interest other coffeehouses in the idea. Parreyor, the ice cream man, agreed to try a jar. Frederic sponsored Parreyor for the first week by giving him ten pounds of free ice each day. After that, he would have to buy it. Since Parreyor's establishment stood opposite the Paloma coffeehouse, Frederic anticipated that Parreyor would draw business away from them as well, which would be an incentive for the Paloma proprietor to purchase a refrigerating jar for himself. Frederic felt the invention would catch on rapidly.

The path of new inventions, however, is not altogether smooth. Introducing refrigerating jars to the coffeehouse owners was not without problems. One mismanaged the business; another thought he knew more about the process than Frederic did and did not heed Frederic's advice. Consequently, Frederic feared that this man would not only lose money but become discouraged with the new equipment. "I must teach him the way I have in view to propose to him to sell cold water & refrigerated fruit together with all his liquors cold."[9]

Frederic also had plans to persuade an ice cream man "to teach all the cooks in the city to make ice cream."[10] If he was to make a living, he had to assist all these beginners in the business of using ice profitably; only if they prospered would he. And prosper he did. Toward the end of May 1816 Frederic wrote Stanwood that "My business is going on here in the best manner. The demand is very steady & I have no interruption." In a rare compliment, he told Stanwood, "I have never had my business so well conducted as it has been done by you."

His busy brain spun off yet another idea. He had a few barrels of apples sent down from Boston packed in ice "to try the effect of the ice on them."[11] They arrived in excellent condition, not more than a couple of dozen apples per barrel having spoiled. He sold them for eleven dollars a barrel. Had the apples been better ones, they would have sold for four dollars more. Frederic jotted himself a memo: "The larger & more beautiful the apple the better price." The fruit business from both countries, he concluded, "must become an object of the first importance in the Ice business."[12]

Here was the start of the refrigerated fruit trade. Already he had recognized the many possibilities of his new business. If fruits could go south, then they could go north. Limes, pineapples, oranges, plantains, bananas, coconuts, mangoes, alligator pears—how the residents of temperate climates would snap up these tropical delicacies! What fancy prices they would pay for these unaccustomed fruits! It would all make Frederic rich! So he purchased large quantities of all of them and packed them into the hold of a supply vessel that had arrived in August. He left fifteen tons of ice in the ship to protect the fruit. Frederic arranged to have cousin William Savage, who was a resident merchant in Havana, look after his business while he was away and departed for New York with his fruit.

During the journey the weather became exceedingly hot and the heat and steam in the hold of the vessel became fierce. The crew removed the fore and aft scuttles to let the air circulate, but such was the heat that they began to worry whether the vessel might take fire spontaneously. After all, there were two or three tons of wet hay tightly rammed in above the cargo. Their apprehensions continued for several days, but as the vessel made its way north the weather cooled and the heat gradually subsided.

Arriving in New York on September 17, 1816, Frederic found that 85 percent of the limes were marketable, as were 35 percent of his 215 barrels of oranges. The rest of the cargo had rotted from the excessive heat. Yet the experiment proved that, under favorable conditions, tropical fruit could be brought to the New York market in saleable condition—and Frederic was determined to do it again. The joker in this particular deck was that the local market was glutted at the moment with native fruits; in the end Frederic lost $2,200 on this speculation. Since he had borrowed the money for the experiment at a very high interest, the loss made him a pauper again.

While Frederic was in New York, one of his father's old war cronies was visiting Boston from his home in Charleston, South Carolina. Gen. Thomas Pinckney and

Judge Tudor were both sixty-six and had met during George Washington's campaign in New Jersey in the winter of 1776–1777. The general went on to glory as governor of South Carolina. He headed a mission to England and Spain and was nominated for vice president of the United States. He had become a major general in the War of 1812 and was now a gentleman farmer with fields and rice cultivated by two or three hundred slaves. Time had been generous to General Pinckney.

That same time had frowned on Judge Tudor, who only saw the dirt of the as-yet unpaved Belknap Street when he looked out his windows. Compelled to live largely on his modest salary, Tudor found himself in a neighborhood that he deemed unsuitable to a man of his class and background—for his neighbors worked as barbers, waiters, and laundresses. Finally, as with General Pinckney, he too was surrounded by black people, as Belknap Street was in the black quarter of the city.

When William, Jr., met the tall, spare, and remarkably upright General Pinckney at a party during his visit, he brought up the possibility of marketing ice in Charleston. Pinckney, who had a good eye for a commercial speculation, said that he would be more than pleased to see Frederic and discuss the subject. Frederic immediately wrote the general, introducing the project of bringing ice to his city, and in particular hoped that the general might be able to use his political influence to promote the business. Since Frederic found himself dead broke as a result of the fruit experiment, his return to Boston had to be surreptitious—anxious creditors lurked everywhere. In spite of the fact that William had assured him in a letter that people in Boston praised his ice business venture, once Frederic arrived home he found no one ready to invest money. While he was home, however, General Pinckney's positive reply to his letter arrived in Boston. General Pinckney indicated that his nephew, Charles Cotesworth Pinckney, Jr., had an interest as well. For once, favorable circumstances made it possible for Frederic to follow quickly on this half of his opportunity

One day, while Frederic was conversing with his friend Francis Lee, the subject of General Pinckney's letter came up. Lee advised Frederic to go to Charleston, and when he learned Frederic was broke offered him an immediate $500 and another $500 in credit. In the end, Frederic took only $300. Francis Lee was a member of a successful family of Boston merchants. He was Frederic's age and closely related to other Boston First Families such as the Cabots and the Jacksons.

Frederic took Lee's advice as well as his money. But as for his departure, it would have to be accomplished in secrecy, as there were four outstanding judgments for debt against him. Having been to prison for debt before, he was not anxious to go again. So, on the first day of November, Frederic unobtrusively boarded the four-hundred-ton *Milo* and sailed from Boston to Charleston. It was fifteen years since he had last visited the city.

Charleston in 1816 was a particularly good market for luxuries such as ice. The city was just emerging from the depression brought on by the War of 1812. With all of Europe at peace, the thriving British cotton mills needed all the fiber they could get from America. As a result, the price of cotton in Charleston had doubled and the city and its port were booming. The population grew as merchants and factors flocked in to partake of the community's newfound prosperity. Frederic Tudor arrived in the midst of this busy commercial scene on November 8, 1816, clutching letters of introduction and a scheme "to raise a subscription . . . from $5,000 to 20,000, build a fine Ice House & put the Ice at a low price."[13] He composed a circular letter inviting the public to subscribe to his plan for bringing ice to Charleston. No sooner had he distributed the letter than he was visited by Charles Cotesworth Pinckney, Jr., who brought with him Langdon Cheves.

Cheves, forty years old, was a stern-looking lawyer with a high forehead and wire-rimmed glasses. He had started out in life without wealth or family name; however, he now had a secure place in Carolina aristocracy. Cheves had just returned to Charleston from a term in the United States Congress. Frederic liked him and thought that he had ability, so he was pleased when Cheves offered his services. Cheves told Frederic to forget about the subscription and instead to secure from the state legislature the exclusive right to market ice in Charleston. In fact, Cheves had already arranged for two men to bring Frederic's petition to the legislature. The next day, Frederic drew up duplicate copies of his application to the legislature, which he had endorsed by the local physician and the city council.

To be on the safe side, Frederic did not put all his eggs in the Pinckney-Cheves basket. That same morning, he conferred with a Boston merchant working in Charleston, Samuel Davenport. Thus began the back-and-forth of business that Frederic so enjoyed. The offer he put forth to Davenport traded one-third interest in the scheme for the cash necessary to begin the project. On Friday morning—the day following his application to the legislature—Frederic again saw Davenport, who agreed to the venture if he could have half the business in exchange for his money. Determined not to yield more than one-third interest, Frederic argued that he would rather cease the effort to bring ice to Charleston—for the present. The interview ended without a decision.

That evening Cheves called again, urging Frederic to leave as soon as possible, no later than Monday, for Columbia, the capital of South Carolina. First, however, Frederic felt the need to explore the business with Davenport, whose decided interest in the project he sensed. On Sunday morning Davenport sent him a note inviting him to come for a glass of wine after lunch; Frederic refused, thus putting pressure on Davenport to meet Frederic's term. The next morning he did so. However, the deal was contingent on Frederic securing a monopoly.

With the assurance that he had a prime investor and the backing of some of the most influential men in the state, Frederic set off for Columbia. It was a long, three-day ride over rough roads. The drinking water was bad the whole distance, and by the time Frederic arrived he was not only fatigued but feeling quite sick. He took to his bed for a few days, unable to keep anything down but a little water and gruel.

When he finally recovered and had an opportunity to look around he found that Columbia was a thriving river town of some two thousand inhabitants. Then he went before the legislature committee considering his petition. The exchange went badly: in an irritable mood, Frederic openly accused the committee of hostility to his undertaking, and the committee was none too friendly itself. One member asked if he intended to kick the legislature into granting the monopoly. Frederic was surprised at the antagonism on the part of the members from Charleston itself. He did not know that the delegation was split politically and that his sponsors were not necessarily in power at that moment.

Frederic did not wait to hear the fate of his petition but returned to Charleston to commence work on the icehouse. Sure of his ultimate success, he wrote Stanwood to go to Central Wharf in Boston to find Joshua Marston together with three other carpenters and send them immediately to Charleston to undertake the work. Just then, the bad news poured in.

First, he heard that the legislature had refused his petition for a monopoly. This released Davenport from his commitment. Then, letters arrived from Havana, stating that the icehouse there was to be removed—what did he want done with the materials in it? Brother William also wrote, expressing his amusement at Frederic's pursuit of monopolies. Frederic was not amused. His agent, Stanwood, wrote that $2,000 in bills on his Havana agent, Fellows, were being protested. And Harry wrote that he was being sued; would Frederic send him money? Finally, when he figured up his costs so far for his own dubious Charleston adventure, they amounted to $134.

What should he do? "I thought for a moment I must sell *my watch and escape home*—abandon my Havana business, this also & sink into utter despair."[14] It was now twelve years since Frederic had begun endeavoring to make a success of the ice business, and at every turn it seemed as if fortune only responded by giving him a good kick in the pants. Would this be the kick that finished him?

CHAPTER 9

I Rolled My Wagon On

AT A TIME WHEN EVERYTHING SEEMED AGAINST HIM, Tudor grimly determined to hang on. As he put it: "I put my shoulder to the wheel & after many a hard struggle I have rolled my waggon on."[1] This spirit was the secret of his success.

Having convinced Davenport to invest even without the monopoly, Frederic had his icehouse built in four months. It was soon filled with ice from the brig *Nancy & Mary*. By the end of the year, he had placed orders in Boston for the manufacture of some thirty small iron tubs, or refrigerators. These "Little Ice Houses," designed for family use, were another of his inventions. On a diet of three pounds of ice per day, one refrigerator could keep drinks, ice cream, and fruit in excellent condition. They sold well in Charleston. Things were now looking good there.

Not so in Havana, however. Frederic learned that David Day, his most faithful and trusted icehouse keeper, had died suddenly in February. Frederic sent his head carpenter, Joshua Marston, to fill the post temporarily. To find a permanent icehouse keeper, Frederic sailed from Charleston on the schooner *Martha* on May 20, 1817, bound for Cuba.

Frederic had plans either to sell out his Havana operations or at least to get a heavy advance of ten to twenty thousand dollars to finance his expansion elsewhere in a better climate. He arrived at the worst season of the year, after a pleasant passage from Charleston of ten days, and took the first boat ashore. Here he learned that yellow fever was rampant and that it had killed many folks—including Joshua Marston.

As a result the two other carpenters he had sent after Marston had turned around and gone home. Furthermore, the twenty-four lead boxes he had them bring with them had been seized by Spanish customs agents. It was not the welcome he had expected.

The yellow fever, Marston's death, and the departure of the carpenters had cut into the sales of his ice. But on the positive side Frederic found the icehouse full and plenty of work to keep him busy. His immediate need was a new icehouse keeper. To fill this post, he found a young man named William Wendell, originally from Boston, who had been in Havana three years. Wendell was used to the climate, appeared to be honest, and best of all, would accept a salary well below what Frederic had paid Day and Marston.

Just a year earlier Frederic had complimented his Boston agent, Stanwood, on the fine job he was doing. That was before he received Stanwood's bill. Now, convinced that he had been bilked out of eight hundred dollars by excessive fees, he told his agent so in no uncertain language. On top of this, earlier in the year Frederic had issued orders to stop all ice shipments for the time being; nevertheless, Stanwood had sent a cargo of ice to Havana.

Frederic vigorously sought a buyer for the Havana ice business. He needed to get out of there to escape the sinister hand of the yellow fever, which was killing people left and right. To find a buyer, however, was not easy. Frederic went the rounds of potential investors, but his agent, Nathaniel Fellows, was not very helpful in supplying the necessary information. It soon became apparent to Frederic that he had only one buyer—Fellows—with whom he would have to make the best bargain he could.

On June 1, 1817, Frederic dined with Fellows. At this point, Frederic found that the more he knew Fellows the more he trusted him. The two bartered back and forth for two weeks before striking a deal. The deal with Fellows turned out to be complicated: it required Frederic's continued association with the Havana business, which put his future there in Fellows's hands. All the while, the pressure was on Frederic to leave town as quickly as possible, particularly since three people at his rooming house had come down with yellow fever. But it was not just the climate and the fever that Frederic disliked; it was the people of Havana, too. As he succinctly put it, "The grossness of this people is extreme."[2]

While the negotiation with Fellows progressed slowly, Frederic was busy writing letters to potential investors in Savannah, his next targeted marketplace for expansion. Savannah was an obvious choice. It was not far from Charleston, and because it was the principal port city of Georgia, the produce of the interior flowed through it, largely rice and cotton. Peace with Britain had brought Savannah a prosperity previously unknown. With it, the residents could afford the luxury that Frederic was anxious to supply. Perhaps he could tap into that wealth and raise a subscription from the

Savannah residents, thus diffusing the risk of his new adventure. On June 19, Frederic left Havana, hoping that he never had to see it again. Seven days later he was in Savannah.

Frederic's plan to organize a subscription to raise funds for an icehouse received the welcome assistance of T. U. P. Chalton, the mayor of Savannah. But, since it was summer and all the wealthy residents had left town, Frederic met with little interest in the subscription. After a few days, he had received only one thousand dollars, so he returned to Charleston with the determination to try again in Savannah later in the season.

In Charleston, Frederic relaxed and socialized. One day General Pinckney invited him to dine with a large party on Sullivan's Island, in effect a sandbank at the mouth of the harbor. Only four miles long, and bereft of even a single tree, the island was used as a summer resort for rich Charlestonians. At least one could catch a breath of cool sea air here. Two or three hundred houses on the island were built on stilts from five to ten feet above the sand. During high seas, the water could roll under the houses while the inhabitants remained high and dry. Everywhere was sand, sand, and more sand. Not only did it cover everything outside, but Frederic found it invaded inside as well—even into the soup and mutton. If these dinners were pleasant for Frederic he also found them a bit of an embarrassment—he was constantly being thanked as the bringer of ice to Charleston.

Frederic's need for funds had by now become desperate. He began writing to anyone who might help him: first, to John Hunter in Savannah, who declined; then to Sam Davenport in Charleston—no reply; next to Sam Conant in Boston. This time Frederic offered to sell a one-half share in Charleston for $2,250—not interested. Finally he wrote to his friend Francis Lee in Boston, who also did not reply. Apparently Lee had heard of Frederic's adversity. Even though Frederic was disappointed in Lee, he did not resent his friend's refusal. It was due, he concluded, to human weakness.

At this junction, nature made up his mind for him. Malignant yellow fever arrived. As a result, Frederic's ice sales collapsed. It was more than time to leave. He booked passage for Philadelphia aboard the ship *General Wade Hampton*. Previous to leaving he wrote to Mr. De Sena, the Portuguese minister in Philadelphia, regarding bringing ice to Rio de Janeiro. When he arrived in Philadelphia, after a five-day sail, he called on De Sena. But the minister had not written due to a rebellion in Brazil. So the hope of expanding his ice business there slipped away.

On August 9, 1817, Frederic set off for New York. As soon as he arrived he wrote to Fellows in Havana: "I am afraid to go home. The underwriters have been sued to recover the lost cargo of ice & I must therefore owe my agent at least $2500 what I shall say to him or what I am to do, I know not. There is also a cargo of ice now thawing at

Boston for which I shall have to pay $3[00]–500. I beg you to consider the urgency of my situation."[3] In other words: send money!

Reluctant to go to Boston, Frederic decided he needed a vacation from the constant pressure of business. What better place than the town of Sandwich on Cape Cod? On the way there, he planned to stop and explore his Martha's Vineyard coal mine.

He set out in a small schooner called the *Fly*. His lease on the mine had two more years to run, but he had no capital to develop the business. He had invited his brother Harry to meet him at Sandwich, but Harry did not appear, and after twenty-four hours alone Frederic was almost ready to flee bucolic nature. When some "pleasant people" from Boston showed up, he ended up having a good fortnight there. Then he headed back to the worries of Boston. One of these was Harry.

During the season of 1817, Frederic had achieved quite a few objectives. He had stabilized the situation in Havana, explored the possibilities of expanding his business into Savannah, and investigated the potential of Brazil. Nevertheless, his finances remained in total disarray, and there was now the problem of what to do about Harry.

CHAPTER 10

What Shall We Do about Harry

BROTHER HARRY HAD NOT GONE TO SANDWICH, as he had more interesting things to do than debate his future with Frederic. Besides, he had already decided his future. He had cast his lot with his brother-in-law, Captain Stewart, with whom he would leave the country in 1817.

Stewart's return to Boston in 1815 coincided with the birth of Delia's second child, who was named Charles. Stewart was not a man who wasted time, and soon after the birth of Charles, Delia was pregnant once more. Now that the war was over, the growing Stewart family sought a permanent residence. The town selected, Bordentown, New Jersey, was conveniently located between New York and Philadelphia. Here, New York stagecoach passengers transferred to the boats plying the Delaware River bound for Philadelphia. Washington, D.C., was also within a two-day's journey. At this intersection, Stewart purchased a four-hundred-acre estate with a twenty-year-old farmhouse on it. He named it Montpelier.

Stewart set about making his farm a great man's estate. He added a second story to the house. Inside he installed marble mantels and fine wainscotting, which gave the place an air of elegance. He planted trees and began to raise fine, imported breeds of cattle. By the summer of 1816, Delia and her family were in residence in Montpelier. Then tragedy struck. Their oldest boy died from accidental laudanum poisoning by his nurse. Then their second son, Charles, almost met the same fate.

Delia was devastated. To help her daughter recover, Delia the elder came from Boston to spend the winter. As for Stewart, he found having one Delia underfoot was more than enough; having two was not a double blessing. Later that year their first girl was born; she was named Delia for her mother and grandmother. Now there were three Delias in Stewart's household, and all were destined to annoy him, Frederic, Robert Gardiner, and eventually the entire British government.

Throughout 1816 and 1817, Stewart made frequent trips to Philadelphia and Washington, where President Madison and then President Monroe used him to consult on naval matters. Madison even offered him a post in the cabinet. Stewart refused. He wanted, with his youth and naval rank, "glory." Delia prized glory as well.

Where was Stewart to find glory? The United States maintained a squadron of warships in the Mediterranean. Isaac Chauncy was their commodore. Since there was considerable friction between the current commodore and his command, President Monroe decided to find a replacement. He offered the job to Stewart. By the spring of 1817, Stewart had made up his mind to accept it. This was Harry's opportunity, too.

The youngest member of the Tudor family, Harry was now twenty-six and hanging around Boston unemployed. So far, all of the family attempts to find him employment had failed. In 1810, when he was nineteen, the family had suggested a legal career, but he had no interest in this, and for once, Frederic agreed. Said Frederic, a poor young man in Boston would only find the law both degrading and disgusting. Far better, thought Frederic, to spend three years in a counting room, where the time would pass pleasantly and one could be sure of success, even though he might have to stoop a little to get started. The business world was "a free & manly way of getting a living." But a lawyer spent his life "receiving half dollars & nine pences from Irishmen, pickpockets & whores."[1]

Frederic had put his advice where his money was. In 1811 he had wanted to expand from his proven base in Havana and add Kingston, Jamaica, as a second outlet. He needed someone to go to Jamaica and start the ice business there. Who better than young Harry? If successful the project would double his business and income.

The Jamaican enterprise had started off on the wrong foot, however, and never improved its traction. To begin with, Harry overslept on the morning of his departure and nearly missed his ship. Frederic was so angry that he almost tore up Harry's commission and canceled the venture. Once he finally reached Jamaica, Harry proved as awkward in business matters as brother William. Discouraging letters reached Frederic from Jamaica, followed by a draft upon Frederic for a thousand dollars. But when the schooner *Active* left the port of Boston on April 11, 1811, with a shipment of ice to Harry, Frederic gave a sigh of relief. At least this time some of the risk of the project had been spread out: $7,500 worth of other people's money was invested in the venture along with his own. This turned out to be fortunate because the *Active* was shipwrecked off Port Royal. Frederic saw a silver lining in the cloud: "I saved the payment of freight at the expense of the cost of the ice."[2]

This Jamaican debacle had made Frederic change his mind about Harry's future as a businessman. Everybody in Boston was losing money in trade and too many stores and shops were either shut up or for rent. Frederic saw nothing but gloomy prospects for himself if a war came, to say nothing of Harry's future. For his part, Harry was happy to disassociate himself from his brother Frederic's business ideas. He was content to be with his mother at Rockwood playing at farming—even if they were not particularly successful at that occupation. Brother William agreed that Harry was "incapable of making the continued efforts necessary to succeed" in anything. "He passes twelve hours in bed & is a first rate player of billiards, smokes, takes snuff & chews tobacco. Of course his appearance corresponds to these practices & exhibits the first stage of the low tavern debauchee."[3] William nevertheless thought that Harry had "fine talents & principles," even though he had seldom seen "a more melancholy wreck of a young man." Perhaps Frederic could find some way to make use of Harry and repair "this heedlessness, sluggishness, encrusting stagnation of body & mind."[4]

By 1817, Harry's financial situation had become desperate. He wailed to Frederic that he needed two hundred dollars immediately or he might have to go to jail. He implored his brother to think of the disgrace that that would bring to the family. Frederic replied tartly that Harry would have to choose between "Brandy & Water or business."[5] He bluntly told Harry that he had "such an alacrity at sinking it was a mere waste of exertion to attempt to raise you up. The moment the prop is removed down you fall."[6] Still, blood is thicker than brandy, and in spite of the apparent hopelessness of Harry's situation, Frederic sent him fifty dollars.

Along with his other faults, Harry was, according to the standards of the time, unpolished. However, there were friends in Boston who were taking care of that fault. They took him out to a practice ball, then to a grand ball at the Hulls' in Charlestown, and after that to a smaller evening party. In this way his friends attempted to turn Harry into a gentleman. Brother William wrote to their mother that "Elizabeth tells him that he must not stretch out his legs, that he must not fold his hands over his head or stick his thumbs under his vest."[7]

It was important for Harry to acquire the look of a gentleman, because sister Delia had a job in mind for him: he was invited to join Stewart's squadron on the Mediterranean cruise as judge advocate. Not that he had any training to be a judge advocate, but a little nepotism can go a long way. And a brother-in-law who can give employment to an idle member of the family is a useful thing to have. On October 7, 1817, Harry left Boston in the stage and arrived in Bordentown two days later. By November 17, he was on board the USS *Franklin*, a 188-foot, three-deck ship of the line, at Annapolis and by November 23 at sea. His first disappointment took place soon after he boarded the ship. He learned that he was not to become the judge advocate. So there he was, without a job, but sailing off to the Mediterranean.

As for Delia Stewart, if she was going to be on her own for two years, she had no intention of being buried down on the farm. Her first thought was to spend the winter in Boston with her family, but her mother talked her out of that. Next she wrote to her husband for permission to live in a boardinghouse in Philadelphia. She argued that the expense would be trifling and her comfort much enhanced. Then, Delia being Delia, she did not bother waiting for his permission but went off to Mrs. Gale's boardinghouse in Philadelphia with her children. Their accommodations were luxurious; each of the children had a personal attendant, the family had its own cook, Delia had books to read, and the Commodore had bills to pay. In April they returned to the farm.

Back home, Delia was in charge. Mother came to stay for the summer, remaining through August 1817. Frederic stopped in on his way from Charleston to his coal mine on Martha's Vineyard. When her mother left, Delia was alone again—or was she?

The same summer Stewart bought Montpelier, another famous personage acquired an estate nearby. On June 16, 1816, the Comte de Survilliers fell in with Dr. William Burns on the road to Bordentown. At the time, the count was living in a rented house in nearby Burlington and was looking for a more permanent residence. Dr. Burns told him that one of his friends, Stephen Sayer, had his estate up for sale in Bordentown. Situated between the Delaware River and Crosswick Creek, it consisted of a large mansion house on 211 acres. It was just the thing. The count bought it and proceeded to develop the house and gardens into an extraordinary showplace, which he named "Point Breeze."

The good Comte de Survilliers, as it turned out, was neither good nor a count. He was an ex-king. The ex-king of Spain to be exact. His real name was Joseph Bonaparte, elder brother to the celebrated Napoleon. After the disaster at Waterloo, he fled France under an assumed name and landed in New York in August 1815. Nor was he a gentleman. In fact an anti-Bonaparte who was traveling in the New Jersey area when he heard Joseph was there referred to him as a "shop keeper" living handsomely off stolen money. Society saw him, however, not as an ex-shopkeeper but as a wealthy ex-king who mixed with his neighbors. Commodore Stewart soon became a close friend.

The count had a weakness for the ladies. His wife and children had remained in Europe, so he was alone, but not lonely. He soon took his major domo's wife as his mistress, along with any other unattached lady he fancied. His friend the Commodore was away, but his friend the Commodore's wife was not. She filled the bill as a friend for the count. She was talented and some thought beautiful. The count filled Delia's bill as well. Rich, a bit old at forty-eight perhaps, but handsome. A somebody who was sophisticated as well, not a rough sailor.

Once his identity was out, the count attracted all the famous who stopped by on their way through Bordentown. This was too good to be true, as far as Delia was concerned. However, to keep up with such heady company cost money that Delia did not have. The income Stewart had left to provide for her proved insufficient. So when she needed money, which was frequently, she sold off anything she could find on the farm. When she had sold everything, the count was ready to provide.

Meanwhile, the Commodore and Harry were innocently on route to England. Harry kept a diary of his adventures. His entry for November 20, 1817, would have pleased Frederic, indicating a sense of developing maturity:

> I have been for some time more rational and seen things as old men see them, than I ever was before; I have lost all enthusiasm, all romantic hopes, the scenes of my future life appear to me naked and bare, divested of the varying hues and fantastic shapes which give to 'dull reality of this world' the picturesque appearance of the clouds at sunset. And while I view myself and my fortune in this clear light of truth, I cannot discover any means by which chance or heaven itself can extricate me from what seems to be my inevitable doom, poverty and obscurity. I shall go out of the world with many virtues and many talents undeveloped.[8]

That he was a full-blown Romantic, and not just pretending, is indicated by a diary entry five days later, when he described a lovely twilight scene: "It is not long since such a situation would have awakened inexpressible feelings in my breast, and my spirit would have travelled on every moonbeam to the top of every curving billow and rode on every flying cloud. These feelings cannot survive the morning of life; and this world affords nothing to replace them."[9] By December 16 the ship anchored off Cowes, and Harry noted that their voyage had taken just twenty-seven days from the capes of Virginia.

The *Franklin*, a seventy-four-gun ship of the line, was closely examined by British vessels in the harbor as she was the first American warship to call there since before the War of 1812. The new minister to the Court of St. James's had traveled with them, and during the voyage the officers, including Harry, dined with him. Three days after they arrived, he went ashore with a proper salute from the guns. The rest of the party, including Harry, were to leave for London on December 21 in two port chaises. They left Portsmouth promptly and arrived in London that night, coming in by Hyde Park Corner. They put up at the Petersburg Hotel in Dover Street, Picadilly. Harry, on this first visit to Great Britain, was very impressed with the country and its comfortable customs. The next morning he became a typical tourist and rushed around to take in all the famous sights. He strolled through St. James's Park, looked at the outside of Westminster Abbey, walked into Westminster Hall and over Westminster Bridge, and finally went to a theater in Covent Garden to see a production of *Belvidera* starring a Miss O'Niel.

On Monday he went into the city by Charing Cross and the monument, through Temple Bar, and down to St. Paul's. He put his head into its dome, but could see little or nothing below on account of the smoke. Then it was down to the Tower of London, which he examined from top to bottom. He was duly impressed by the two hundred thousand muskets and three or four hundred thousand other arms in the Tower's military collection. He stopped last at the armory of ancient kings and gaped at the crown jewels. He returned to his hotel through East Cheap, but could not find the Boar's Head pub that he sought. That night, he saw the actor Edmund Kean at Drury Lane in Shakespeare's *Richard III*. The poet John Keats, writing to his brothers that day from Hampstead, reported that he had seen Kean in that play. Keats thought that he had given an excellent performance. Harry left us no critique on Kean's acting. Harry celebrated Christmas Day by attending services at Westminster Abbey. Ultimately, he decided that if he possessed a large income he would not mind living in this London.

On December 27 the party returned to Portsmouth, and on the last day of the year the Commodore entertained a Russian admiral who was also in port. That gentleman observed that the U.S. Navy was a thousand years ahead of the Russian navy and five hundred years ahead of the British Royal Navy. That must have pleased the Americans. Shortly afterwards, they set sail for the Mediterranean and on February 5 arrived in Syracuse. Up to this time, Harry had been acting as the judge advocate since the regular judge advocate had not yet joined the ship. When he came aboard at Syracuse, Harry was left with nothing to do but enjoy the voyage; near its end, however, when the Commodore deposed the regular judge advocate for ignoring one of his orders, Harry found himself reappointed to the position for the balance of the cruise. The remainder of the voyage fulfilled all of Harry's hopes for the experience.

He spent the whole of the next year entertaining as well as visiting the exotic ports of North Africa. Although he had not expected to find yellow fever in Spain or plague on the Barbary Coast, he remained in good health and spirits, even when the squadron was quarantined. He wrote to his mother that, "had fortune pondered ever so long to contrive what good turn she could do me, she never could have found a better than . . . sending me upon a two year excursion to the Mediterranean."[10]

So it might appear to young Harry, but his brother Frederic held a less positive view of the trip. As Frederic had written their father a year earlier:

> It appears by one of Harry's letters that he has the intention of returning early in the spring and I am sorry to see he is talking about seeing remark-

> able places, fine arts, etc. During the winter—what his intentions are I know not but in his present situation habits & views, it appears to me he is utterly unfit to commence as a practicing lawyer in Boston; especially as he is without that kind of regular, business industry, so essentially necessary. I have already tried to aid him in the arrangement relative to the Rockwood estate & I was sorry to find him so weak as he turned out in that transaction. Seeing however that he necessarily must want assistance I have been thinking what I could do for him.[11]

By the time Harry returned to Boston with Commodore Stewart in April 1820, Frederic had made up his mind. He sent his brother to Rockwood to be a farmer!

Harry proved to be a poor farmer. One of his first acts after his voyage was to have most of the trees at Rockwood cut down, including an enormous pine tree "which stood alone on the top of the Hill"[12] and which Frederic loved. As Frederic explained to his mother, "Everything is bleak & bleak."[13] So Harry continued to make a mess of things, and even though three years had passed, his future was still unresolved. As far as his parents and siblings were concerned, they still faced the question: What shall we do about Harry?

CHAPTER II

Striking the Second Blow

WHILE HARRY WAS ON HIS TOUR OF EUROPE, Frederic was still struggling to establish his ice business on a firm foundation. His stay in Boston during the summer of 1817 was a short one because of his creditors, and when he left for New York he "was again obliged to leave . . . in the manner of an escape."[1] Not that he was without funds, as he received remittances from Fellows in Havana, but he had a better use for this cash than to pay off his debts. In this mood he wrote to John Hunter in Savannah and engaged him to act as his contact there until he could set up a permanent establishment. "I have determined to make a beginning under the expectation that the subscription will eventually be nearly or quite filled."[2]

From New York he went to Charleston; it was a long voyage of twelve days. During these endless, boring days he worried about his prospects in Savannah. Was there really a market for ice there? Savannah was only a quarter the size of Charleston and during the summer most of those with money left. He calculated that there would only be three months of good ice sales. At Charleston, on the other hand, all the wealthy planters came into the city in the warm season, and in spite of the fact that the fever had sent away many of the local residents in the summer of 1817, ice sales were good. But perhaps three months of an excellent market would be enough—at the moment, Savannah was booming.

Delightful weather greeted Frederic on his arrival in Charleston. "To see the roses in full bloom in the gardens & green pease & string beans on the table at dinner is pleasing as well as refreshing."[3] He was in a wonderful spirit. During the year since his last stay in Charleston, he had put on fourteen pounds and been exercising regularly. Clearly he felt that his "waggon" was rolling onward and upward.

When winter arrived, and the permanent population of Savannah had returned, Frederic decided to begin his pursuit of capital there once again. Here, however, he was received "with condescension & complaisance," which caused his good mood to vanish.[4] "This state of things," he wrote in his ice diary, "makes me more haughty than it is decent for me to be. . . . Whether I succeed or not here I do not intend to leave the place with the character of a humble unsuccessful solicitor. I mean to have it understood that what I ask is to confer as well as receive a favor."[5] He shared this attitude on December 18 with his local contact, John Hunter, who at first hardly wanted to see him. At the conclusion of their meeting, however, Hunter had changed his tune—he now intended to help Frederic push forward his plans.

The new year, 1818, found Frederic back in Charleston, summing up his situation in his diary. In the end, he had left Savannah empty-handed. None of his plans had borne fruit. But he did not let himself feel defeated and wrote in his diary in a bold hand: "He who gives back at the first repulse and without striking the second blow despairs of success, has never been, is not & never will be a hero in love, war or business."[6]

Frederic elected to spend the winter at Charleston. Now thirty-five, in excellent health "although care & anxiety have shed a premature growth of gray hairs upon my head," he firmly "resolved to push forward upon success & to endeavor to reap every advantage which the business shall offer to me."[7]

In New England, the weather was warm most of the winter season, so warm that he was unable to cut additional ice to send south. One shipment, which went on the ship *Luna*, was all he had to send to Havana. Thus Frederic worried about what would happen to his business in Havana if an accident befell the *Luna*. Sixty-three days after it sailed from Boston it had still not reached Havana. He became convinced that it had sunk in a storm. He was almost correct. After only four days at sea, *Luna* lost its masts; after forty-six days, it limped into the island of St. Barts, far to the east of Cuba, where the vessel and its cargo were sold. Back at home Frederic somehow found enough ice to ship out a second cargo on the *Cicero*. Unfortunately, that ship foundered—the fate of many wooden ships in those times.

In the midst of all this gloom, his brother-in-law Robert Gardiner wrote him a letter in which he shared his current philosophy of life. This, in turn, put Frederic in a philosophical vein. He wrote Gardiner: "It is more than ten years since I became satisfied in my mind of the absolute worthlessness of our existence here & the difficulties I have passed through . . . have not had a tendency to lessen or soften this opinion."[8] He then went on to dismiss the religious beliefs of both the Arians and the rigid Calvinists, especially those who subscribed to the Hopkinsian creed. His own view was "that too great sacrifices of present felicity should not be made today for the benefit which is to be derived to us tomorrow."[9] In the end he had faith not in the golden rule but in wealth. That was an individual's first necessity and it alone provided "full enjoyment of this life."[10] It alone brought a man respect. And that was very important to Frederic Tudor.

Havana might be a disaster that year for lack of supply, but the sale of ice in Charleston doubled, and the sale of his small refrigerators did as well. This gave Frederic enough capital to test the Savannah market. He had several shipments of ice sent to his agent there, a young man named Paddleford, as an experiment; he also considered and was interested in the feasibility of building an icehouse there. Later, when Frederic evaluated this project, he decided that the undertaking in Savannah worked pretty well and so he instructed Paddleford, who he felt was doing an excellent job, to look about for a place to build the icehouse.

With the approach of summer and the danger posed by the various diseases associated with this season, Frederic decided to return to Boston. At the end of a busy summer back home, he concluded that he must make one more trip south to establish firmly his business there. Yet, somehow the visions of success that had been so vivid in Boston Harbor had a way of turning into mirages once he arrived in the South.

When Frederic arrived in Savannah on December 3, 1818, he found that Paddleford had not yet found an icehouse site. John Hunter, who had joined Paddleford during the search, offered them a lot he owned for $500. Frederic, however, remembered that he had been offered this same site the year before for $200. After grumbling about this in his diary, he poked about himself and found a site for $200. So much for Mr. John Hunter!

On the social side, Frederic had come into Savannah as an unknown. He did not have family friends in high places, as he did in Charleston. Consequently, Savannah's elite, perceiving him as no more than a seller of ice, ignored him. He felt that as a gentleman and a stranger to the community he deserved far better treatment. But perhaps they did not ever realize that he was indeed a gentleman. Their attitude disturbed Frederic greatly, and he lashed out against them in his ice diary. Charleston society was more polished, he thought. Charlestonians were an older, richer, better-bred society, and had proper reverence for old gentility. Savannah's leading citizens, he consoled his ego, who thought they epitomized fashion, did not even know how to treat respectable people—namely one Frederic Tudor. Then he confessed to his diary, "I have been surprised to find how much I have been affected by so insignificant a thing."[11]

Could Frederic's sour attitude have stemmed, in part, from poor health? In January 1819 he came down with jaundice, which he attributed to exposure to damp weather. The jaundice turned his body "a delightful gold color."[12] A week later he credited his sickness to "over exertion & anxiety."[13] He had been working hard on his icehouse, the construction of which he watched closely because he did not want to lose any of the time of the laborers. The pulverized charcoal used for insulation made the work dirty and dusty—and dangerous, too, because it could easily catch fire. "I have been driving on here with 30 workmen of different kinds for nearly two months past & have nearly accomplished a fine brick fire proof building capable of holding between 12 & 13,000 square feet of Ice. Enough to keep all Georgia cool for some time."[14]

He was still feeling very isolated and upset at the way Savannah society treated him. His only friend seemed to be his business associate, Harlen Kimball. As he grew to know Kimball, Frederic expressed anger about the way he was being ignored. Kimball was sympathetic. When he compared Kimball to his man in Havana, that rascal Nathaniel Fellows who was always badgering him, there was no contest. As he put it, "The excellence of Mr. Kimball's character is very striking."[15]

Frederic had started business in Savannah at an interesting time in the city's history. Between his initial visit and this current stay, the city had begun to undergo a dramatic transformation. This was partly due to the unprecedented prosperity Savannah's planters were enjoying. They were growing rich and so turned their attention to rebuilding their city. During Frederic's first trip, for example, he had noticed that everything looked temporary and that the buildings were almost all wooden. Now brick buildings showed up throughout the city. They owed their existence not only to the increase in wealth but also to the arrival from Liverpool, England, of an attractive and witty twenty-three-year-old, William Jay.

Jay left England for Savannah in 1817, the year of Frederic's first visit. His move came about through a family connection: his sister had married Robert Bolton, a Savannah merchant stationed in London, and one of Bolton's kin, Richard Richardson, needed a new house. Jay received the job. He prepared the plans in England and came over to Savannah to supervise the completion of the building. Frederic, when he saw the house under construction, found it admirable—fit for an American city. It was said around town that Richardson's house had cost him forty thousand dollars. Before long, Jay was besieged with requests for new houses.

Not only did Jay design houses, he also planned a new Presbyterian church and a theater; both buildings were finished by the time of Frederic's 1819 visit and just in time for a financial panic that swept the country that year. Then, early in 1820, a fire destroyed the business section of the city. Jay made suggestions concerning the rebuilding after the fire, but his patrons no longer had the funds to employ him. So Jay moved to Charleston. Frederic thought it all too bad for Savannah because "from magnificent house will rise more dignified manners."[16]

By early February 1819, Frederic had received 160 tons of ice, which filled two-thirds of his new icehouse. He was ready for business. Despite a recession, by May 1819 Frederic pronounced his speculation in Savannah a success. He was selling more ice here than in Charleston. He commenced sending ice up the Savannah River to Augusta by boat. He also sent it up the Altamaha River to the flourishing town of Darien some sixty miles inland. Soon the people of nearby Beaufort, South Carolina, were anxious to get ice.

On the morning of the Fourth of July, Frederic sat aboard the brig *Almira* on his way home to Boston writing in his diary. "I leave Savannah with no inconsiderable satisfaction as everything goes with tolerable smoothness. But best of all, 'I think I shall when I once more place my foot on land quit it no more.'" It had been a most successful season. The prospects of his three establishments—Savannah, Charleston, and Havana—were promising. He hoped to extend his enterprise to yet another city—New Orleans—in the fall of 1819. His success was assured, of that he was confident. Most important of all, the "vagrant voyaging life" was to end, with no more "severe sacrifices of personal convenience." All this he had accomplished before his thirty-sixth year of age.[17]

This great success he was eager to share with his father, the confidant of so many letters over the years. When he arrived in Boston a rude shock awaited: his father had died on July 8, while Frederic was still at sea. "He died without any call to the Physician or trouble to nurses. He was a little (as was thought) indisposed four days preceding his death & while laying on the bed, conversing with his accustomed hilarity & pleasantry suddenly gasped & expired: dying as he always wished he should without trouble to others or pain to himself."[18]

The effect on the family was considerable. They all shed tears for the loss of their parent. But the mark it left on Frederic was deeper. He lamented this loss "more acutely than I should do any person now in existence." Part of his whole desire for worldly success came from the anticipation of sharing it with his father. "He is dead & with him much of what can make life to me agreeable."[19] Nevertheless, the second blow had been struck, and for the moment forgetting death and depression, it appeared to have been most successful. It looked as if Frederic was about to become a hero in business. Would he be a hero in love and war too?

CHAPTER 12

The Worthless Cousin and the Unfortunate Schemer

FREDERIC SEEMED TO COLLECT PROBLEM PEOPLE. As if his own family members were not difficult enough, he reached into the large Cabot family and pulled out Stephen Cabot. Five years younger than Frederic, he had had a speckled career. He was related to many prominent Boston merchants including his father, the very successful Sam Cabot, Jr. He worked for two of his cousins, the merchants Henry and Francis Lee, but proved unsatisfactory. Indeed it was Henry Lee who referred to him as "our worthless cousin."[1]

This was the man Frederic chose in the spring of 1817 to be his representative in England, where he still hoped to obtain a monopoly to sell ice in Jamaica and other British West Indies possessions. His assessment of Stephen Cabot to brother William was a lot more complimentary than Henry Lee's. "Mr. Cabot is a connection . . . of Sam Williams who is under particular obligations to his father. He has also a very particular friend who had weight & influence where it may be useful & he is a gentleman who will do honor to any recommendation or introduction you may or can give him. He will also probably have letters from the British Minister etc. etc."[2] Frederic held this good opinion, however, before Stephen worked for him.

Stephen went to Charleston in April 1817 to receive instructions directly from Frederic. These included information about his brother William's fruitless trip on the same purpose to Europe in 1806. Frederic's relationship with William, like every other member of his family, was very much an on-and-off thing. In 1817, it was off. That spring, Frederic wrote to William that "Our good will towards each other may now be considered at an end, in consequence of the construction you have thought proper to put on my best intentions."[3]

By his "best intentions" Frederic meant an annuity he kept proposing to set up for William, which never materialized due to Frederic's continued shortage of funds. Now, however, he needed William to get documents for Stephen to take abroad. So good relations or not, Frederic proposed a treaty: "As you have decided that we cannot be friends, let us be decent in our disagreements."[4] William was "decent" and gave Frederic what he wanted, but he told his brother that he thought applying to the British government was a waste of time. The war with Napoleon was scarce two years past, international trade was still at a standstill, and British ship owners had lots of empty holds and would not welcome any proposals calling for American vessels to be engaged in trade and shipping. He suggested that Frederic instead approach the French authorities, where he felt there was real possibility for success. During his stay in Paris in 1806, William had won an "exclusive patent" for the islands of Martinique and Guadeloupe for ten years. This had now expired, but perhaps it could be renewed.

Stephen went off to England in the spring of 1817. Frederic received his first report from him while he was in Charleston that July. It was full of complaints. Frederic sent back a soothing reply, and to encourage Stephen he listed all his current successes—putting as good a face on everything as he could—and his plans for the future, which included New Orleans and Brazil. He went so far as to suggest that Stephen might just be the man to open up this new territory for him. Frederic heard nothing more from Stephen until October, when he reported that William had been right. The British refused to give an exclusive patent, but as William had suggested, he decided to try his luck in Paris. That gamble would cost Frederic, if he failed, about five or six hundred dollars.

When Frederic arrived back in Charleston that November, he found another letter from Stephen, who, contrary to Frederic's expectation, had succeeded in obtaining a ten-year exclusive privilege for Martinique and Guadeloupe. Maybe he was not such a worthless cousin after all. By March 1818, Stephen was in Martinique. The exclusive privilege he obtained in Paris had to be ratified by the colonial governments, which they did at Martinique. Then he went to Guadeloupe on the same mission. By June he was back in Boston. Frederic was on his way back, too.

Upon his arrival there, Frederic found Stephen quite depressed, with good reason. That January, Frederic had written to Stephen's father, Sam Cabot, Jr., that in spite of Stephen's expectation he did not intend to go forward with the West Indies project that winter. He gave as an excuse that to build icehouses there in the winter would risk the danger of poorly constructed structures; the real reason, however, was his lack of money.

What to do with Stephen, now broke and unemployed? Poor Stephen had used his own money to pay for his trip to Europe and the West Indies, and his mission had been successful. Stephen's friends were rightly furious at the way Frederic was treating him. Frederic, however, did not have the means to help him, so Stephen had to cool his heels, remain unemployed, and depend on his friends for charity. Frederic wrote in his diary: "C[abot] wished me to explain to his friends. I told him I would not & that his own best [interest] was to rely on me & treat all jesting, as well as sober advice, of persons (necessarily ignorant) on the subject of ice with entire indifference & scorn."[5]

Frederic followed this advice himself. "I put all their opinion at a non plus. . . . I walk & bowed & smiled & talked like other men when they feel within them that they stand firm & need neither the assistance, the good wishes or money of anyone."[6] He even took a trip to Sandwich, Cape Cod, for several days to fish, swim, exercise, and relax. This lifted his spirits and prepared him for the busy and stressful summer. Still, the pressure was on Frederic to do something to aid Cabot. Fortunately, that summer he received $5,600 in insurance money from the loss of the *Luna* and *Cicero*, plus another $5,000 in returns from Davenport. That meant that he could proceed with building the Martinique and Savannah icehouses after all. Accordingly, he made an arrangement with Stephen to manage the business in Martinique. Stephen would get three-eighths of any profit they made as well as $2 a day.

From his counting room, which Frederic had hired at Wheeler's Point on the Boston waterfront, he directed this new venture in Martinique. He purchased wood in Maine and shipped it to Boston to make frames for the new icehouse. Other materials were assembled so that a complete package could be shipped out together with carpenters, who would supervise its construction with local labor. Along with the Martinique icehouse, Frederic gathered enough materials for one in Savannah. The total cost was $15,000. As usual, he was short; he only had $10,000. He pressed Fellows, in Havana, to remit the balance.

With the decision to go forward in Martinique, Frederic contracted Silas Marean a one-quarter interest if he would advance $5,000. As an inducement, Frederic guaranteed that Mr. Cabot would be there as his personal supervisor. Also on the spot would be his man John Wade Damon, whom Frederic valued highly, felt to be honest, and depended upon. Unfortunately, once again Frederic was wide of the mark. Damon was, in the end, to cost him many thousands of dollars and much aggravation.

Stephen sailed on October 25, 1818. Frederic had returned south to supervise another venture that August. Not until January 1819 did he receive news that Stephen had arrived safely in Martinique and had located the right site for the icehouse. Damon was busy supervising its building. On March 29, the schooner *America* brought Stephen his first cargo of ice. A second cargo in the brig *Albert* left for Martinique the day the *America* arrived. Early sales were small but were improving. When Frederic returned to Boston from Savannah in July, not only did he find that his father had died, he also found Stephen there as well. Stephen was in a buoyant mood—the ice business in Martinique was a great success. Therefore, he insisted he should now have a greater share in the business. But Stephen soon learned what it meant to deal with Frederic Tudor; his pay remained the same.

A new problem diverted the men from this debate: the stock of ice in the Martinique icehouse threatened to run out in the busiest part of the season. Where could one find ice in July? Certainly not in New England's ponds or rivers. But there were places on the globe where ice remained year round, one of which was not too far from New England: Labrador. Stephen hired a Maine captain to sail there and bring back ice for Martinique. Captain Hadlock left Castine in the brig *Retrieve* on August 13, heading north. He ran his vessel along the shore looking for a suitable iceberg to capture. Several were too large for their purposes, but by September 11 they saw a likely prospect grounded in forty fathoms of water. They hove to beside it.

Shortly they commenced cutting and loading its ice, until a gale sprang up. They weighed anchor and made for a nearby harbor. When the gale subsided, they found another iceberg near them, and they started to cut ice from it. The work was not easy. These ice islands stood high above the water, they were unsteady—a single misstep could land a careless cutter in frigid water—and it was difficult transferring the ice from the bergs to the vessel. To make the work easier, part of the crew worked on the berg, prying large blocks of ice loose with crowbars and axes and then sliding them into the water, after which the rest of the crew hoisted them aboard ship. It was ingenious, but by cutting on only one side of the iceberg they unbalanced it. When they were nearly loaded, the berg suddenly rolled over. A spur of ice projecting twenty to thirty feet from it rose under the vessel and lifted it about six feet, starting a leak. The captain thought he would have to unload his ship in order to save it, but after pumping for about a day the leak subsided. The crew finished loading from the same berg. Fully loaded, Captain Hadlock's vessel arrived in Martinique in late October. He received $1,700 for his efforts.

Before he left Martinique for Boston in the autumn of 1819, Stephen had drawn on Frederic for $1,200. When the bill was presented, Frederic refused to pay, as he had not authorized it. But the creditor was waiting with an arrest warrant for debt when Stephen arrived in Boston. Obviously, Frederic could not let Stephen go to jail, so he was forced to pay.

Stephen now pressed Frederic to proceed with an icehouse for St. Thomas in the

Danish Virgin Islands. Frederic agreed and early in November Stephen set off for the island with the icehouse. It turned out to be a bad time for new initiatives: the depression that had started in 1819 was well established by the spring of 1820. Frederic's business suffered. To make matters worse, Stephen overspent on St. Thomas. Frederic had by now advanced $5,000 for the operations at Martinique and St. Thomas and had received nothing back. Perhaps, the gossips said, Stephen's attention was diverted by a brown-eyed local lass. After all, he was an eligible bachelor. The rumor around Boston insinuated that he was considering matrimony. As for every occasion, Frederic had advice—one bachelor to another. It was short and sweet: if you marry a lady from abroad, that's where you should live!

The continued poor sales at Stephen's establishments bothered Frederic. His representative was obviously doing something wrong and Frederic thought he understood what it was: he was trying to exploit the wrong market. So Frederic explained his standard strategy: "The [ice] creams are the first great object & thereafter *cold* drinks at the same price as warm." Frederic advised Stephen to get one or two barkeeps to accept free ice and serve cold drinks to their customers at the same price as warm—the ploy that had worked in Havana in 1816. "A man who has drank his drinks cold at the same expense for one week can never be persuaded to drink them warm again. . . . When we have persuaded 100 persons by means of our *same price* plan . . . these 100 will soon carry with them 100 more & that the ratio will compound faster than we can calculate."[7]

Nevertheless Stephen ignored Frederic's advice and refused to sell cold drinks at the same price as warm drinks. Frederic's letters grew more and more insistent, his handwriting larger and larger, and his main points were illustrated with finger-pointing hands. To help Stephen understand his idea further, Frederic related his experience during his stay at Mrs. Woodrouff's boardinghouse in Charleston:

> I had constructed one of the jars of tin & placed [it] in the dining room for the purpose of holding Ice water which I told them I intended to drink myself. This was the subject of ridicule to the household & *everyone* of the boarders declared they would not touch the water & endanger their health. As I calculated how long their resolution would last, I had the jar made to contain 4 gallons. I found that the high resolution & firm determination was soon overcome without any persuasion of mine & that after a time every man drank the water & no other and that 4 gallons was not enough.[8]

But poor Stephen just did not get it. He believed that selling to the rich alone would produce a suitable profit. Frederic attacked this idea vehemently. Ice, he proclaimed, should be sold to everybody! In Savannah, when the slaves starting drinking cold drinks he knew that he would succeed.

To emphasize his point further, Frederic claimed that in the 1820 season in Charleston, of the $6,000 worth of ice he sold to butchers and others to cool produce, only $1,000 went to rich patrons. What more proof did Stephen require? Yet it did not sink in and so Frederic ordered him home. Stephen instead sailed for St. Thomas full of ideas for expansion, all of which would cost his boss more money, money he did not have. Ignoring Frederic's further letters to spend as little as possible, in November 1820 Stephen wanted to extend the business to Guadeloupe. Frederic objected that he had paid out $18,890 so far with no return and none expected for a year. Clearly it did not make sense to pour in more money.

Stephen still paid no mind. In December 1820, he wanted Frederic to ship fresh poultry and other game to St. Thomas. Frederic rejected the idea, based on his previous experiences. He had practical experience with frozen produce in Savannah in both 1818 and 1819. At that time, he had Stanwood ship him some fresh provisions in a frozen condition. It was not a complete failure but hardly a success. On the other hand, the same year a boat came into Savannah with fresh fish preserved in ice. That worked. The key was to pack fish immediately in ice after caught. With the correct precautions, he thought such a trade could be established with profit. Thus did Frederic Tudor anticipate the frozen food business by a hundred years.

Stephen was not listening, but it hardly mattered any more. In February 1821 Frederic wrote him: "The last 12 months has changed the face of my affairs so greatly that from being as I thought a rich man I am almost a Bankrupt. . . . To proceed any further is impossible."[9] The business crawled on through the summer of 1821. Then, Silas Marean, to whom Frederic had given a mortgage on the Windward Island icehouses, foreclosed, which effectively closed down the business. As for Stephen Cabot, he stayed on. He ended up in Haiti at Port-au-Prince. Because of local law, he was unable to marry his girlfriend, Zamie Feche. However, this did not stop them from producing Joseph Clark Cabot in 1823. Staying in Haiti where Zamie ran a retail provision business, Stephen joined her in it. He died eight years later. When it came to summing up, Frederic, that "unfortunate schemer," reckoned he had lost some twenty thousand dollars trying to prove that Stephen Cabot was not the Lees' "worthless cousin."

CHAPTER 13

Inevitably and Unavoidably Rich

FREDERIC WAS NOT ONE TO BROOD UPON HIS DEFEATS. Instead, he turned his attention to getting his ice business started in New Orleans. Persistence in an enterprise was second nature to him. And now he had a lucky stroke from a most unexpected place. His brother William, who had been so dependent upon him for financial assistance, proved to be more of an asset than Frederic ever imagined.

William had returned to Boston from England in 1814, broke and with no prospects. The Anthology Club had disbanded, although the Boston Athenæum, which it created, was going strong, so he had nothing to keep him in the city. But he had a new venture in mind. He would write a book and do it from the Maine residence of his brother-in-law Gardiner. So he went to "Oaklands," as Gardiner called his estate, and spent a comfortable year. As it turned out, Gardiner was glad to have him, for he found William's sense of humor lively. William must have been an expensive guest, however, for as his brother-in-law learned William liked living well.

During the time in Maine, William—writing with a cat next to his arm—produced *Letters from the Eastern States*, a series of long essays on such topics as religion, government, literature, social life, and customs. It was eventually published to some small success. When William returned to Boston after completing the manuscript, and while he was waiting for its publication, he decided to try for a political career. In May 1815, he became a candidate for the lower house of the Massachusetts legislature. Running unopposed, he was elected for a two-year term. He thought of running for Congress, but a better-known candidate emerged, and that was that.

So William, at the ripe age of thirty-six, decided to study law. In January 1816 he was admitted to the bar, but he did not set up as a lawyer. He continued his unremunerative work in literature. With the *Monthly Anthology* defunct, William and some of his friends from the old Anthology Club created a new magazine to review literature, the *North American Review*. William was the editor and chief contributor. By March its subscription list and reputation were showing signs of good, albeit slow, growth. William hoped that in a year it might be financially viable. Given its concentration on New England affairs, spiteful people called it the *North Unamerican Review*. Unfortunately, William's monetary expectations for the magazine did not materialize, and so his editorship ceased. Nothing he did seemed to flourish.

Even in love William was not a success. During the spring of 1816 he courted a young woman, but it was a hopeless quest from its start. Only William would have pursued it as long as he did. Still there was one place he was not a failure: in society. Ah, there he was a success! His lack of resources, however, limited him. In the fall of 1816 he wrote Frederic to ask for money. Frederic was not much better off, but he did have credit. So he borrowed three hundred dollars, gave William fifty, and left for Havana on the ship *Milo*. No one came to say good-bye, and that hurt him.

In the Massachusetts legislature, William was appointed to the prison reform committee and, in the spring of 1817, went to Baltimore to study the state prison there. Baltimore did not impress William. After investigating the penitentiary there he went on to Washington, arriving on Friday, April 17. The White House had been burned by the British during the recent war, so the president's temporary residence was next door to the hotel where William lodged. Immediately upon arrival, William called on President Monroe in hope that he might be asked to take a government job. Finding Monroe out, he left a letter of introduction that his father, the Judge, had written and his own card. Since the presidency in those days was hardly the burdensome task it is today, he was able to see Monroe the next morning. The visit did not produce a job.

In the spring of 1818, William had a new project. In 1790 there had been great interest in the construction of a canal across the narrow neck of Cape Cod, from Barnstable to Buzzards Bay. This would spare coastal shipping the dangerous passage through Vineyard Sound and around the exposed coast of the Cape, the scene of many shipwrecks. A legislative committee turned the idea down; they said the passageway would freeze in winter and choke with sand in the summer. But by 1817 a new wave of interest surged. The five thousand coastal vessels sailing around Cape Cod each year were all potential customers. Also, two years earlier, a steamboat line had been established between New York and the Connecticut shore. With a canal, steamboats might easily make the journey all the way to Boston.

It would be a mammoth undertaking, costing perhaps as much as $500,000. In

November a committee formed to gather data. The membership included the cream of the Boston business community, along with William, who, his mother claimed, was really the instigator of the plan. A bill was introduced in the legislature, of which William was still a member, to incorporate the "Navigation Canal Corporation." The bill passed the Senate, but the House recessed before taking action.

Even before formal incorporation, ten thousand shares of stock were offered to the public in January 1818. As no money was required, buyers made a mad rush for shares. The share value increased 5 percent immediately. At this point, William decided to visit Washington to see what interest he might encourage there. The journey took ten days. He stayed two weeks and then headed home, stopping in Philadelphia to visit friends. But what about the Cape Cod canal? William thought that he might petition Congress about it. But there the matter rested. A government survey would plot a route in 1825, and several private companies made efforts in the 1870s and 1880s, but not until 1907 would digging actually begin. Not all the Tudors were as persistent as Frederic.

Meanwhile, Frederic had been dreaming of cooling drinks in New Orleans for some time. It was a logical extension of his current business. In 1818 New Orleans was

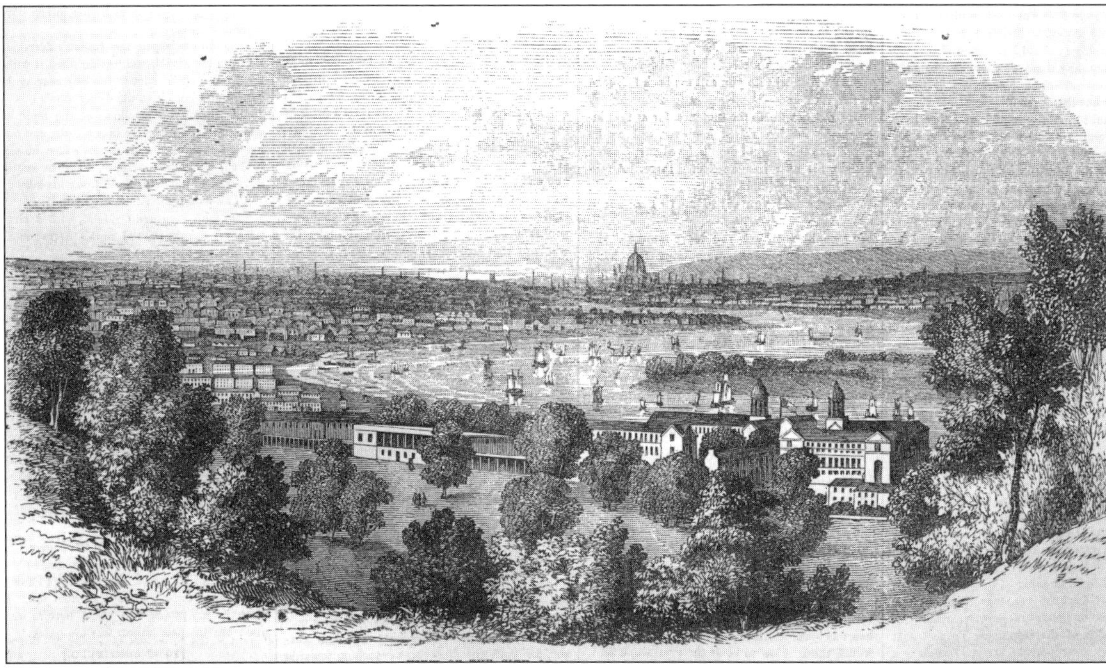

View of the City of New Orleans
Gleason's Pictorial Drawing-Room Companion, *1852 (vol. 2).*
Collection of the Massachusetts Historical Society.

crammed into ninety blocks, hemmed in between the river, two lakes, and a great swamp. This confined the city to a narrow crescent on the banks of the Mississippi River. One hundred ten miles upriver from the Gulf of Mexico, it was the logical place for ships from all over the world to dock and exchange goods with the flatboats and steamboats from the interior of the country. Down the river came produce from the homestead farms of Ohio, Illinois, and Pennsylvania. Back up the river went molasses, sugar, cotton cloth, tobacco, and the varied manufactures of Europe. Upwards of thirty thousand people handled this trade—and they attracted Frederic's interest, for it was said that they had four delights: dancing, dueling, gambling, and drinking. The last would make his market—cooling those drinks.

On his way home from Charleston in September 1816, Frederic stopped in New York to sell a load of fruit. While there he met a Dr. Lucius Woodbury, who showed great interest in his idea of opening an icehouse in New Orleans. Their lengthy discussions resulted in a deal wherein Woodbury would go to New Orleans and start the ice business there. Frederic was to get 5 percent of the sales in return for his advice. During the winter and spring of 1817, Frederic wrote long and detailed letters in which he told Woodbury all that he had learned after ten years of selling ice. From Woodbury there was only silence. Frederic wondered what was happening. When Woodbury had arrived in New Orleans, he later told Frederic, he found that they had their own way of making ice and so did not need to buy it. Quite disillusioned, Woodbury returned to New York.

In the summer of 1817 when Frederic was passing through New York again on his way home, he happened to meet Woodbury on the street. Frederic described the meeting:

> He appeared considerable wrathful & told me he intended to call me to account. I expostulated with him & asked him if he could seriously deny his having deceived me we talked some time in the course of which I told him I should not recall what I had said & although I had never put my personal courage to any particular test I thought I should not fear him in any way he chose to call on me. The business, however, ended in nothing.[1]

On the day Frederic left New York he wrote Woodbury a threatening letter saying that, as far as New Orleans was concerned, he would go it alone. He added that he was determined to do so because Woodbury had broken their agreement. Where Frederic was to find the money to fulfill his boast was another matter.

While in Boston that summer, Frederic thought better of his threat. What if Woodbury called his bluff and started operations there on his own? After all, Frederic had revealed to him just how to do it. Before he left Boston for the South again, Frederic fired another salvo at Woodbury indicating that he was "desirous to know whether you have really the intention of meeting me as a competitor there. This will be the ruin of both our undertakings. I would rather give you the five percent which you propose to give me to withdraw rather than this state of things should take place."[2]

On his way back south, Frederic again passed through New York. He went to see Woodbury but found he had gone to New Orleans—an ominous portent. Yet when 1817 ended, to his surprise, Frederic received a cordial letter from Woodbury. Whatever Woodbury's motive for this change of position, it did not work. Still angry that Woodbury had deceived him, Frederic fired back an angry response. Frederic never heard from Woodbury again—his threat seemed to have evaporated.

Then appeared Richard Salmon, an Irishman from Philadelphia, who decided to sell ice in New Orleans. By the time Frederic learned of his existence Salmon had already visited Boston and arranged for a cargo of ice to be shipped there. His operation followed the pattern of Frederic's innovations, almost exactly. Salmon had secured permission to distribute ice from the city council of New Orleans. The ice was to be distributed from the icehouse, but the proprietor would furnish pails for carrying it home to avoid excessive melting. In addition, he was preparing refrigerators similar to Frederic's, which he called "cellerettes." So far so good, it appeared, but Salmon's second cargo of ice did not materialize. His sales amounted to only ten dollars a day, and to continue his operation in New Orleans required another three thousand dollars, which he did not have available. By the fall his creditors had forced him into bankruptcy and in December 1819 Richard Salmon died, a victim of yellow fever.

The road was now clear for Frederic. Unfortunately, his great success in the 1819 ice season slowly evaporated by 1820. The depression of 1819 deepened, and by August 1820 Frederic was crying the blues again. "There is now what is called 'hard times' in full operation everywhere & it effects my business extensively."[3] His nest egg from the 1819 sales had vanished, going mostly to his creditors. And breathing down his neck were Cabot's bills. In addition, he still had to support William. Deeply gloomy, Frederic escaped to Sandwich to renew his spirits. At the end of August he was ready to attack the largest potential market in the South—New Orleans.

To build an icehouse there and to commence operations would require about $10,000. Where could he get so large a sum? He began running everywhere in search of the money. To brother William's friend William Amory—he declined. To Thomas and Edward Motley, successful merchants who had come to Boston as poor country boys at the turn of the century and had made good. Hoping to borrow $3,200, Frederic engaged them in intense discussions, but in the end since he could offer them no security they too declined. Their refusal upset him deeply. For the next forty-eight hours he went about in a state of mental excitement such as he had never known.

At first he felt he could make no more effort after being turned down by the Motleys. Yet, as in the past, the disappointment had the effect of spurring him on to increased endeavors. It so happened that one of his Savannah connections, a Mr. Hills of Johnston & Hills, was visiting Boston. Frederic wrote Hills with the request that they guarantee his note to the Motleys. The next day he met Hills on State Street, where the Boston merchants met each day to transact business. Hills began their meeting by offering $500, far less than the sum Frederic needed. By the end of the meeting, Frederic thought he had talked Hills into standing to the full amount required. Four days later, however, when Hills went away for a trip to Salem and Portsmouth, the arrangement was still not complete.

On September 16, nine days after their first meeting, Frederic heard that Hills planned to return home directly without stopping off in Boston. The rumor turned out to be a false alarm. On September 20 Hills was back in Boston. Before breakfast (and while still in slippers) he called on Frederic with his acceptance. Shortly thereafter, Frederic handed the bill to Motley and received $2,775. Success, but this was not enough, especially since he had to pay $850 to Davenport against his claims. But it was a first step. Where could he find another $3,000 to commence the project?

That same day Frederic met his friend Tom Lee on State Street and walked with him as far as Boylston Market. Cannily Frederic backed into the subject of New Orleans, telling Lee he wanted his advice and assistance but not his money. After a lengthy talk, Lee consented to look at the papers Frederic had prepared on the operations of the Charleston and Savannah icehouses. Frederic hoped that Lee would help him raise the necessary $3,000 if he sold him a three-tenths interest in the New Orleans house. But he realized that Lee had to be handled gingerly.

When Frederic met him on September 22 Lee was cool to the idea. The next day he took a long walk with Lee, carefully avoiding the subject. But Frederic was unable to play cat and mouse much longer, and on September 25 he asked Lee directly if he would help him raise money for his New Orleans venture. Lee refused. Worse, he had so little confidence in the scheme that he would not come in himself at all. With this rebuff Frederic turned inward: "I shall now set out to trim my vessel, adjust the sails & regulate the ballast, economize & bring to perfection those concerns which are already established & rest satisfied on the subject of New Orleans with having attempted everything which could be possibly thought of & having failed."[4]

It was at this low point in Frederic's pecuniary contrivances that brother William finally proved his financial value by providing the solution to the money problem. William suggested some people who might be interested in the New Orleans scheme, which set Frederic off once more, despite his earlier determination to repose in his shell. In the first month of this new tack, Frederic chased down William's friends to no avail. On October 26 he wrote in his diary that he "had as many minds & changes of determination in this thing as there have been winds in the north."[5]

On Saturday morning, October 28, William appeared once more at Frederic's counting room on Wheeler's Point. But not to borrow more money as his brother thought. Not at all. William had a plan. If Frederic would go security for him, he could borrow the $3,000 needed from some of his friends and take a part in the business. Frederic agreed at once and suggested that William apply to some of his younger and more active friends instead of the older, wealthier ones whom William had first mentioned.

First on the list was Thomas Lee, Jr. Before long, Frederic was dining with him to explain the entire proposition. Lee held out the possibility that William's friends might be interested if they thought that it would do William any good. If Frederic was the persistent Tudor, William was the popular Tudor. He had many friends who wanted to encourage his literary work. Frederic spent the rest of that afternoon drafting a proposal that he sent to Lee's house that evening. According to this arrangement, William's friends would lend him enough money to invest in the New Orleans enterprise if Frederic would guarantee to provide William an annuity to meet his living expenses. It was an odd idea, but it seemed to work.

The following week was an exciting one for Frederic. "In the course of the week past much has been accomplished. N. Amory, T. Lee Jr., Dwight & T. H. Perkins have agreed to let W. have with my endorsement $2000 & tomorrow I shall have that sum in hand."[6] All at once the Tudor brothers had an embarrassment of riches. Brother-in-law Gardiner now offered to endorse notes for the $3,000. Frederic refused but thanked him for his kindness. He did, however, allow Gardiner to provide the last $1,000. With the money in hand, Frederic could begin the real business. He spent the next weeks preparing the new enterprise. The carpenters finally received orders to build frames for the New Orleans icehouse.

For some time, Frederic had been discussing the possibility of employing Harry again in his ice business. Since his return from the Mediterranean, Harry had been vegetating. After much indecision, Frederic finally decided to ask Harry to run the operation in New Orleans. He was to stay until July 1821, to superintend the erection of the icehouse and to start the business. Frederic agreed to pay him $500 for the season. There was one problem, however. Harry was still destitute, with two arrest warrants outstanding against him for a debt of $800. Frederic had to go surety for those debts before Harry was free to sail. So in one stroke, he provided for both of his brothers.

Harry left for New Orleans on November 9. Frederic filled his days with getting the icehouse frame loaded on a vessel, collecting the materials Harry would need to put it up, and hiring carpenters to do the work. Finally, at noon on November 19, the *Phoenix* sailed out of Boston Harbor with the icehouse parts and the carpenters. Should

Harry have a quick passage to New Orleans, should he swiftly find a suitable site for the house, should no accident happen to him, should he make good arrangements, then perhaps in a year or less Frederic could turn his ice business around.

Harry arrived in New Orleans as planned—after which, of course, the problems began. First, some of the people they had relied upon for financial assistance in New Orleans disappointed them. So Harry had to do some fast footwork to pay the freight cost on the materials that arrived on the *Phoenix*. Duly impressed, Frederic thought that his brother had managed this crisis just right.

In fact, quite by chance, a curious accident had assisted Harry. He met Charles C. Whitman in New Orleans. Whitman, as a child some twenty years before, had lived in Lynn, Massachusetts. Judge Tudor had known the parents, since the Tudor farm was in the adjoining town of Saugus. Taking a liking to young Charles, and wanting to assist his poor parents, the Judge had paid for Charles's education. Eventually, Charles became apprenticed to a gilder in Boston. In time Whitman had gotten ahead in life and now had the opportunity to render assistance to the son of his old patron. He lent Harry five hundred dollars to meet his immediate expenses. Piously Frederic noted in his diary that this ought to be a lesson to Harry. "It shews what industry is capable of effecting & how wasteful is luxurious indulgence in which all our family were educated."[7]

Being five to six weeks away from New Orleans by letter meant that news of that operation lagged some time behind the events, a great disadvantage in mercantile operations. Early in March, Frederic knew that Harry had erected the icehouse. He also knew that Harry had managed to purchase a small stock of ice from a Marblehead sloop and had started selling it. The brig he had sent to New Orleans should arrive shortly, assuring a regular supply of ice. To average ten dollars per day in sales would be sufficient for the first season. Frederic eagerly awaited the first report.

Frederic had to wait until July 12, 1821, in fact. That day, he learned that the undertaking exceeded all expectations: sales averaged forty dollars a day! Immediately a rosy glow spread over everything. That he had to close out the business in Savannah, St. Thomas, and St. Pierre, or that he had no receipts from Havana, where the office manager had been murdered in a robbery and his successor had died of the fever, with Mr. Fellows sick and in the States, all these difficulties were inconsequential. New Orleans was a great success and Frederic was exultant. He even praised his brother: "Harry has conducted that undertaking in a very admirable manner."[8]

The large market afforded by New Orleans and the recovery of national prosperity proved to be critical to Frederic Tudor's pursuit of riches. At last what he had sought for so long and which had constantly eluded his grasp, was his. This last venture would save all the rest. Finally he was to be, as he styled it, "Inevitably and unavoidably rich."[9]

CHAPTER 14

My Wagon Mired in Mud

In Frederic's life there was no standing still. His too-busy brain kept churning out new enterprises. Kept awake one night, he made a memorandum of an idea that popped into his head. Why, he argued, could not one produce a continuous source of power by harnessing the energy of the tides? No sooner did he think this than he decided it could be done and leaped to the conclusion that nobody could do it better than himself. Without bothering to work out any of the details, he determined that this would be an important invention, and so he wrote a note to remind himself of the time when he first made this valuable discovery. It did not occur to him that Uriah Cotting had already tried the scheme unsuccessfully in damming up the Back Bay of Boston. Nor did he follow up on the idea.

In another brainstorm, he decided to establish a flour mill in partnership with brother-in-law Gardiner. Wheat could be cheaply shipped from New Orleans to Boston on the return voyage of his ice ships. Like many of his fancies, it came to nothing. There was an article on capital punishment he intended to publish, but later he decided it was not the subject on which he should first break into print. All the time, he filled his notebooks with miscellaneous philosophical ideas that flashed in and out of his mind.

The end of April 1821 found Frederic sick, so sick that he neglected all his business. He had taken cold at a party and it had prostrated him. Never had he had such a severe attack before. By May 11, however, he was feeling better and wrote his brother-in-law Gardiner that news. While Frederic did not realize it, this illness provided a disquieting sign of what was to come.

During the autumn of 1821, the years of effort he had put into starting his ice business finally caught up with him. Just as his labors appeared on the verge of reward, the bottom fell out of his world. He suffered a complete collapse—what we call a nervous breakdown today.

To his rescue, as ever, came Robert H. Gardiner. To Gardiner it seemed no more than a severe attack of fever, perhaps a recurrence of Frederic's old malaria. In fact, brother William wrote their mother that Frederic would be better as soon as money came in from the West Indies. Since none of Frederic's family were in Boston at the time of his illness, Gardiner came down from Maine to look after him. Frederic's doctor told Gardiner that he considered him "very ill."[1] Although a regular nurse was in attendance, the doctor advised Gardiner to remain in Boston and watch over his brother-in-law until he recovered.

Generously, Gardiner agreed. Frederic required constant monitoring, so Gardiner spelled the nurse, taking the early night shift from eight in the evening or so until two or three in the morning. Night after night, he watched over his brother-in-law, giving him the frequent rubbings prescribed by the doctor. He also sat with Frederic during the day, breaking only for a short walk outside in the fresh air.

Finally, Frederic became convalescent, and his sister Emma came down from Kennebec to see him. The doctor advised freedom from all care and anxiety as the only immediate remedy for Frederic's condition. This would never happen unless somebody reliable and trustworthy took charge of the Boston end of the ice business. Emma suggested that perhaps her husband, Robert, could do so while Frederic took a long rest. Frederic's reply to Robert was typical: "What a fool you must be to make yourself my druge and allow me to go off to take my ease and recreation."[2] Gardiner thought this response "droll." In a letter to his mother a few months later, Frederic was more appreciative: "It is needless for me to say to you how much we are all & myself in particular indebted to the wonderful active kindness of Robert. I can not say what would have become of me but for his stepping in to relieve me at this time."[3]

Well on the road to recovery by January 22, Frederic thought a southern sea voyage would be helpful. Southward meant Havana, where business complications persisted. Since Fellows was still in Philadelphia, Frederic's only icehouse keeper in Cuba was a man he did not know, William Carlisle. To remedy this problem, Frederic thought of John W. Damon, the young man who had assisted Stephen Cabot in Martinique. Damon, a carpenter by trade, had been hired in 1819 to go out with Cabot and help erect the icehouse at St. Pierre. He had proven so capable that he was induced to remain and run the ice operation at St. Thomas. In February 1821, when it was clear that the Martinique venture would fail, Frederic invited Damon to work for him. Soon after, Frederic decided that Damon was the man to fill the gap at Havana. By November, Frederic wrote Carlisle of his decision: "I have no reason to complain of you but simply that I am not acquainted or known to you & in supplying your place with Mr. Damon I merely place a man in charge of my business who knows minutely how I wish to have it conducted."[4]

Frederic's letter of instruction to Damon of December 14, 1821, gives an insight on how the ice business operated and was probably typical of the arrangements he made with other icehouse keepers in his employ.

> I wish you per agreement to proceed from Boston to Bath in Maine & there oversee the loading of the Brig *Cabbossee Contee* . . . being particular that the ice is well stored & that the bulkheads are tight so that no air passes over the ice on the passage to waste it. . . . The expense of your journey to Bath you will charge me; but not your board there or any other expense. On your arrival at Havana you will call on Guthroz & Morland & inquire of them whether they are willing to receive the consignment on the terms of my letter to them . . . & in case they do not you will advise with Mr. Fellows or Mr. Wm Savage in case I should not be there. As soon as the ice is stored in the House the tan [tanbark][5] is to be got on shore. . . . This tan is expected to be of use in the future construction of a new House. . . . You are to endeavor as soon as convenient to make an arrangement with Mr. Carlisle to go to Matanzas [a province of Cuba] for the sale of ice at that place. The plan of the cold drinks is to be attempted in Havana on the instructions you have heretofore had. The price of ice is to be continued as heretofore & no credit to be given to anyone. Mr. Fellows is to have ten pounds of ice daily & he will inform you to what other persons it is to be given & the quantity to each. The collector is the principal person & one or two others who must necessarily have ice without paying for it. I have already told you the precautions that will be necessary respecting money to be received in Havana. It will be well you should in all your letters to Mr. Gardiner give him the information of the quantity in height remaining in the House & you would do well to write with tolerable regularity to him giving statement of sale *three times each month*. . . .
>
> The poor condition of the Ice House in Havana will render it useless to send any acct. of the run of water. Any defects in the House attend to & remedy as well as you can & be particular to have a good covering of shavings on the top of the ice. It has herefore been customary not to have any charge of labour in getting out ice. You must put me to as little expense of this kind as you conveniently can: but in case ice should be sent in considerable quantity to Matanzas more expense of this kind will be necessary than otherwise; but in this & all other cases I shall depend on your endeavors to reduce expenses as low as possible. *Small expenses* which occur *every day* amount to a great

> sum at the *end of the year*. . . . Your compensation will be for all your personal services & for everything you may do for me as well as your board & passage home ten per centum on the gross sales of ice & this ten pr. ct. I wish you to receive from time to time in Havana at your convenience & as you wish.[6]

On January 23, 1822, Frederic wrote to his mother, who was living in Washington then, that his cargo of ice from Maine was at sea, that Harry and another ice cargo was on the way to New Orleans, and that he was off to Havana. The ship *Bearing*, on which he traveled, carried guns and blunderbusses for defense against pirates active around Havana. Pirates were not a casual matter, and piracy in the Caribbean—especially around Cuba—had recently increased as opportunities for privateers (legal pirates) declined with peace among the former Spanish possessions. The U.S. Navy would finally suppress piracy in the region in 1822–1825. Indeed, one of Frederic's cousins, William Savage, had been on a ship in December 1819 that was boarded by a gang of pirates. They had stripped Savage, forced him to lie on the deck for several hours with only a blanket to cover his body, and then almost killed him. Before they left they robbed him of his ring, gold watch, and other valuables. Fortunately, this did not happen to Frederic and he arrived safely in Havana on March 1.

Frederic had left his brother-in-law Gardiner to look over the Boston end of the business, which consisted largely of managing the finances of the operation. As it turned out, it required Gardiner to advance considerable sums of his own capital to keep the business liquid. Gardiner never charged interest on this loan nor did he take any compensation for his services.

Frederic had planned to remain in Cuba only six weeks. Then he would join Harry in New Orleans, travel up the Mississippi on horseback, and finally head home. His plans changed, however, and he stayed on in Havana much longer; the Tudor who went up the Mississippi was Harry. In 1822 this was no parlor car tour. Since trains had not yet arrived in this country, Harry took one of the new Mississippi River steamboats. At Cairo, the boat left the Mississippi, turned right onto the Ohio River, and puffed its way for another six hundred miles along the border between Kentucky and Indiana toward Louisville, where the river was crowded with steamboats and rafts. Here at the falls of the Ohio Harry changed to a smaller steamboat and continued upriver to Cincinnati, then a community of twelve thousand inhabitants. At this point in his journey he gave up traveling by boat and made the seven-hundred-mile trip to Boston by horseback. For Harry it was another romantic adventure.

For Frederic, the original six weeks in Havana stretched into over a year, to his satisfaction. By April 1823, the business in Havana was doing well, and Damon was performing to Frederic's satisfaction, so it was possible for him to return home at last, once again vowing never to come back to Havana.

CHAPTER 15

Taking Care of William

FREDERIC AND HARRY WERE NOT THE ONLY MEMBERS of the family traveling during the summer of 1822. Delia Stewart had accompanied her husband in the USS *Franklin*, flagship of a U.S. Navy squadron of five vessels sent to visit South America and then to explore the Pacific Northwest, go to China, and come home by way of the Cape of Good Hope. Stewart, on his return from the Mediterranean cruise in April 1820, had been furious at the dilapidation of his estate caused by Delia's ungovernable extravagance. The conventions of naval life, however, dictated that Delia accompany him on his social engagements, which she did. They included a stay in Washington during the winter months of 1820. Although the situation may have angered Stewart, it did not bother Delia: this was the social life she enjoyed.

Their 1822 sojourn in South America stemmed from a series of events that began five years earlier. In 1817, the federal government had sent Capt. James Biddle to the West Coast to lay claim to the Oregon Territory. On his way up the coast of South America he stopped in Callao, Peru, for water. The colonists in Argentina and Chile had successfully revolted from Spanish rule, but Peru was still controlled by Spain. Biddle returned to Washington and reported the confused state of things in South America. He told Washington that, at the time of his visit, the revolution had reached a stalemate and pirates swarmed the coast, operating as privateers with Spanish licenses. Both sides had declared blockades without sufficient naval force to enforce them. This was really an excuse to plunder shipping—especially American ships, which were not particular about which side they sold their goods to as long as there was a sufficient profit.

Based on Biddle's report, President Monroe decided to send a squadron of warships to protect American shipping there. Such an assignment called for prudence with firmness, diplomatic discretion, and a stern countenance. The president offered the assignment to the one person he thought had these attributes, Commodore Stewart. However, Stewart was not sure he wanted it. If he went, he would take Delia and the children—he had no intention of leaving Mrs. Spendthrift on her own this time. Clearly, this was not Delia's cup of tea, and she complained long and loudly about it to her brothers. Harry advised her sententiously to take lots of books about the places she would be visiting and to keep a daily journal. In no way was his sister interested in staying in her cabin writing journals or reading books. She liked parties. In the end, Stewart accepted the commission and arranged to leave in June.

During all this time, William had been trying, without much success, to earn a living. He kept out of debtors prison only by borrowing money from his friends, especially brother Frederic. Perhaps his literary activities would be the source of wealth and fame. In March 1821, his book *Letters from the Eastern States* was finally published. Frederic commented on the $2.25 price: "pretty high. I am told its exterior appearance is respectable."[1] So much for Frederic's interest in literature. The book had a mild success, but it brought William no money.

Perhaps politics offered the road to success. Yet his work in the Massachusetts legislature seemed to lead nowhere. Maybe some diplomatic post might suit him. His frequent applications to President Monroe had brought no appointments, but Monroe was well meaning. When Stewart spent an evening alone with the president in May 1822, shortly before he was to leave for South America, they had discussed William's situation and, while the president expressed his friendship for the family, he still had no job to offer. Passing the buck back to the Commodore, Monroe suggested that Stewart find a post for William in his command. Although Stewart knew of no vacancy at present in the Pacific, he invited William to come along on the voyage. A job might come up that William would be capable of handling.

When William heard this proposition he was indignant. He considered it an insult. But it presented him with a problem, for John Quincy Adams, Monroe's secretary of state, was also trying to get him a job. How could William explain to Adams the refusal of Stewart's offer and still keep the possibility of a government job? William the writer found the perfect excuse. He was busy writing a biography of the American patriot James Otis. If he went to South America with Stewart, this project would be indefinitely postponed. "You will perhaps smile," he wrote Adams, "at the naivete of a author in thinking so much of his book, but it was this agreement which chiefly prevented my going out in the *Franklin*."[2]

Frederic had opposed William accepting Stewart's offer. He thought William was better off sticking to the ice business in New Orleans. To keep him financially afloat William had the annuity that Frederic promised to pay him from the profits made in New Orleans. The South American scheme would occupy William for three years. In Frederic's mind that was a long time for a man now forty-two and still without a settled career. So Commodore Stewart sailed away without brother William aboard. He did have, however, his wife, Delia.

In spite of her original fears, Delia found the trip exciting. As the wife of a commodore, she was fêted wherever she went, and limelight was to Delia the sunshine of life. Observations she might have put into a journal found their way into long letters home—such as the earthquake that hit Valparaiso shortly before their arrival. It destroyed all the houses except the wooden ones.

In her letters to all members of the family she was ecstatic about the happiness she found on her journey. Not only was she happy, but she had the power to make all who moved in her orbit happy—or so she declared in a letter to William. By *happy* Delia meant rich. She wrote to William that she knew "of an individual here who would assist with capital to any amount for commercial speculations whose fortune is colossal beyond all we hear of in the U. S.—and I know for a certainty that in less than a year either of my family, either or all of my dear brothers could realize one hundred thousand dollars a piece."[3] Much as they were aware of Delia's rich imagination, which shaped events to suit her fancy, this was too bald, too unequivocal a statement for any of them to disregard. Delia's August letter should have reached the family members in Boston by November or December of 1822. It fell on fertile ground.

William's second book, *The Life of James Otis*, published in the spring of 1823, was a critical success. William Lee, writing from Washington on May 8, 1823, told William with how much delight he had read the work: "too much cannot be said in its praise."[4] The southern papers, he reported, were full of extracts from it, by which fact, he added slyly, "it is much admired and has placed you 1st among our writers."[5] But William might have reflected that no royalties came to him from extracts in the newspapers. In reply, Lee was advised that William had now decided to join Stewart in Peru. Lee answered that he would see if he could secure an "official character" for the trip from President Monroe.[6]

John Quincy Adams had spoken highly of William's book and had on an earlier occasion mentioned making use of William on a mission to Spain. Adams had the ear of the president and Lee had the ear of Adams, not that these ears had been very productive in the past. Lee was aware of William's motives for the trip, and he admitted that the chances for speculation in Peru appeared to be good because of the Greek War of Independence. But he knew that William was "too kind and too pure to buffet along among the rascals of this world. Oliver Goldsmith would have made about as good a trader as you."[7] William was just not up to the "dirty tricks" of the business.[8] By the end of May 1823, things were warming up for William's appointment. Lee had seen

Adams "last night," he wrote William on May 28, and added: "If you were his brother he would not take a greater interest in your welfare."[9] But William had already involved himself in another project.

On the morning of April 17, 1822, William had seen an announcement in the *Boston Patriot* newspaper that "a lot of ground including the monument erected to the memory of General Warren and the remains of the breast work thrown up on the eve of the battle fought" on Bunker Hill was advertised for auction on the first of May. The paper hoped that "some patriotic gentleman of wealth will purchase and preserve it." William was no "gentleman of wealth," yet he was patriotic, and he could hardly sleep that night for thinking of the dangers that threatened the sacred spot. The next morning he learned that the notice had been inserted by Gen. Henry Dearborn of Roxbury. William interviewed him but found that Dearborn had no money either with which to buy the land. Could they find such a man? William turned to Daniel Webster, who offered no money but—a good politician—lavishly blessed the project.

The logical choice of a rich rescuer for the sacred spot was Warren's nephew Dr. John Collins Warren, also a friend of William from the Anthology Club, and General Warren's closest living relative. Warren was most sympathetic to the nephew, and on May 1 he attended the auction and bought the property. During the winter of 1822–1823, he held several meetings at his house at 2 Park Street to discuss what to do with the property. It was agreed that some suitable monument should be erected there. William had discussed the project with his friend Col. T. H. Perkins, and early in the spring of 1823 the colonel invited the concerned parties to breakfast at his house on Temple Place to talk about forming a society to perpetuate the memory of the great battle. Webster, Warren, William Sullivan, George Ticknor, George Blake (a well-known Boston lawyer), and William made up the group around the colonel's dining table. After debating the various possibilities, they rode over to Charlestown to view the actual site.

Then William, together with Webster and Boston's mayor, Theodore Lyman, sent personal letters inviting their friends to a meeting at the new Exchange Coffee House. Twenty-six gentlemen showed up and enthusiastically endorsed the idea of a memorial to Boston's only full-scale battle of the Revolution. They formed an association with a five-dollar membership fee and all present joined. At this price, even William was able to join, and he put up five dollars for his friend Colonel Perkins, who was at the moment in England on business. Shortly thereafter, on June 7, 1823, the Commonwealth charted the group. Within a month, circular letters solicited funds. At the formal organizational meeting, William was elected secretary of the Bunker Hill Monument Association.

Throughout June 1823 William continued on edge, waiting for news of his appointment in Peru. He took lessons in Spanish as he waited and hoped. At the end of the month, he wrote again to Secretary Adams. By this time, Adams must have been tired of William's pressing him for work. A year earlier, he had written to Adams to solicit the job of commissioner of bankruptcy newly created by the Congress. At that time his application was seconded by a long list of Boston worthies, including Judge Joseph Story, Chief Justice Isaac Parker, and Daniel Webster. In the end, he did not receive the job.

Out on the coast of South America, Stewart turned out to be a poor tightrope walker. He favored the Spanish government over the revolutionaries. Secretary of the Navy Samuel Southard received complaints from the various local governments as well as from individuals regarding Stewart's obvious favoritism to his own countrymen and others who they felt were breaking the law. In less polite terms, Stewart was being accused of gun-running to the Spanish forces.

Apparently, Stewart was in serious trouble. The United States agent in Peru, John W. Prevost, compounded the case. Prevost and Stewart did not get on, and their antagonism was exacerbated by Prevost's strong support for the revolutionaries. In August 1823, Washington ordered Stewart home. Shortly afterwards, in September 1823, William's appointment as United States consul to Peru was announced. William Lee suggested that William could leave with Comm. Isaac Hull, who was replacing Stewart.

> I hope you will go with Hull. It may be less expensive . . . and more to your interest for Hull knows nothing of business and after getting a leaf out of Stewart's book may wish to join hands with you. . . . I must write Stewart as I have been to work for him in parrying some attacks on the subject of his making money. Adams is his friend though he has all the complaints before him. It is said he made 100,000$. I wish it was 1,000,000$. He had better know the facts in order to be prepared for them when he arrives.[10]

So off William went to pursue that gleam of foreign wealth that had eluded him at home. Foreign wealth had apparently rubbed off nicely on his brother-in-law Stewart. In a letter Delia revealed that "Commodore S . . . has been fortunate here far beyond my most sanguine expectation. Of course this will not be mentioned for somehow it happens that respecting a command in the Pacific there appears to be a great deal of jealous scrutiny."[11]

Frederic, too, had become successful in his ice business. And now that Harry was assisting Frederic, perhaps he would prosper as well. So it was definitely the eldest brother's turn to become "inevitably & unavoidably rich." William would have to leave the monument on Bunker Hill for his friends to complete. At the age of forty-two he was off to seek his fortune—down in the regions where Frederic had found his.

Thomas Thompson (1775–1852)
The U.S. Ship Franklin, with a view of the Bay of New York
Oil on canvas.
30 x 65 in. (17.2 x 165.1 cm)
The Metropolitan Museum of Art, The Edward W.C. Arnold Collection of New York Prints, Maps and Pictures, Bequest of Edward W.C. Arnold, 1954. (54.90.289)
(The Franklin is the three-masted ship just right of center.)

CHAPTER 16

Plotting Her Last Plot

While Delia's letters were full of her delights, they were silent regarding some of the most dramatic parts of their life in Peru. The most difficult part of Stewart's assignment was to keep himself and his command from becoming entangled in the complicated political situation in which he found himself. While Stewart was skillful at being neutral despite his inclinations otherwise, Delia was not. Toward the end of September 1822, the USS *Franklin* was at Callao. The revolutionary forces had seized control of the city and the Spanish government had fled. While in town one day, Delia was accosted by a Spanish officer disguised as a peasant, who begged her to permit him to escape to the safety of the *Franklin*.

Although reluctant to become involved, Delia asked Lieutenant Mayo, an officer from the ship who was in town with her, if he would take the stranger as a servant. Mayo declined—he already had a servant. The stranger left, but Delia requested Mayo not to mention the incident to the Commodore. A few days later, just as the *Franklin* prepared to leave Callao for Quilco, the stranger came aboard and asked to see Delia. This time, he had a note from a friend, which said that the stranger's name was Madrid and recommended him to Delia's protection. She sought the advice of Eliphalet Smith, a merchant aboard the vessel, saying that if the man was sent ashore he would surely be killed by the revolutionaries. Smith said that Madrid would have to go ashore if the boat that had brought him was still alongside the *Franklin*. But it had already left, and so, accidentally, the die was cast.

Delia called in the cabin steward, Peter Birch, and told him to hide the man in his pantry, where Madrid stayed until a chance for escape offered itself. Later, when the victorious rebels learned that Madrid had escaped via the *Franklin*, they demanded the surrender of the fugitive. Stewart, unaware of what had gone on, was able to say in all honesty that he knew of no such individual aboard his ship. When the vessel reached Quilco, Delia faced the problem of spiriting Madrid off the ship without her husband seeing him. Peter Birch was given the job of smuggling him off in a boat provided by Smith. Since Stewart was on deck, Madrid had to squirm his way to freedom through a port in the ship's side.

Delia's secret was well kept from the Commodore, although everyone else aboard the ship appeared to be aware of it. Perhaps Stewart would never have learned about it, except that over a year later Madrid paid a return visit to Delia to thank her for saving his life. Stewart accidentally discovered the man's identity and the reason for his visit. His rage was unbounded, for besides his indignation at his wife's deception he realized that his professional reputation had been jeopardized and that dismissal from the navy might be his fate. And certain rumors may also have exacerbated his rage, rumors apparently unfounded, that Delia had accepted a bribe of thirty thousand dollars for secreting the fugitive and that she had fallen in love with him.

Commodore Hull in his flagship, the USS *United States*, joined Stewart's squadron in the harbor of Callao on Sunday, April 11, 1824. There was a round of salutes, and at 11:30 that morning Commodore Stewart and Delia made a formal call on Commodore Hull and his wife. Mrs. Hull took an instant dislike to Delia. "She is too selfish and odd. . . . She lives for admiration and the follies of the world."[1]

On the voyage back to the United States, Stewart punished Delia for the Madrid business by refusing to speak to her. She was compelled to take her usual seat at table without the least notice from him. The *Franklin* docked in New York on Sunday, August 29, 1824. New York was in the throes of a two-week's celebration of the arrival of General Lafayette, the "nation's Guest." The *Franklin* and her crew joined in by giving Lafayette "a national salute" when he went by the navy yard the next Sunday. Stewart and Delia met the general at some of the many parties and balls held in his honor. Stewart seemed to forget the events of the past few months and behaved, in public at least, as if nothing had happened.

But Stewart, it appeared, had other problems. He found himself deep in controversy regarding certain alleged misconduct during his time in Peru. John Prevost, the local consul, had accused him of a number of offenses. Prevost had been recalled to prove his charges against Stewart and to be tried himself for charges preferred by different merchants against him. The rumors about Stewart's misconduct had been floating around for some time before his return and one of Stewart's first actions was to write a vehement letter of denial to the newspapers.

What were the accusations? First, that he had been involved in contraband trade while in Peru, which had brought him considerable private profit. Second, that he had violated American neutrality in the internal revolt in Peru by giving refuge to a certain deposed official on board his warship. Other charges were of a lesser nature, such as failure to exercise his gun crews and inflicting cruel and unusual punishment on one of his staff. When Stewart's public denunciation of the charges failed to end the agitation against him, he decided to face it head on by demanding a court martial. An immediate trial was impossible as it would be several months before Stewart's principal witness, a Mr. O'Sullivan, could return from South America. In the meanwhile, he could do nothing but wait.

Delia spent the first few weeks back at home in Boston with family and friends. When she returned to Philadelphia, she found Stewart was in good humor. He had been invited to spend the winter in Washington with General Lafayette. Delia was eagerly looking forward to this, since Lafayette was the prime social "catch" of the season. William Lee, having heard that Stewart's house and farm were in disorder due to the family's absence, had invited the Stewarts to share his house with them while they were in Washington.

For Delia, this proposition never came to be. Delia even had her clothes packed and ready to go when a letter arrived from Frederic for the Commodore. It was in effect a bill for debts that Delia had incurred over the years without her husband's knowledge. Frederic wanted Stewart to pay for his wife's obligations. As the correspondence between Frederic and Stewart continued, Frederic revealed in full the details of Delia's conduct in Europe years earlier. All the pent-up resentment between Frederic and his sister poured forth. These letters, Delia wrote to William, who was now in Peru, have "done me the most serious injury" for "Comm S . . . shews them about everywhere as a justification of his barbarous conduct [to me]."[2]

In an attempt to help her husband's cause, but more to ingratiate herself with the Commodore, Delia wrote long letters to the president, the secretary of the navy, and Secretary of State John Quincy Adams explaining her involvement in the affair for which her husband stood accused. As far as she was concerned, the incident on the *Franklin* "scarcely deserved a momentary consideration—yet so deep is the hatred of Prevost to Commodore S. that by the most artful misrepresentations he has contrived to make it a subject of national important." Then she boldly claimed "All ships of war either English or French or American in the Pacific have given occasional asylum to persecuted individuals who have fled to them for safety."[3] Her letter generally derided the vices of Consul Prevost, extolled the virtues of Commodore Stewart, and closed with an expression of her "ardent desire" to converse with Adams personally. Of course this meant that she would have to go to Washington, but Frederic's interference in her affairs made this unlikely, as Stewart was increasingly annoyed with her. Accordingly, she asked Adams as a "favor" to write to Stewart "and urge him to take me on to Washington with him."[4] As far as Stewart was concerned, Delia had plotted her last plot. He stormed off to Washington alone, leaving his wife and children in a boardinghouse in Bordentown.

There was still the matter of the court martial. In spite of her apparent willingness to help her husband, Delia really wanted nothing to do with it. Earlier in the year, when she and Adams were in New York together, she had not taken the opportunity to discuss the matter with him. Later, she attributed this silence to her emotional state over the whole issue. Stewart selected as his lawyer the Philadelphian Joseph Hopkinson, whose father had been a signer of the Declaration of Independence. Delia wrote Hopkinson in February 1825 that a court martial should be avoided because it would be time consuming and costly. Later in July, she wrote him that she was concerned that her name might be dragged into the proceedings. Nevertheless, her husband expected her to be there and to testify for him.

By August 1825, Delia and her children were in Nahant, the seaside resort near Boston, visiting her mother. The Commodore received word in Washington at the time that his principal witness, Mr. O'Sullivan, had died, so there was no longer any reason for delay of the trial. He asked for an immediate hearing. August 18, 1825, was the date selected. In Nahant, Delia's family urged her to go to Washington to testify for her husband. She resisted. Robert Gardiner commented, "She was like a timid animal in the presence of a powerful force ready to devour it, against whom it has no power of resistance, and whom fear has deprived even of the power of flight."[5] It was as if, thought Gardiner, she was trying to escape some calamity. But the calamity was not to be avoided.

Since Hopkinson was to be deprived of Delia's direct testimony, he determined to have her give a deposition before a notary in Boston, which took place on August 9, 1825. When the trial concluded on September 4, Stewart was found innocent of every charge brought against him. Furthermore, and most significant, the court appended a ringing defense of the Commodore to its acquittal. Not one circumstance had been brought out, it firmly declared, that should impair the confidence of the court, the navy, or the nation in his honor, in his talent, in his patriotism. He was without question a distinguished officer. When William learned of the verdict in Lima he thought it just and fair. He wrote to his mother saying "I trust De. will make a vow never to meddle with serving any one again but refer all appeals to those who are responsible. Her nature is so imbued with a generous noble credulity that she is unfit to meddle in the affairs of the world."[6]

The stay-at-home Delia had to learn the outcome of her husband's trial from the newspaper. Not one word had she received from Stewart except through his lawyer.

But she consoled herself with the fantasy that as soon as the trial was over, her triumph would begin. Her husband would come to Boston to the plaudits of its citizens, sweep her into his arms, and a blissful new existence would begin for them. "Alas," moaned her mother, she is "unconscious of the dreadful whirlwind's sway."[7] Now, with little thanks to her, Stewart had been exonerated. Finally she faced the truth that there would be no exoneration for her. She had to gather her children about her and return to her home in Bordentown to "meet the dreadful wrath of her husband which she had done so much to provoke."[8]

Unwilling to face this alone, she invited a friend to travel with her and give her moral support. The friend, a Mrs. Elizabeth Blight of Bordentown, a wealthy widow, was fond of intrigues and had conceived a violent dislike for the Commodore. She was more than happy to be Delia's ally in the coming battle. She proved as helpful as her name indicated. When the party arrived at the Commodore's estate, Montpelier, on December 8, 1825, they found the owner away. He was only a mile down the road, however, staying with a Mr. Field. Delia and Mrs. Blight lost no time in moving into Montpelier. Then she dispatched an abject fawning letter to "My dearest husband," pretending to wonder why he was not at the manor house and why he had not written her: "I have been unable to account for your silence—it has been hinted to me that you were displeased with my having gone to Boston to visit my beloved, my aged, and I alas must add my infirmed mother."[9]

Scarcely a year before Delia had described the "aged" and "infirmed" paragon of a mother as looking younger and infinitely happier than before Delia had gone to South America. But that was in a letter to brother William. True, their mother was seventy-two years old in 1825, but this vigorous woman was to live another eighteen years and die just short of ninety. Delia went on to ring all the changes on this theme of an aged parent. Then there was her sister, her "only sister." In this period of such great anxiety, she needed such "kind attentions" under the roof of "my widowed parent."[10] Delia was living in a soap opera of her own creation and had a wonderfully dreamy attitude toward her problems. As her mother said, "Whatever she desires, she thinks possible, whatever is possible becomes probable—what's probable settles down into certainty."[11]

Just in case the claims of filial affection would not melt her husband's hard heart, Delia dangled the lure of sex: "Hasten then to me my dearest husband. . . . If by words or acts I can prove to you my poignant regret at having caused you even a moment of uneasiness I shall forget my sorrows—I shall live to prove that I have no dearer object than your happiness. . . . Adieu! Forgive love and console your affecte Delia."[12]

Stewart's reply was like a blast of ice water. It was an order to get out of his house and a declaration that he would never again sleep under the same roof with her.

Immediately, she rushed a letter off to Frederic asking him to hasten to Bordentown and protect her. Choosing Frederic to come to her aid was most curious. For at the same time she was appealing to him for assistance, she was blaming him in her letters to William for all her difficulties. And indeed Frederic's letters were of great use to the Commodore, for whenever one of Delia's friends protested to him of his treatment of his wife, he merely showed them her brother's letters. If Stewart thought he knew the worst of his wife, however, someone should have told him that he had not seen anything yet.

CHAPTER 17

The Dreadful Whirlwind's Sway

Did anyone in Delia's family try to understand her or ever reflect upon why she behaved as she did? Perhaps two persons did: her mother to some degree and her brother-in-law Robert Gardiner, the more objective of the two. In a letter to her son William written early in 1826 Delia's mother said: "This unhappy child my William was cradled in illusion—while she was pursuing the different objects of her own choice with an intensity which seldom occurs to a young girl the South Boston bubble (to us) was the prevailing theme with the male part of the family. . . . She thought the end of life was to be wealthy—to accomplish herself in order to enjoy good society—to diffuse blessings on such as were less fortunate—instead of play, after she laid aside her dolls which she loved with maternal fondness."[1] In other words, the men in her family taught her their goal in life—money—and she proved to be an excellent learner.

Gardiner, who had been the one who had taken care of Frederic during his recovery from his mental breakdown and who was now to help Delia as her marriage unraveled, wrote years later in his recollections: "I most sincerely pitied her situation. It was impossible for parties so entirely opposed as those of the Commodore and his wife to have the mutual affection necessary for the happiness of the married state, yet I was conscious that the evils had been greatly aggravated by her course of conduct."[2] Obviously her personality was a difficult one and her marriage with Stewart was a mistake from its start, but just as obvious was her need to receive from her brothers—especially Frederic—some degree of compassion. That never came.

What came was the breakup of the marriage, one marked with bitter and unkind acts on both sides. Frederic noted in his diary on December 15, 1825: "News from Phila. The Commodore determined to separate from his wife." At this point Frederic forwarded Delia's appeal to him for protection from Stewart to his brother-in-law Gardiner, saying that his business was such that he could not possibly go. He added, moreover, that Gardiner was a more suitable person to manage the matter. Delia's mother, then staying with the Gardiners at their Maine home, joined her pleas with his wife's, and shortly, Gardiner was headed south.

Once in Bordentown, poor Gardiner found himself thrust into a hornet's nest. None of these hornets took an objective view of the situation. Each was determined only to sting the other. Gardiner had the bad luck to be in the middle. On the legal theory then in force that the house belonged to the husband, Gardiner instructed Delia to move with her children into other lodgings, which he located for her. He then tried to deal with the lawyers and the Commodore to work towards a settlement of the difficulties.

Delia did not want a separation or a divorce; Stewart did not want a reconciliation and vowed he would never listen to a word on the subject. For a lawyer he retained Joseph Hopkinson, who had represented him at his court martial. During Gardiner's first interview with Hopkinson he was told again that any reconciliation was impossible. The Commodore would consider a legal separation only. Further, he insisted that his wife must give up all control of the children. He would pay her eight hundred dollars a year to live on, but only if she guaranteed that he would not find himself billed for any of her present or future debts. Gardiner replied he would tell Delia of the Commodore's proposal but would also recommend that she not agree to it. Delia was indignant, especially at the prospect of losing her children.

Gardiner urged Delia to get legal counsel and suggested another important Philadelphia lawyer, his friend William Meredith. Delia agreed, and Gardiner set off for Philadelphia to engage him and to outline the case. No sooner was he out of her sight than Delia set off for Philadelphia by another route to see Meredith herself. Gardiner explained her action in his recollections: "This was evidence that altho' she had accepted me as her friend and protector, she did not give me that confidence to which one in my situation was entitled. She was aware that there was much in her conduct which I did not approve, and she feared lest I should let Hopkinson [Meredith?] know of that disapprobation."[3]

The purpose of Delia's hasty visit to Philadelphia was to tell Meredith first-hand of her woes with the Commodore—some real but some probably fanciful—and to beg for his "assistance to intercede with Mr. Hopkinson to spare her children to her."[4] After Gardiner and Meredith had talked the case over they went to plead Delia's cause with

Joseph Hopkinson. They succeeded to the extent that he permitted her to take the children to Gardiner's home in Maine.

Meredith now made a counterproposal to Hopkinson. Delia should have entire control of the children, have her debts paid, and receive a larger alimony. Hopkinson refused, and Gardiner said they should go to court. If they did, Hopkinson said he would share with the court two facts: that Delia had borrowed money from her neighbor, Joseph Bonaparte, without her husband's knowledge—and he suggested that perhaps sexual favors might have been involved; and that Delia had gone late at night to a house of ill-fame.

The sad tale of Delia and Charles now becomes a dreadful whirlwind's sway. Delia denied Hopkinson's charges only to have to admit later to their truth. She had visited that house, she explained, only to have her fortune told, and she had lied about the loan so as not to incriminate herself. She made, however, her own charge in return: Stewart, it was reported by some, was staying at the home of a Mr. and Mrs. Field in Bordentown, and it was suggested that he was very friendly with Mrs. Field. At this point Gardiner retired from the situation and returned home to Maine.

Delia wanted him to take her children with him for fear that Stewart might take them from her. Reluctantly Gardiner agreed that she could send them to Maine after him and that he would pay the expenses. He arrived home to find the children already there. Stewart now threatened to sue Gardiner for kidnapping his children, since he had never agreed to Hopkinson's allowing them to leave Bordentown. Eventually it was arranged for the children to remain with Gardiner and his wife.

Delia remained in Bordentown, living with Mrs. Blight, who loaned her money from time to time. She also borrowed from her mother and Gardiner. She spent her time writing letters to anyone she thought might help her keep her children, including the president of the United States, John Quincy Adams.[5]

In the spring of 1827 Delia's mother came to stay with her, and they all moved to a boardinghouse in Princeton, New Jersey. Life here was said to be pleasant for the two ladies with their combined income of twelve hundred dollars a year. Delia usually frustrated Stewart's attempts to see his children. When grandmother Delia asked for permission to take her granddaughter to Maine for the 1827–1828 winter, the Commodore said no and, according to his wife, spoke of kidnapping his daughter. So, in panic, the household fled to a new boardinghouse in New York.

Delia continued to write long letters to her brother William about the wrongs done to her by "Commodore S"—and almost everyone else, especially Frederic. William wrote back and occasionally sent her money. However, he was still in business with Stewart and had just gratefully accepted a generous loan from him. Frederic sent no money to either his sister or his mother. He felt that any money sent to his mother would be spent by his sister, and he felt that he needed to protect his mother's small yearly income.

On a characteristic impulse, Delia suddenly decided that Secretary of State Henry Clay could be of assistance to her. So off she went with her household to Washington, where the social season was in full swing. This move, after the last few years of seclusion, put Delia back in her element. Invitations came from everywhere. Her mother wrote William that his sister's "spirits rose and she received the most unequivocal marks of esteem & *homage* from the various *diplomats* there collected."[6] One of the invitations was to a dinner party at the White House where the president arranged for Delia and her mother to sit on either side of him.

The next day she had a private meeting with the president. Adams wrote about it in his diary. "Her objective was to prevail upon me to write to Mr. Hopkinson of Philadelphia and urge him to induce her husband Commodore Stewart to make some adequate provision for her."[7] Adams replied that he would reflect on the matter. To his diary he commented: "They have been these two years or more separated after great imprudence and not a little misconduct on both sides. On her part inexcusable extravagance and disgraceful expedients to raise money for which he had been made responsible, on his part, harshness, intemperance and licentiousness."[8] She later had a talk with Henry Clay.

Delia lingered on in Washington until June 1828, when the heat made her mother ill. Where could she recover? Not in Boston, as Frederic did not wish to see either of them. And indeed Frederic's anger toward his sister was ferocious. In a letter to his brother Harry, Frederic raged: "The necessity I feel of protecting myself against Mrs. S. renders it proper that I should inform her which I request you to do, that if she comes here I shall have nothing to do with her or with any person who gives sanction to her proceedings & is aiding or abetting her. This whether that person be old or young—sick or well, a relation or a stranger."[9]

Where could they go then? It turned out to be Nahant, a seaside resort some fifteen miles north of Boston, where Mrs. Tudor had a cottage. So off they went.

CHAPTER 18

The Three Delias

ALONG WITH THE REST OF FASHIONABLE BOSTON, the Tudor family had made occasional visits to a one-square-mile tidal island that thrust like a fist into Massachusetts Bay a dozen miles north of the city. This resort, then a part of the town of Lynn, was called Nahant. After serving as a cow pasture for the farmers of Lynn for nearly two centuries, it was "discovered" by a Tudor family friend, Thomas H. Perkins. He built a cottage there in 1819 so that a grandson of his might have a healthy place to spend the summer.

For many years before that, those who had leisure would come to Nahant in summer for a relaxing day by the sea. Some might stay for a few days with one of the four Quaker families resident there, all of whom augmented their meager income from fishing and farming by opening their houses to the summer visitors. Perkins was quick to see the possibilities of Nahant as a place for his rich Boston friends to spend their money on summer vacations. Proper exploitation demanded a hotel and a way to get there quickly and conveniently. The newly developed steamboat provided an easy solution to the latter problem: soon enough, a steamboat ran between Boston and Nahant. Within four years Perkins erected America's first seaside resort hotel, which opened in 1823. Nahant's history as a pleasant place for the rich and famous to wile away the warm summer days began.

Upon his return from Havana in 1823, Frederic hired a house at Nahant for the summer. The experiment proved so successful that he hired a cottage for the next season as well. With Frederic came his mother and Delia Stewart, newly returned from

South America. Since the place was filled with fashion and the fashionable, Delia thought it better than any other place she had ever been too. But, more important, her brother Frederic treated her in a friendly manner. This was in 1824, before Delia's breach with the Commodore.

That summer, their mother decided to build a cottage of her own at Nahant, although Delia was quite content with the one that they rented. Mrs. Tudor purchased a good piece of property in the middle of the resort from Daniel Breed. She planned to build a simple cottage, using the proceeds from the annuity Frederic paid her for the building the family owned on Court Street plus contributions from the rest of the family. The foundation was dug in the fall of 1824, and the cottage was fairly well completed by the following year.

Two things altered the original plan drastically: the family was not forthcoming with contributions and Frederic took charge of the building operation. Under his direction, the simple stone cottage became something more substantial and elaborate. As a result, the cost of the project exceeded everyone's expectations, and since Frederic was the only member of the family footing the bills, his mother's simple cottage became a country seat by the seashore for himself. Once started, he could not be stopped. All the energies he had once bestowed on Rockwood, until that estate was sold, he now focused on Nahant. And the project held one additional attraction for him—he could mold the whole establishment after his own ideas.

In the spring of 1825 Frederic began traveling back and forth to Nahant. He hired a young man, David Day, early in April to do most of the farm work. When the ground permitted, Frederic started his garden. Two-year-old asparagus roots were put in on April 9. A week later in went peas, lettuce, and beans. By April 22, he was excited to see the asparagus poking two inches above ground. Now, like any novice gardener, he started to plant everything he could lay his hands on. He sowed parsley, onions, radishes, tomatoes, squash, turnips, carrots, beets, and green peppers in what he still called his mother's cottage garden. Then came sweet corn and potatoes and, shortly afterwards, more asparagus roots—this time three years old and from Gardiner's farm in Maine. On May 5 the proud farmer cut a mess of asparagus from the garden and had the delight of eating his first produce.

Besides walking or riding to Nahant, Frederic sailed there in his boat, the *Ohio*. The boat was particularly useful because it could carry all kinds of necessaries: people, provisions, furniture, and household goods. Sometimes it brought a carpenter with locks and fastenings, once a lightning rod, and another time Harry's canoe. The trip from Boston could be as long as four hours if the wind were light, and it could involve some rowing if the wind failed. The fastest passage recorded that summer was on July 7, when Frederic made the trip in one hour and forty minutes. Whether long or short,

Nahant
Lithograph, n.d., by Mary Jane Derby.
Pendleton's Lithog. Boston.
A/B64/N1/V.g. (no. 3).
Boston Athenæum.

the time spent was pleasant. Frederic and his friends even used it to go fishing. All in all, Frederic took great pleasure in playing the role of a country squire at Nahant.[1]

That first season of 1825 in the Nahant cottage was a busy one with family gatherings. Delia Tudor was in residence, and the entire family came to visit. Delia Stewart hid out there during her husband's court martial. She had her two children christened there on September 3, 1825, by the Reverend Dr. John Silvester Gardiner, with Frederic and Mrs. Thomas H. Perkins, Jr., as sponsors. The Commodore was significantly absent. It was also in this cottage that the three Delias sought refuge during the difficult summer of 1828. Frederic, in order to keep the peace, confined his visits that summer to day trips. Once he stayed at the hotel for a night. His sacrifice of his summer in Nahant was not appreciated by his sister, however. He complained to his diary, "It may be put down as true charity to give to the thankless who have little claim but poverty. From the first I have heard no word of thanks." But with regard to his mother, she "has exhibited a grateful heart for a bounty which has often been a great inconvenience to me."[2]

The settlement with the Commodore, which dragged on for three years, came to an end late in 1828, when Delia finally accepted the arrangement that Gardiner had worked out for her in 1825. The Commodore agreed to pay her debts and allow her eight hundred dollars a year. In addition, the agreement stipulated that Stewart would not be responsible for any future debts Delia might incur. It turned out, however, that the list of bills she had submitted represented only a small part of what she actually owed. She had been afraid to list them all. So these remaining liabilities went unpaid. The allowance from Stewart was paid over to Gardiner, not to Delia, who paid from it any bills she acquired. When the final divorce papers were signed at the beginning of 1829, Delia's new life began. She had custody of her daughter, Delia, but not her son, Charles, who remained with his father. Delia also had the companionship of a house in Washington, and there the three Delias settled. Between them they had an income of thirteen hundred dollars a year, which paid their living expenses and a bit more. It was a very pleasant income for those times.[3]

In faraway Peru, William was kept abreast of all these dramatic changes in long and distressful letters from his sister Delia. William had arrived in Peru early in 1824, just in time to greet his sister and the Commodore before they sailed back home. In fact, Delia reminded him later that he had actually been on board the *Franklin* when the fugitive she was accused of concealing had come aboard to thank her for saving his life.

William was swamped with letters from his friends and family at home, including one from Col. Thomas H. Perkins, who informed him of the latest developments with regard to the Bunker Hill Monument. He told William also of Stewart's request for a court martial to settle the charges against him arising out of his South American duty, of the summer cottage at Nahant that his brother was building, and of his own house at Brookline.

William found that making a fortune in Peru was as illusive a thing there as it had been back in Boston. He explained it to John Quincy Adams in September 1824 that

> The state of the country & my unwillingness to make engagements that would detain me several years from home, have made me decline forming

> any commercial engagements here. The small means I could command I have employed through the agency of others in some moderate speculations which have hitherto been fortunate. The Consulate does not yield enough to pay for a clerk, judging from what it has yielded the fees would not amount to 300$ a year.[4]

Williams's position paid no salary. He was expected to earn his keep on the commissions he charged American merchants for the transactions that he undertook for them. Since the real money was to be made in smuggling, not in legitimate trade, he received few payments. Soon after his arrival, he importuned his politically connected friends at home to secure him a salary. He wrote Colonel Perkins to see if some branch bank could be set up in Peru, but this did not materialize. Whatever William set his hand to did not turn into gold. The Midas touch was not his.

By May 1827, after three years in Peru, William was heartily sick of the place, its lack of culture, and—in his view—its ignorant inhabitants. No one was more anxious than he to return to his native country, which he expected to do in the spring of 1828. In addition, complaints that he neglected his consular duties drifted in to Washington. These complaints derived mostly from a venture William undertook.

Soon after he arrived in Peru he became involved in a mining effort in the Cordilleras, which took him out of Lima for weeks on end. He had as his vice-consul Stanhope Prevost, son of the United States agent John W. Prevost, who had been Stewart's antagonist. Stanhope was a merchant, and whenever William was away, Stanhope refused to act on anything controversial, fearing to hurt his own mercantile business. Commodore Hull complained bitterly to William of his long absences from his duties and warned him of the consequences.

By mid August 1826, the political situation in Lima was chaotic. William advised Commodore Hull to have his family ready to leave at a moment's notice, then unwisely left for his mines in the mountains. Hull complained again in September, and his complaints undoubtedly reached Washington. Before long William was notified of a change of assignment. President Adams found a place for him on the other side of the continent, in Brazil, where William might be induced to pay more attention to government business. His new job as United States chargé d'affaires paid $4,500 a year, about equivalent with the earnings of the manager of one of the large textile mills near Boston. In addition, he received $10,000 for the two and a half years he had spent in Lima. William was at last a man of comfortable means. It certainly paid to have friends in high places. He left Peru in December 1827 and made a most leisurely journey down the coast, not even reaching Valparaiso, Chile, until April 1828.

Shortly after his arrival in Rio de Janeiro, William wrote Daniel Webster, now secretary of state, that he hoped to have a treaty signed between that country and the United States. He anticipated that once such a treaty was in place he would resign. He had no motive for staying. He was tired of South America. Promotion was uncertain and the salary was—he said—far too small. This was an amazing statement, given that he was receiving more money than he ever had in his life, but probably quite true for one with a spendthrift sister who helped herself to his salary.

Back in Washington, former president John Quincy Adams, after a pleasant evening entertaining Delia and her mother, reflected in his diary that William's mission to Brazil had been of great value: "He has obtained a settlement of many of the complaints of commercial depredations, and has concluded a commercial treaty so advantageous that it has been ratified by the present President, by and with the advice and consent of the present Senate. Tudor unadvisedly asked and urged last summer permission to return to the United States. . . . His health has been much affected by living in tropical climates."[5]

William never did return. He was not to see the United States or his family again. March 9, 1830, a Tuesday, was a cold day in Boston, with a northwest wind. Frederic busied himself loading a brig with ice for his southern markets. On this day, in Rio, William died. The cause was an infection of the urinary tract that he had had for several years.

The news, or at least the first intimation that all was not well, did not reach Boston until April 28. On that day Frederic noted that he had a letter from Rio dated March 7 which mentioned "the extreme illness of my Brother William as that there was no hope of his recovery. There will be but one sentiment in the family on this disturbing event & amongst as extensive acquaintance a very general regret. He was born 28th Jan. 1779. He is therefore in his 52nd year."[6] This dry entry hid Frederic's real feeling of loss.

At William's death, his mother and his sister Delia asked former president John Quincy Adams to write an obituary notice. He agreed and on May 3 called upon the two Delias seeking biographical information concerning William. They had almost no facts to give him, and that night when he attempted to start the obituary he found himself "obliged to generalize everything" and soon had "to stop in utter dissatisfaction."[7] Further conversations with the two Delias proved unproductive. Delia Stewart was only interested in the publication of an immediate obituary in the newspapers, while Delia Tudor tried to make Adams list all of William's titles. She also asked him to show that William had cleaned up the mess in Rio made by the previous consul. Adams refused.

More confusion ensued. Adams had asked Alexander H. Everett to write a biographical notice on William for the *North American Review*. The two Delias approved.

But when Everett indicated that he planned to consult with Frederic concerning the early part of his brother's life, which he would need for the narrative, the two Delias objected. Indeed, they did not want Frederic's name mentioned at all. As the months rolled along and the year became 1831, the two ladies' interference dominated the discussions concerning the biographical notice. They insisted that the piece might include William's letters, biographical notices on all the members of the family (except Frederic), and a translation in verse from Virgil's *Georgics* prepared by the youngest Delia. Mrs. Stewart also wanted to include any good words William had written about her. Then they did not want the biographical notice published in the *North American Review* but instead in a book of his miscellaneous writings. The two Delias saw the book's profits as a way to pay off their debts.

John Quincy Adams made his last diary entry about the biographical notice on March 23, 1831. When that plea disappears, it is replaced by Delia Tudor's request for help securing from Congress a pension based on her husband's Revolutionary War service and compensation for her as a result of the work William, Jr., did in South America. With Adams's aid she eventually got the pension and forty-five hundred dollars for William's services to his country. As for William, no biographical notice about him ever appeared in the *North American Review*.

CHAPTER 19

Of Salt, Double Dories, and Love

HARRY DID SUCH A GOOD JOB SETTING UP the New Orleans icehouse in 1822 that Frederic employed him regularly in the business from that time on. In the spring of 1825 Frederic sent him to Savannah on an icehouse project. Harry returned to Boston early that July in time to accompany Frederic on an inspection of the coal mine on Martha's Vineyard in August. Frederic had not given up the idea of mining coal; he had only postponed it until he had available capital.

So they sailed from Nahant in the *Ohio* at quarter past eight on the morning of August 10, 1825, with George Johnson from Nahant as pilot. Nine and a half hours later, they arrived at Sandwich on the north side of the Cape, where they spent the night. The next day they had the *Ohio* taken by wagon overland seven miles to the south side of the Cape. Carting the boat took all afternoon, but it saved the long and dangerous sail around the hook of Cape Cod. Off they set again. It was dark before they decided to stop for the night. Not seeing any houses in the vicinity, they anchored the boat near the shore, cooked an excellent supper—fried eggs and coffee—then went to sleep under an awning they had erected.

On Friday they set sail at four in the morning and arrived off Gay Head on the Vineyard just before noon. With the help of two Native Americans, they dragged the boat and baggage on to the beach. Saturday was spent at Gay Head as the three of them were tired—so fatigued, it appears, that Frederic's diary does not mention that they looked at the coal mine that had been the original purpose of the trip. They did not launch the boat for the trip back until quarter after nine on Sunday morning, and it was 8 P.M. when they arrived at Sandwich, as they ran out of wind and had to row part of the way. Frederic and Harry stayed in Sandwich to relax and recuperate, then returned to Boston in the coach while George Johnson sailed back aboard the *Ohio*.

Harry was a frequent visitor at Frederic's vacation estate that summer and fall. Although the last guest had long since left Nahant, Frederic and Harry were still there on October 15. That day there was a rainstorm from the southeast, and overhead the green plovers and ducks were flying to winter quarters. Harry, in spite of the storm, was employed "in making experiments on evaporation & arcana of salt works & salt making."[1] Nahant was nearly surrounded with water. Salt water. In 1825 salt sold for forty cents a bushel. So it was logical to add salt-making, which was already well established in Cape Cod, to farming at Nahant. Harry started the project, but within ten days, as might have been expected, Frederic took it over: "Today completed two vats 15 feet square each & put water (sea) upon them in hopes of having them tight, by the swelling of the stuff tomorrow."[2]

The salt experiments continued. On November 2 they tried using cloth to aid in the evaporation by "capillary attraction," though it was late in the season for any satisfactory results. Later that month, Frederic carefully recorded all the details in his diary. As his enthusiasm grew, so did the scope of the salt project. By December he proposed that Harry take a one-quarter interest in the new venture, but to Frederic's annoyance his brother refused. The winter was now upon them, and so Frederic put away his new salt toy until spring. Harry was sent to New Orleans on ice business. By the time spring 1826 arrived, Frederic's interest in salt-making had cooled, leaving it to Harry alone. He moved its operations from Nahant to Hull, just south of Boston, and continued his salt business for some years to come during the summers.

Frederic got caught up in one of his former interests: boat design. He reckoned that he could get "swift sailing stability cheapness & convenience" from a boat made up of two hulls, rather like a catamaran, which has two parallel hulls that provide the ability to stay upright even under full sail.[3] Frederic designed his using two dories, the beach fishing boats used in nearby Swampscott and along the North Shore. The dory has a relatively narrow, flat, rockered bottom, straight flaring sides, and a nearly double-ended shape with a very narrow triangular stern. By connecting two dories, side by side, with a cross deck and a sailing rig, Frederic thought to produce a stable craft that would sail fast because its two hulls had little wetted surface. Frederic arranged to have a prototype built by a local firm, Tufts and Taylor's. On Tuesday, April 16, he was busy inspecting their work. That Saturday afternoon, the two dories were carted to Nahant, soon connected together, and fitted with a mast and sails. It took six men to carry the boat to the water. In this first test the boat sailed no faster than any other boat—but it did sail. Obviously, Frederic still had improvements to make. So he had the boat refitted with more keel aft, an enlarged sail, and a deck constructed between the dories to cut down on the spray.

Much to Frederic's pleasure, "The talk of Lynn & Swampscott is about the double dory. About half saying the plan will not do—most of the others in doubt & a few saying that the plan will do."[4] Ten days later Frederic took her for a second test sail but was again not completely satisfied with her speed. On June 2 he was at Tufts and Taylor's giving "instruction for a new double dory . . . to be 20 feet long . . . to be rigged a sloop."[5] The project now took on a new and commercial aspect. It was rumored that the steamboat service between Nahant and Boston was to be terminated. If his new vessel proved satisfactory, he hoped to have her replace the ferry to Boston. A bit later, he thought better of this idea.

During the summer of 1826, Frederic continued to be fascinated with his double dories, the larger of which he had named the *Gemini*. In June he held his own regatta off Nahant. His two double dories raced against the hotel's small sailboat. The *Gemini* won the day.

In November 1826, Harry went back to New Orleans to build a new icehouse, and Frederic settled into another winter of superintending ice shipments. By now, his business had grown so large that he could no longer manage it alone. So that fall a new assistant appeared in his life: twenty-four-year-old Nathaniel Jarvis Wyeth. He hired Wyeth on November 1 at a salary of five hundred dollars a year to supervise securing the ice from Fresh Pond in Cambridge, which was at this point Frederic's primary ice source.

Wyeth's family had owned land in Cambridge since 1751, part of which bordered on Fresh Pond. Just before the turn of the century, Nathaniel's father built a hotel on the bluff overlooking the pond, and being a pleasant carriage ride from town, it quickly became a popular summer resort for Bostonians. On January 29, 1802, Nathaniel was born in the hotel. The Jarvis in his name came from his mother's father. Exactly twenty-two years later, he married his cousin Elizabeth Jarvis Stone, two years his senior. The family expected him to go to Harvard College, as had his father and older brother, but for some reason he did not. Instead, he worked in his father's hotel until Frederic hired him.

Wyeth took charge of cutting the ice, storing it, carting it, fitting out the vessels, and loading them. Frederic continued to operate all other phases of the business. For the five hundred dollars a year he paid Wyeth, Frederic got a bonus—Wyeth's extraordinary inventiveness. The ice business was not new to Wyeth, as his hotel had an icehouse, and as manager he harvested ice from Fresh Pond for his own use and to sell to local retail merchants. Wyeth, always thinking of ways to better the ordinary operations of the business, had invented a horse-drawn ice cutter in 1825. The invention solved two problems Frederic had struggled with for over twenty years. The original manner of cutting ice by hand into blocks of random sizes was slow and expensive, and loading them in a ship was no easier. Wyeth's contraption speeded up the process immensely and assured that every piece was cut to the same size. The hand-cut blocks had tended to shift during the voyage; uniformly sized blocks, stacked neatly, would stay put.

Frederic could not find enough adjectives to praise Wyeth. He was "active & Intelligent." He was "of singular excellence." He was "just enough of a schemer & inventor to be valuable."[6] After Wyeth's superior performance in the 1826–1827 season, Frederic continued his employment the next winter. With Wyeth and the weather both on his side, how could 1827–1828 not be the best season ever?

By the spring of 1827, Harry was still in New Orleans. With the activity of his ice business completed for the season, Frederic turned his attention once again to Harry's salt project. By now, a saltworks had been constructed at Hull, and Frederic sent his boatman, Pette, to work there. Going to Hull to check on the saltmaking became one of Frederic's regular activities over the next couple of months. Usually it was an excuse for a day of fishing. He thought of ways that the process could be improved, but he did not wish to get too involved. When Harry came home in July he returned to his salt operation and Frederic was relieved of that responsibility.

Nathaniel Jarvis Wyeth
Courtesy of the Northwest Room, Spokane Public Library.

In the fall of 1827, Frederic sent Harry off for the winter on ice business to Charleston, South Carolina, and Augusta, Georgia. His main task was to erect a new icehouse in Charleston. Harry sailed from New York on November 22 and arrived in Charleston five days later. Land for a new icehouse had already been purchased for forty-six hundred dollars. It had a dwelling house on it, which took two weeks to raze, and in another ten days Harry had laborers digging the foundation and carts leveling the ground.

By January 5, 1828, the brick walls of the icehouse were far enough along to allow Harry to take the coach to Augusta, Georgia. He spent two weeks there getting the existing icehouse repaired, and then he traveled on to Savannah. Rather than putting up a new building in Savannah, Harry rented a two-story store and fitted it to hold ice. By February 7, he was back in Charleston to check on the progress of the new brick icehouse. Frederic kept a steady stream of letters flowing to his brother in which he lectured him on his views of business methods. His advise can be summed up in a sentence: "to produce the most perfect results . . . attention to perpetual & perfect discipline, is necessary."[7] Woe be to those who deviated from his instructions—including Harry. With his brother, however, Frederic employed the carrot as well as the stick. "The very admirable doing of yourself for me last year at New Orleans" was the carrot of praise.[8] But the stick of rebuke quickly followed: "your going contrary to my instructions & allowing Beamis to get drunk & brag about 9-10m sales *would be my ruin*. But I see again some disposition in you to doubt my judgement & *to act against positive instructions*. This will not—cannot be admitted. . . . It is absolutely necessary that I should be *obeyed*. I *must* be a dictator." He ended his tirade with "Do this & please. yrs. affectionately. F."[9]

While the three Delias were staying in Nahant during the summer of 1828, Frederic forsook his cottage to avoid embarrassing confrontations. He spent his summer on boat excursions to Hull and the islands in Boston Harbor with Harry and some of his bachelor friends from Betsy Lekain's boardinghouse. Come November, Harry was off as usual to build a new icehouse, this time at New Orleans. The spring and early summer of 1829 were especially busy for Frederic. Ice shipments extended longer than usual. There were fewer sporting excursions and only two trips to Nahant during the whole of July. The second trip, however, was to be momentous.

On July 29 he went down by steamer to attend a ball at the Nahant Hotel. There the forty-seven-year-old bachelor danced with little intermission from eight until midnight with a charming twenty-nine-year-old widow from Philadelphia and Bordentown. She had been born, in 1800, Elizabeth Hopkinson, the daughter of Joseph Hopkinson, the same Joseph Hopkinson who was Commodore Stewart's lawyer in his separation from Frederic's sister Delia. Elizabeth had first married John Keating, Jr., who died in 1824 and left her, with her sweet blue eyes and soft brown hair, a most enchanting widow.

Within two years of widowhood, it was rumored in Philadelphia that she had plighted her troth to William Biddle, but she was still the Widow Keating when Frederic met her in Nahant in the summer of 1829. She obviously charmed Frederic, as four days later he took Mrs. Keating and a party of ladies for a carriage drive. Then there was an excursion with Mrs. Keating and a party of ladies as far as Framingham, where they all dined. The ladies continued *en route* to Saratoga, while Frederic returned to Boston. The next day, he wrote to her in Saratoga. The letters continued through the fall and winter of 1829 and right on through the spring of 1830. On June 15, 1830, he took passage for a trip to Bordentown to visit her. As he wrote Harry when he returned: "My affair with Mrs. Keating is status quo anti bellum & whether it will ever come to any thing time must determine. . . . It is a hard thing for a lady of 30 to assimilate with new friends & new habits."[10]

Frederic was back in Boston on July 1, 1830, and planned a trip to Saratoga to see his lady in August. On August 7, he confided to his diary that he had "finished with a fair lady my contract for divided empire."[11] Mrs. Keating's brother-in-law came to Nahant early in September to work out the details of the marriage. By October, Frederic was busy preparing his Nahant cottage for another occupant. On November 5, things were settled and he could note that he had bid his adieu to a free life.

But he had taken that adieu too soon. By the end of the month, he had learned that his affair at Philadelphia was over. A banking friend there had told him about it, and Frederic wrote him on December 9 that the rupture had been determined by the lady, not by himself: "The lady is universally admitted to be a very fine woman. The cause of the rupture, I incline to believe arose very much from the circumstance of the implied necessity of leaving her home & residing in a strange city. Other reasons I leave to be given by herself—Ladies in these matters have entire authority."[12] On the same day he wrote Mrs. Keating, asking the return of all his letters to her; he received them back on December 23, a somewhat unwelcome Christmas present! On that merry day, he wrote in his diary the laconic phrase "Free life no marriage."

Those words—free life no marriage—and his abortive affair with Mrs. Keating raise the question of Frederic's sexual life. Clearly a man as passionate as Frederic Tudor was not likely to remain celibate until married, and when he finally did, the lack of a sexual appetite was not the complaint uttered by his wife. Indeed, she considered him too randy and insistent. A marginal note in his diary written by his wife after his death indicates that before his marriage he had had a long-term affair with another woman. Since she provided no name, one can only speculate who Frederic's companion might have been. The main candidates suggested by Frederic's diaries are Betsy Lekain, his landlady for so many years, and Mary Groves, his Nahant housekeeper for ten years before his marriage. After September 1, 1834, when Frederic lists his household as of that date, faithful Mary Groves is missing, never to reappear again. There is no evidence whatsoever that when Frederic finally wed he ever strayed from his marriage bed.

Meanwhile brother Harry continued to make salt in the summer and supervise the construction of Frederic's growing chain of icehouses in the winter. By 1831, his salt operation was producing a hundred bushels a day, but as a commercial venture it did not make him inevitably and unavoidably rich. In a letter written in August 1845, James L. Homer described the saltworks as "an object of some interest to visitors at Hull. Mr. T. may be considered an amateur salt manufacturer, for he certainly cannot make much money by his works."[13] As to the double dory, it went the way of Frederic's other failed ideas. He sold the vessel and abandoned the project. But there always proliferated in Frederic's head other worlds for him to conquer.

CHAPTER 20

The Winter That Rotted in the Sky

THE WINTER OF 1827–1828 MADE FOR GREAT UNEASE FOR THE head that bore the crown of the Ice King. When Frederic opened his almanac diary to inscribe his notes for November 1827, he found this advice from its editors: "Now my friends, put your affairs in order and prepare for an attack. Old December will soon approach with a fierce battalion of snow, sleet, cold wind and tempest. . . . Yes, come on my farmer warriors, and be ready for the onset."[1] Frederic farmed the frozen waters of New England rather than its soil, but ice had to be ploughed and harvested as carefully as any other crop. The difference was that he harvested his crop while the land farmers were huddling about their firesides.

As winter approached, Frederic's prospects looked especially favorable. Since his return to Boston in the spring of 1823, his ice business had gone well, expanded, and become organized to the point that by March 1827 he had finished harvesting ice for that season. His ice trade was two decades old now. Frederic calculated the total shipments of goods from the port of Boston in 1826–1827 at three thousand tons, of which he had shipped two-thirds. His strongholds—New Orleans, Charleston, and Havana—took most of that stock. Competitors, who had sprung up once he had established the trade, shipped to such places as Wilmington, Delaware; Norfolk, Virginia; and Martinique. One even dared to ship to Charleston; Frederic met him with a price war.

The ice trade flourished only because Boston was the port of entry for southern cotton destined for the textile mills that surrounded the city. Since the South imported no goods from Boston, vessels on the return trip had to go in ballast, which sometimes meant a hold filled with rocks. Thus, ship owners were prepared to give ice cargoes a low rate. By the same token, Boston had the ice trade almost entirely to itself: the other principal ports—New York, Philadelphia, and Baltimore—shipped farm produce from their back country to the South. The mountains in western Massachusetts blocked Boston from produce grown west of the Hudson River, and the soil east of the mountains was too poor to support large-scale agriculture. Consequently, the growing ice trade could make a substantial contribution to the economy of New England only.

Since temperature was of the essence, Frederic kept a constant eye on his thermometer and recorded the temperature daily. November 1827 was remarkably cold for so early in the season. It looked to Frederic that this winter promised a good crop of ice for cutting.

December began with the temperature hovering annoyingly just above freezing. If one day it dropped to 32 degrees, the next day it shot to 52. Frederic's hopes rose on December 8 when the temperature dipped to 30, but for much of the month it stayed at 36 or just above. Indeed, on the fifteenth it was 48. That day as he walked the nine miles from Boston to Fresh Pond in Cambridge, a walk he made often and one he very much enjoyed, he perspired freely. So far this month he had harvested no ice; instead, he was busy ordering bushes and vines to sell in Havana. It seemed more like spring planting time than winter.

He conferred with Wyeth about a new invention: an iron and steel ice cutter that could cut blocks four inches deep. Wyeth also had made a model for an improved ice-loading machine, and Frederic ordered one to be made. On December 20 the thermometer registered 20. Frederic began to feel in the mood for business and signed agreements with Ephraim Spear, a shoemaker aged twenty-five, to take charge of the icehouse in Savannah and with John Beamis to do the same at Augusta. Spear was to get sixty dollars a month and Beamis eighty.

On December 22 the temperature fell to 15 degrees—the coldest it had been so far this winter. The next day it fell to 6. Finally, real winter had come. The day before Christmas Frederic could walk across Fresh Pond on ice five inches thick. Three days later it thickened to eight inches, and a light snow was falling. But the next day, up went the glass to 36, with an easterly rain carrying off the snow. Two days later he walked out to Fresh Pond to see a demonstration of Wyeth's newest ice-loading machine. It failed to meet his approval and the workers returned the older method. When Frederic walked out at noon on December 30, the thermometer, which had read 20 in the morning, read 38. The weather was, as the almanac had predicted for December, changeable—always a safe call in New England.

Ice Cutting at Fresh Pond in Cambridge
Ballou's Illustrated Drawing-Room Companion, *Mar. 17, 1855.*
Collection of the Massachusetts Historical Society.

New Year's Day 1828 came, and Frederic, with a friend from the boardinghouse where he lived, walked to Fresh Pond with skates in their pockets. At the icehouse they put on their blades and coursed about the pond for an hour. Frederic had not skated for years, but he greatly enjoyed any exercise. He came back to Wyeth's hotel and dined on pickerel from the pond. Several men could be seen fishing through the ice. One had caught several pickerel weighing at least twenty pounds.

Wyeth had begun cutting ice for his own icehouse, even though it was only six inches thick. Although Wyeth was in charge of Frederic's ice business, he continued to harvest ice for retail ice dealers in Boston. A number of other people were also cutting on the pond, but Frederic felt it was still too thin for him. Perhaps he could begin after three or four more days of cold weather. It was not to be. The remarkable mildness continued. On Sunday, January 13, he put on his overshoes and walked to Wyeth's. The mud was so deep in many places that he had to walk across the fields. He found Wyeth wandering about the woods "in all the lonely perturbation of invention & contrivance."[2]

Wyeth's fertile brain was developing improvements for his earlier creations. "I have from time to time given him several hints, particularly respecting the ice cutter which I first suggested to him."[3] Seeing him thus busy with his schemes, Frederic, thinking of the day of rest, could not forbear noting in his diary that "for minds highly excited & in great activity there is no Sunday."[4] Through the month of January, Frederic made arrangements just as if this were an ordinary winter. He dickered with ship owners to hire their vessels to supply his icehouses in the South. He had his men ready to commence work as soon as the temperature could produce ice of the required thickness.

His consolation for the warm spell was the old proverb "the winter never rots in the sky."[5] On January 22, the old proverb seemed true, as the thermometer plunged to two above zero, the coldest day of the winter. Frederic exulted: "The frost covers the windows, the wheels creak, the boys run, winter rules & $50,000 worth of ice now floats for me upon Fresh Pond."[6] The next day, he commenced cutting and testing Wyeth's new rig for hoisting ice into wagons. Instead of walking, he rode a chaise to the pond with his icehouse keeper from Havana, John Damon, who was on holiday in Boston. They saw the new device in operation. Inspired by this burst of activity, he then walked to Charlestown and started to arrange for fitting two vessels at Deven's Wharf to receive the ice.

Just when things started to go along normally, the weather moderated again. At the wharf they had fifty cords (sixty-four hundred cubic feet) of ice piled outdoors, trusting to the cold weather to preserve it. Then the thermometer soared to 43; the next day it rose to 60. Wyeth grew very concerned. One vessel had been loaded with seventeen cords of ice, but another ninety-three cords were sitting in a shed at the wharf. And Frederic had six vessels waiting to be loaded and no ice. On Saturday, January 26, Frederic went to discuss the matter with Wyeth. But weather is as weather does: talking about it has no affect on it.

The next day, a Sunday, the thermometer obligingly dropped to freezing, but the pond was so thawed on the edges that no wagons could be loaded. The roads were so muddy that even carting was nearly impossible. Yet Wyeth was not a man to be frustrated easily by Nature. He was, Frederic wrote admiringly, "equal to a difficulty which to common minds seems insurmountable. He was on the pond without hat or coat. He had forgotten that the Therm. was at the freezing point. In his yet unsettled plans he found warmth or circulation from the calm-seeming but in fact vigorous action of his mind."[7]

Wyeth developed a new scheme for loading the wagons. He had the workers cut an extended canal in the ice leading to the icehouse lift. They would then float the ice blocks over to the lift, draw them out of the pond, pass them along a staging yet to be built, and slide them along this to the wagons waiting just under a declivity of the hill. Wyeth would keep a team of two horses to help pull the wagons up the hill.

On that last freezing Sunday in January, Wyeth cut ice that had been in the shade of a hill through the preceding day of the great thaw and so had not melted as fast as other ice in the pond. Although it was only seven and a half inches thick, Wyeth believed he could get thirty cords into his icehouse before nightfall. When the thermometer rose to 36 the next day, the snow melted into slush. Traveling became quite bad. Still they managed to cart fifteen loads over to Charlestown.

Frederic began walking to Charlestown two or three times a day from his boardinghouse in Boston. Not only was it good exercise, it also encouraged Wyeth, the workmen, and the captains of the vessels, who wanted to get their ships loaded and under sail. The longer they sat in port, the less money they would make.

Every time the temperature dipped below freezing, Wyeth kept his men at work, sometimes straight through the night. They could not afford to lose a moment. Now knowing that this would be a treacherous winter, they would cut ice whenever and wherever they could. Wyeth performed what seemed to be miracles. The ice they were loading on the vessels now came directly from the pond. In the meantime, Wyeth kept putting ice into his own icehouse. He tried to keep a steady two hundred cords available there. He would cut even when the temperature was at 60, provided that the sky was overcast. During the day they would load the teams, and during the night they would fill the icehouse. Frederic, to be on the safe side, wrote to his brother-in-law Gardiner to ask him to build a temporary icehouse at the Kennebec; if filled in advance, it would have an additional supply of ice for the hungry maws of their southern icehouses.

Frederic had agreed to pay the teamsters who were taking the ice from Cambridge to Charlestown an extra fifty cents per cord during the bad traveling. Three teamsters had already agreed on a fixed price calculated for an ordinary winter, but Frederic gave them the extra payments, too. Because of the bad roads, Wyeth proposed to try gondolas to sled the ice along; however, he had no luck finding them. Frederic talked of using rafts or a canalboat to bring ice to Charlestown. They had to do whatever they could to avoid delays, for ship owners punished Frederic with a charge known as "demurrage" when they had to wait for their cargoes beyond an agreed-upon period (this detention was also called "demurrage").

Yet the key to this winter remained the weather, which continued to be against them. On February 7, Frederic wrote in his diary that the skies were "weeping." Such rain was deadly. Frederic had twelve out of fifteen teamsters on hand, but it was the worst day for moving ice that he could remember. Everywhere there was mud, and driving through it exhausted both the horses and the drivers. Sometimes the frost still in the road softened and the wheels of the wagons sank down into the ruts up to their hubs, at which point the drivers had to abandon the ice on that wagon and add his horses to the new wagons coming along.

There were little triumphs, however. Wyeth came in to see Frederic on February 8, a day when the temperature hit 26, to report that he had found ice nine inches thick on the south side of the pond. A steep hill had shaded the area. The previous night he had taken in forty cords of excellent ice. Frederic suggested rafting this ice to the icehouse rather than hauling it around the pond. He took Wyeth to Charlestown to order the boards to build these rafts, then he went to the pond to see how bad the roads were, particularly on Wyeth's property.

The day before, Wyeth told him, just to draw six feet of ice in a load had taken sixteen oxen and horses. Frederic was able to canoe to within one hundred rods of Wyeth's icehouse, where just four days before there had been ice strong enough to support a horse. When Frederic sat down to lunch, a neighbor showed Wyeth and Tudor a sprig from a cherry tree on which the buds had started to swell. That night, Frederic wrote again to Gardiner, asking him to cut an additional 250 cords at Kennebec. Finally Frederic had to start paying demurrage to the ship owners for waiting so long.

Back at the pond on February 10, Frederic found the ice-cutters had built a fort of about one hundred cords on the north bank. Some of the opposition cutters had built two forts, though neither as large as Wyeth's. Now most cutting took place at night, because by eleven or twelve o'clock in the morning the ice was too soft. For more than three weeks there had been no Sundays and no nights off at the pond. Men cut when the ice was hard enough. They slept and rested only when they could not cut. Even then only small amounts could be harvested—ten cords one night, fifteen cords another. It was costing Frederic a lot of money to harvest his ice this way; furthermore, the ice his men did cut was of very poor quality. By the middle of the month the ice was so broken at Fresh Pond that the work there came to an end.

With their prime source of ice gone, Frederic and Wyeth began to look around at other ponds. A man was sent to look at Jamaica Pond; he reported that the ice there was also all gone. Wyeth visited Spy Pond in West Cambridge (now Arlington), hoping he might be able to cut 40 to 50 cords there. Steadman, one of Frederic's competitors, offered him 100 cords of ice from his icehouse at $7 per cord on three months credit. Frederic countered with an offer at $4 per cord; when the thermometer zoomed to 50, he offered $6 per cord. Steadman held out and the next day Frederic agreed to take it for the original $7 but got the credit time doubled to six months. With this ice in hand, Frederic could have the brig *Atlas*, which had been standing by, loaded for shipment.

Frederic and Wyeth inspected Spot Pond in Medford and found that the 100 cords of ice Steadman sold them had come from there. So Frederic told Wyeth to buy ice from Steadman's icehouse and, if he refused, to take a crew out to Spot Pond and cut some for themselves. Meanwhile, Wyeth found a small pond in Malden that other ice-cutters had not discovered. The ice was said to be nearly a foot thick. Instantly Wyeth swung into action. He and twelve hands arrived to start cutting on the evening of February 17. Wagons would arrive in the morning, eight or ten of them, plus whatever carts they could scare up in the neighborhood. Frederic agreed to pay his teamsters an extra dollar a cord as an inducement to work faster.

Inspecting the pond that evening, Wyeth became quite excited about the treasure trove he had found. It was not more than five miles from Charlestown, and it looked

Ice Cutting at Spy Pond in West Cambridge
Gleason's Pictorial Drawing-Room Companion, *Feb. 18, 1854.*
Collection of the Massachusetts Historical Society.

as if there might be as much as 500 cords of excellent ice in it. Nestled in the hills, it had been protected from the sun and the winds. Frederic offered Wyeth an extra commission of a dollar per cord for every cord over 100 that he could get from the pond—partly to offset a request for ice that Wyeth had received from his brother in Baltimore.

The mild winter had created a shortage of good ice in many places where the ice trade had been built up. Local stocks in all major cities were poor, and they turned to more northerly climates for the luxury commodity. With a view to cashing in on the scarcity, Frederic asked Gardiner to increase the quantity of ice he was cutting at Kennebec from 600 to 1,200 cords. On February 18, with the thermometer at 38, Frederic inspected his new pond. It appeared that none of his competitors had found it. It was called Swain's Pond and Frederic thought that it might contain 1,000 cords.

At three o'clock in the morning, the pond's neighbors had their first intimation that they were being invaded by the ice-cutters. When Wyeth had arrived with his crew at midnight, they discovered in the narrow land leading to the pond a large rock that obstructed their passage. They blasted it with a charge of gunpowder that must have startled the good farmers out of their warm beds in confusion and fright. By morning the wagons appeared.

Frederic, driving down the lane in his chaise, was amused by the sight of old and young women, boys, and girls gazing through the windows at the curious traffic that suddenly packed their quiet country lane. So narrow was the lane that Frederic had to move aside to make way for the loaded ice wagons heading out; he was obliged to drive into a little orchard belonging to a farmer named Arnold Shoemaker. That gentleman came out to put back up the bars that Frederic had taken down to gain access to the orchard. When Frederic promised to make good any damage Shoemaker had suffered, the man replied that he and his wife had been up half the night tending the workmen who had been hurt. Frederic offered the man twenty-five cents.

At breakfast that morning the owner of the land around the pond appeared to find out what was going on. Frederic immediately purchased for $10 the right to cut bushes, fell trees, and pile ice on the man's land. They discovered another fellow who had cleared some snow to cut thirteen cords, and to get rid of him Wyeth agreed to cut the man's ice for him and load it on the man's wagon if he would pay a quarter of the land right fee. So for $7.50 Frederic had bought all of the ice at Swain's Pond. He meant to harvest as much as he could, even if the abominable state of the roads forced him to increase the teamsters' pay by half to persuade them to continue.

Wyeth had planned to work the men through the night and sleep only through the middle of the day, but that night it rained. When Frederic inspected the pond the next day, he found that the rain had reduced the surface by a good two inches. He ordered a cart sent from town with three hundred yards of sailcloth to shade at least a small part of the ice. So badly had the rain damaged the ice that it looked now as if they might not be able to cut more than one hundred cords. Not only had the ice been hurt by the rains, the roads had become even worse. Frederic broke both of the springs of his chaise in passing a rut. The carts sent to Charlestown failed to reach the wharf. The teamsters wearily had to conclude that the roads were impassable and that no attempts could be made on the morrow. The moderation of the weather continued and even the sailcloth was of little help in preserving the ice. One horse broke through the pond and had to be rescued.

Something needed to be done. Frederic remembered another possible source, Long Pond, and he and Wyeth went to see it. Only a very bad road led to it, but nevertheless Frederic instructed Wyeth to harvest the ice. At first Wyeth demurred, but he finally agreed that they might get fifteen cords. This was just the kind of battle Frederic relished. It was Frederic against nature. The struggle promised to be expensive, but he had Wyeth and his competent crew of twelve workers. Frederic felt like a general marshalling his troops for a grand assault. They needed only to keep up their courage for a few more days and they would triumph.

In the meantime, he recruited help elsewhere. Letters went to a man in Bath, Maine, whom Frederic instructed to cut ice for him. Two others were designated to cut if the first man did not. Gardiner was pressed to have a large supply of flat ice cut up for possible sale. If anybody could outwit nature, Frederic was determined it would be he. However, nature is not outwitted even by the most determined. Despite old proverbs, this winter did rot in the sky. On February 21 Frederic finally admitted defeat. When he went to Swain's Pond, he found Wyeth and his men at Wait's Tavern "at their ne plus ultra."[8] They had gone as far as they could and they knew it. Wyeth told Frederic the ice in Long Pond was no longer worth cutting either.

Frederic had one scheme left. "I asked Wyeth if he was equal to the occasion & whether he was ready & willing to change his *latitude* & go north until he found Ice. He promptly answered that he was."[9] Frederic wanted him to go to Kennebec. There was ice in Maine, and Wyeth could cut to his heart's content and to the satisfaction of Frederic's wallet. Frederic offered him his expenses and 10 percent of the profit made from Kennebec. To save time training new men, Frederic told him to bring his present crew with him. They were to leave as soon as all the ice in Spy Pond had been harvested.

Secrecy about the expedition obsessed Frederic. Wyeth and his crew had to sneak out of town without the competition discovering what was afoot. They did so on the morning of February 26. Immediately, as was to be expected, the thermometer dropped to 22. Frederic hoped that moonlit nights and the snow on the ground would slow the arrival of spring. He urged Wyeth, now at Kennebec, to try to cut a hundred cords a day and not to stop until he had cut twelve hundred. And then he was to press on again. The same request went to Gardiner. In spite of Frederic's worries, his competition, Steadman and Coolidge, showed no concern about Wyeth's disappearance.

The temperature continued to skip around the freezing mark, and a few loads were brought in from Cambridge and Malden by the men Wyeth had left behind. Word came from Wyeth that he was cutting lots of ice. Frederic wanted him to cut even more—the price of ice was soaring. Steadman was now asking twelve dollars a cord for the same ice that Frederic had thought overpriced at seven.

Enough ice was now available to Frederic that he could continue to fill vessels and dispatch them southward. He tried a new system as he loaded the brig *William Smith*. The ice was passed in at two hatches instead of one, using two gangs of hands. He had begun to have the vessel fitted to receive ice, which meant insulating the hull, on a Wednesday at 1 P.M. and had completed it the next day at 3 P.M. Workers loaded the ship with 110 cords (equivalent to 330 tons) of ice; it took thirty hours to fill the hold and another twenty-eight hours to protect the ice with hay and to make the ship generally fit.

He appeared to have solved his ice supply problem at last, but Frederic was kept busy nevertheless with a variety of minutiae. Money was tight in Boston at the time, so he found it difficult to secure the capital he needed. Undaunted, he talked with William Gray about purchasing Gray's Wharf, a subject he had broached about a year before. This time Gray seemed much more amenable. Frederic also hired a young man named Carneau near the end of March to act as his clerk, thus relieving him of some of the burden of routine correspondence and bookkeeping. Meanwhile, the price of ice continued to rise.

In Richmond, Virginia, it sold for $100 a ton or $30 a cord. Applications for ice came to Frederic continuously from other places. He hoped to realize $5 per ton profit on the Kennebec ice. Wyeth returned from Maine on March 24. On the next day, he reported to Frederic that he had collected two piles of ice measuring 1,132 cords and that Gardiner had cut another 1,412 cords, for a total of 7,632 tons of ice for sale. In Boston, they now had available 520 cords from Bath, Maine, for a total reserve of 9,192 tons. At a profit of $5 per ton this represented the potential of $45,000 to Frederic's wallet. The winter, however, was not through with them yet.

Wyeth went to New York, Philadelphia, and Baltimore to sell ice. On May 12, Frederic noted with relief that the ship that had sailed that day completed the regular winter's work. All still appeared satisfactory. Frederic's $45,000 pile of ice had been stacked riverside on Gardiner's land, awaiting transfer to the south for sale. On May 16 Frederic went to Nahant—the summer season had begun and workmen awaited his instructions about painting and yard tasks. That day, the ice stored in Maine met disaster.

First, an overflow tide caused some of the ice in one of his piles to fall. This was quickly put on board a ship and sent to Philadelphia. By May 20, the news from Maine was worse. Gardiner's ice piles began to melt at the bottom, and as a result, started to fall down. On the first of June, the news from Maine reported the loss of at least two thousand cords. It was a serious financial setback. Frederic automatically looked for solutions—if not for this season, at least for the next. He put into action a major lesson he had learned from the winter of 1827–1828: since there was no place in the Boston area where he could have an exclusive right to cut ice, he needed to build his own pond.

On July 22, 1828, Tudor picked up Wyeth in a chaise and they drove out to look over the springs in Chelsea to consider the possibilities of establishing there an artificial pond. He did not mention the subject again in his diary until the spring of 1829. On April 21, he and his brother Harry took a walk over to Chelsea to have another look at the springs. These were about ninety feet above sea level. On the other side of Chelsea Creek lay Noddles Island, a dumbbell-shaped island some two and a half miles long, with the creek on one side and Boston Harbor on the other. Frederic visualized an aqueduct that would stretch from the springs across the creek to the island, where he would construct his artificial pond and a wharf on the harbor side. From pond to ship was the scheme of Frederic's fertile mind. A month later, on May 25, he took Wyeth to see the island. Frederic now wrote to the owner of Noddles Island, D. S. Greenough, about purchasing it, but he received no response. By September, he and Wyeth were still looking for a place to build an artificial pond. They scoured Cambridge, but each place they saw only showed the superior advantage of Noddles Island.

One persistent problem in the ice business was the difficulty of harvesting thick ice early in the season. Frederic made his first attempt at this in the fall of 1829, when he turned his attention to a patch of water directly in front of the icehouse at Fresh Pond. According to his theory, confining the water in this patch with a wooden fence would result in early and thick ice. Wyeth confirmed the idea, and they picked a place free of springs and weeds for the experiment. They did not follow through, however, because Frederic feared that his competitors would imitate an idea he could not patent. Nevertheless, he continued to study the problem, and by January 1830 he had a simple solution.

On January 17, the ice at Fresh Pond was frozen but only three inches thick, too thin to be of any use. Why not, he suggested to Wyeth, try to double it by "passing one sheet [of ice] under the other & cutting round so as to let it rise a little." Wyeth agreed to try the plan that night. It worked well enough so that two days later they decided to try it on a larger section, a square fifty feet on a side. On January 22, Wyeth reported triumphantly that on a pond covered with only four and a half inches of ice, he had produced a block of ice nine inches thick. "The joint appears firm & more extended operations are ordered," Frederic noted in his diary. Three days later, they were getting ice twelve inches thick. "The union appears perfect."[10] By January 29, they had two hundred cords of ice cut, loaded, and shipped south.

By the 1831 season this new method had become standard. In February Frederic noted that the blocks were now, on occasion, twenty inches thick. Although that season was only thirty-five days long, it was quite profitable. Next they tried doubling the doubled ice. In the season of 1833, when Fresh Pond ice was only five inches thick, they doubled it twice and had ice as thick as twenty-one inches for the icehouse. So the winter that rotted in the sky still produced some benefits for the ice business.

CHAPTER 21

Ixion, King of the Lapithae

IXION WAS A KING OF THE LAPITHAE, as every learned schoolboy ought to know. In Greek mythology he aspired to the love of Hera, Queen of Heaven, sister and wife of Zeus. As punishment for his arrogance he was bound to an endlessly revolving wheel in Tartarus. Why Tartarus? Because Hell was not sufficient punishment for Ixion's sin. Tartarus, so the *Iliad* has it, is as far below Hell as Heaven is above earth. These are not precise directions, but they were easy enough for the great Zeus to find. To this odd myth Frederic turned for the name of a venture that began in 1828. Why he picked the name Ixion he never said.

The adventure had its origin in 1633 when one John Oldham of Dorchester went on a trading journey to the Native Americans across the wilderness of central Massachusetts. He brought back to Boston samples of "some black lead whereof the Indians told him there was a who'e rock."[1] Three years later, John Winthrop, Jr., the son of the governor, was granted the land in Sturbridge containing this black lead. Not much was done until 1658, and even then the mining was a difficult operation. "The rock had to be broken by fire on the rock face, quenched with water and then worked out with gads and bars."[2] Finally the ore had to be taken to Windsor on the Connecticut River by packhorse for eventual transshipment to London.

Winthrop died in 1676 and for the next 125 years the property in Sturbridge was involved in lawsuits by the heirs. Even after the suits were finally settled nobody worked the mine until Frederic Tudor. His active interest commenced on July 21, 1828, when he sent his friend, fellow boarder, and prospective partner E. R. Dorr to

Sturbridge to examine the mine. Frederic had known about it since 1823, when he was told by Capt. Joseph Dixon that in the hill called Tantiusque near the town of Sturbridge, Massachusetts, there was a bed of plumbago, also known as graphite. On August 8, Tudor and Dorr bought the property, which ultimately became an estate of 127 acres. They obtained tools and hired Captain Dixon to superintend the project. Ten days later, Tudor and Dorr visited their new holding. Dixon had six men at work.

The partners spent Tuesday, August 19, trying to solve the immediate problem of too much water in the mine. Frederic then returned to Boston for a few days. Soon, however, he came back to see how the work was progressing. The water problem had been overcome by a siphon and blasting had begun, so there were samples to be examined. Frederic planned to establish a factory at Avery's Wharf in Boston to manufacture black lead vessels, known as crucibles, which he could sell to foundries for melting metal. On September 20, 1828, he received his first shipment of lead from the mine. Three days later workers started to make the crucibles but, as with all new ventures, things did not go smoothly, for none of them fully understood how crucibles were made. Eventually they had to hire a potter to spin them on his wheel. By November 7, five hundred large ones were finished and ready for baking.

Frederic went back to Sturbridge five days later. Since there was still too much water in the mine, the pump had to run constantly. Frederic wondered if a windmill would do a better job, so he purchased one for $150 and asked Nathaniel Wyeth to set it up. Wyeth, who agreed to take time from the ice business, came to Sturbridge. In his usual efficient manner, Wyeth had the windmill busily pumping away at the accumulation of water. Work, which the flooding had forced to a stop, commenced again. When Frederic returned to Boston, he had additional good news: a new vein of lead had been discovered.

The first crucibles were baked on November 17 and, after two days of finishing, were completely done. They looked good, but just how good were they? Two brass founders who had bought them reported favorably and declared that they were better than the imported Dutch ones they had been using. Things looked promising. Then Frederic discovered that Dixon was involved in "some underhand work & double dealing . . . for the aid of his son."[3] He reacted immediately—closed down the entire operation and fired Dixon and everyone else.

Three days later Dixon and his son appeared at Frederic's counting room at Wheeler's Point. The captain declared his entire innocence of wrongdoing, while his son on the other hand simply muttered threats. Frederic told them that he required assurances that they would not repeat their double dealings again. After they left, he concluded that they were not prepared to give him what he wanted. Shortly after Christmas, the Dixons began earnestly to try to smooth over their trouble with Frederic. But it was too late—he had decided that the Dixons had to go. On January 1, 1829, he formally ended the relationship.

Dorr experimented with the crucibles that Dixon had made and decided they were not strong enough to do the job for which they were designed. Rather than tarnish the firm's reputation, Frederic decided to break up all five hundred of them, grind them down, and begin anew. Frederic was determined to sell only superior quality crucibles. He had labored from the end of July to the end of February and now had only experience to show for his efforts. When the deep snow at Sturbridge blocked all the roads in the neighborhood of the mine, the operation shut down for the rest of the winter. Perhaps Ixion was the right name for the project, for Frederic seemed to be bound to an endlessly revolving wheel, which traveled much but went nowhere.

Work resumed in the spring. The factory in Boston moved from Avery's Wharf to a place behind Foster's Wharf. The first batch of crucibles they made without Dixon appeared to be excellent. Atkinson & Rollins, a New York firm, agreed to act as the marketing agents for the crucibles. But, Frederic wondered, would there be a demand? By April 14, 1829, the agents had sold two hundred dollars worth of vessels, and a week later Frederic heard that ore in London was selling at a price that would give him a profit of seventy dollars per ton. Unfortunately, the London market was at present oversupplied, so he shipped samples of his lead all over to have it examined, hoping to find a market for it. Some went to Marseille, some to Havana, and some even to Canton. Optimist that he was, Frederic even shipped them to London.

At the factory, Dorr invented a new machine for kneading the mixture. It was an apparent success. They now employed four workmen. By the spring of 1829, Frederic had invested three thousand dollars in the project. Wyeth brought a wagon out to Sturbridge loaded with materials: bellows, anvil, vise, grindstone, lead pipe, and such. The miners produced nearly a ton of ore daily; on good days they dug almost twice that amount. The Boston factory kept busy too. By mid July production had caught up with the demand. Frederic found this project an exciting one and spent increasing amounts of time at the factory. He had competitive black lead imported from Liverpool, England, for examination. His seemed better. While this concern advanced rapidly, however, the American economy was declining. On September 19, Frederic noted in his diary "many factories failing. I hope *one* at least may be conducted with caution enuf to weather the storm."

By the fall, internal problems also developed. Tudor and Dorr had a falling out, and on October 17, Frederic told Dorr that he wanted to dissolve their partnership. Two days later Dorr agreed to Frederic's terms, which allowed Frederic to ask Wyeth to take charge of the mine, its production of ore, and all its workmen. He offered Wyeth a quarter of its profits and debts. The good Wyeth agreed and went to work immediately. As with the ice business, his inventiveness soon resulted in improvements. One of these, however, was the reduction of workers' wages by 25 percent.

In May 1829, Wyeth had gone to New York on private business but had found time to consult with their agents, Atkinson & Rollins. He asked them to be more active in marketing the firm's vessels. At home he divided his time between the mine and the manufactory in Boston. In August, Wyeth went to Martha's Vineyard to look at clay specimens. Things were going well until Wyeth fell ill, which slowed production to a crawl. Finally Frederic had to step in and take charge. He even had to work with his own hands.

Frederic now received bad news from England, where he had hoped to sell ore; the test shipment fetched only ten pounds per ton. At the same time Frederic received a sample of Borrowdale ore, which was said to be worth four thousand pounds a ton. Frederic thought after he examined it that his own Sturbridge ore compared favorably with the Borrowdale ore. Nevertheless, the firm had but few orders for their crucibles. To add to this woe, a November storm tide flooded the factory. Obviously that was one of the hazards of its location at Foster's Wharf. Indeed, in the spring of 1830 a second storm tide again flooded the factory with twenty-eight inches of water, forcing Frederic to close it for several days.

Orders came in slowly. Four months of advertising efforts in Baltimore, Philadelphia, New York, and all New England brought only one hundred dollars in sales, and this with agents in the field pushing the product. Like all salesmen, they were confident that business would develop, and so they fed Frederic's hopes.

Wyeth experimented to improve the quality of the crucibles. He thought to extract the quartz from the lead by grinding the quartz and washing it in water, so that the heavier impurities would sink and the fine lead could float free. Then he could compress the purified lead together with an adhesive glue into pots. The purer lead would yield a stronger crucible; when tried for melting bar iron, it stood the test. If this worked, they anticipated a demand for their pots for the manufacture of cast iron. Frederic and Wyeth now rested their hopes on this new experiment. If the pots could perform as expected and sell for the price needed, a new market would open to them. The pots, however, did not perform as expected. A purchaser in New York found that all of the twenty he used broke when put into fire. In addition, Frederic faced competition from pots made from Worcester coal.

Then a disaster hit at the mine. On October 13, 1830, a mass of overhanging rock fell, crushing two workmen to death and crippling a third for life. Frederic gave each man's family sixty dollars in compensation. When sales showed no signs of improving, Frederic shut down the mine for the winter and laid off one member of the small crew at the factory. The man was such a good worker, however, that Frederic sent him to his New Orleans icehouse. At the same time he asked him to solicit Ixion orders from the western foundries.

Over the winter of 1830–1831 Ixion received orders for $300 worth of crucibles, and there was news of the sale of lead in London at a fair price. Accordingly, Frederic sent Wyeth to Sturbridge to resume mining, and the Boston factory commenced operations again. In June a shipment of pots went to New York and Wyeth undertook a sales trip to the South during the summer. His reports from the field were encouraging. The potential market was a large one: in New York and Philadelphia there were possible sales of $5,600 a year, in Boston maybe sales of another $2,800 or so, and perhaps $1,200 or more in the rest of the twenty-four states. When Frederic added these figures up he saw $10,000 a year. All of this could be his, he thought, once the supply of imported pots from Holland was exhausted. When Wyeth returned from his trip he was aglow with praise for Ixion pots and broached to Frederic the idea that he buy him out—which, of course, only made Frederic all the more enthusiastic about the business and its prospects.

Eventually, however, the enthusiasm of both men waned. Wyeth determined to make an overland journey to Oregon and left Frederic's employment. As a result, Frederic incorporated the company and took in his selling agent, Parish & Co., as a stockholder. Things were going so well in the business that he decided it was a good time to spread the profit and the risk. Sales continued steady. However, the general economy of the Boston area began to slow in 1833 and the banner year Frederic was hoping for did not materialize. By November there was little demand for the product and the work force at the mine was reduced.

Ixion's work force usually started making pots in April or May and closed with the coming of the cold weather for little could be done during winter. Since the manufacture of the melting pots was conducted in an unheated shack at Wheeler's Point, mining could not occur after the ground froze. This made the Ixion business ideal for Frederic. His ice project occupied him over the winter and his crucible business over the summer. Unfortunately for him, however, Ixion sales continued to decline. At the 1835 stockholders meeting Frederic announced that they were down by one-half from the previous year. Nevertheless, the stockholders decided to let Frederic fix the situation. It was an unwise vote on their part, for while the market improved by the fall, Frederic's attention had turned elsewhere. At the next annual meeting John W. Fenno was appointed agent.

Sales seesawed up and down, year by year. As a result, at the 1838 annual meeting Frederic proposed dissolving the corporation, but he could not get the holders of the Parish & Co. shares to agree on terms he found acceptable. So Ixion struggled on. Mining at Sturbridge continued under Frederic's management until the middle of the century. It was finally shut down not because the mine had become exhausted but because the market price for graphite had fallen too low to cover costs. And so the Ixion enterprise ended like many other ideas Frederic hatched—a failure. No matter, Frederic's attention had now strayed to a more exciting arena: speculating in coffee.

CHAPTER 22

New and Untried Paths

HALL J. KELLEY WAS A FORTY-ONE-YEAR-OLD jack of all trades from New Hampshire. He worked as a teacher, a surveyor, an engineer, and a reformer. A good citizen, he was busy in such enterprises as the Boston Young Man's Education Society, an early Sunday School in New England, and (not forgetting the fair sex) the Penitent Female Refuge Society. In 1828 he invested all his earnings in a canal scheme in western Massachusetts that went bust the next year. But nothing daunted the redoubtable Hall J. Kelley. He had dreams for all seasons. When one failed him, another was ready to take its place, accompanied by equal enthusiasm on his part. Settling the Oregon Territory was one of Kelley's dreams.

Shortly after the publication of Nicholas Biddle's authorized history of the Lewis and Clark Expedition in 1814, Kelley started to agitate for American occupation of the territory then belonging to no country. He applied to Congress without success, though the United States did claim the territory in 1817. So he decided to take matters into his own hands and formed, in Boston, the "American Society for Encouraging the Settlement of the Oregon Territory." In 1831, Nathaniel Wyeth caught Kelley's "Oregon fever" and joined the colonization society, not only for patriotic and adventurous motives but also because he scented profit in the expedition. "My plan," he wrote his brother, "is to go out there and carry with me what property I can spare after leaving a support for my wife. . . . After finding what can be done in the fur trade, or other business, write to friends . . . to send me the means of doing business."[1] Wyeth wanted his brother, Dr. Jacob Wyeth, to join the expedition as its surgeon.

Soon, however, he began to lose confidence in Kelley's abilities and decided that if he were ever to get to Oregon it would have to be on his own initiative. Once he had made his decision, he moved with his customary efficiency and dispatch. At the same time, he was operating both the ice business and the Ixion concern for Frederic and was moving into a new house. His wife, who was an alcoholic, was a constant problem for him. On September 19, 1831, Frederic noted in his diary that Wyeth was making arrangements to separate from his wife, Elizabeth, "in consequence of her habit of drinking. He had been a long while greatly distressed by this domestic trouble." Clearly this was a motivation for Wyeth to put three thousand miles between himself and Elizabeth.

Wyeth's plan was simple. Fully confident of his own ability to overcome any unforeseen situation, he would lead the expedition across the continent. He would also send a vessel laden with provisions around Cape Horn to supply the expedition when it arrived on the coast. At the mouth of the Columbia River he would establish a trading post, collect furs, and salt salmon, which produce would be sent back overland via posts that he would have set up on his way out. This would mean that ships would not have to remain for two years or more on the Pacific coast before they returned home. Wyeth had no doubt that they would all make money and could return home in five years quite comfortably fixed.

Frederic apparently did not hear of the scheme until Friday, January 6, 1832. "Wyeth announces to me his determination to leave my employ in consequence of his domestic inquietude. It is a great loss to me."[2] The following Sunday, he spent part of the day "writing a long letter to Wyeth . . . in hope to dissuade him from going to the Pacific with fur trading party across the continent."[3] It was no use. Wyeth was determined to go. Frederic tried to tempt him with money offers into changing his mind, but more money, as nice as that might be, was not what really interested Wyeth at this point in his life. His imagination sought romance and adventure. And, for him, that could only be found right now in Oregon.

It was a busy January for Wyeth. He enlisted men for his expedition and sold shares in his joint stock company. By early February, he had signed up twenty-three men. He put a good amount of his own money into the project and got subscriptions from his uncle and elder brothers, Charles and Leonard, while brother Jacob joined as the expedition's surgeon. Even Frederic offered to help underwrite the expedition. Wyeth was trying to raise five thousand dollars, and Frederic agreed to go surety for half the sum in exchange for Wyeth's ice machinery patents.

On Saturday nights Wyeth and his company met at his house to plan for the expedition. To a young second cousin, John B. Wyeth, a blithe seventeen-year-old who had signed on for the adventure, it seemed as if "nothing was forgotten and every thing necessary provided."[4] Wyeth turned his inventive skill loose on his new scheme and designed a "*unique* contrivance, half boat, and half carriage" which some classical scholar called the "*Amphibium*." The wags among the Harvard students renamed it the "*Nat-wye-thium*."[5] Young John Wyeth described it as

> a boat of about thirteen feet long, and four feet wide, of a shape partly of a canoe, and partly of a gondola. It was not calked with tarred oakum, and payed with pitch, lest the rays of the sun should injure it while upon wheels; but it was nicely jointed, and dovetailed. The boat part was firmly connected with the lower, or axletree, or wheel part;—the whole was so constructed that the four wheels of it were to be taken off when we came to a river, and placed in the wagon, while the tongue or shaft was to be towed across by a rope. Every thing was as light as could be consistent with safety.[6]

On the first of March 1831, dressed in uniforms of woolen jacket and trousers, cowhide boots, and broad belt equipped with axe and knife, the men left Boston to camp on one of the islands in the harbor for a ten-day training session to prepare themselves for the journey westward. At the end of the encampment they sailed to Baltimore. There the amphibiums and crew were put on board the Baltimore and Ohio Railroad, which had recently opened, and rode the first sixty miles. Then the journey got tougher, as they had to drag their wagons over the mountains to Pittsburgh, where they arrived on April 8. From Pittsburgh, they went by steamer to Cincinnati and then down to St. Louis. The average American map of that period did not show much beyond St. Louis. Intelligence concerning the remainder of the journey had to be gleaned from experienced mountain travelers. The first advice they received was that their wagons were impossible, so Wyeth sold them. For the first time, they saw real Native Americans and heard tales of their raids. At this point, some of the crew began to wonder why they had joined the expedition.

Up the Missouri River they went by slow steamboat. Those adventurers with second thoughts began to drop away from the expedition, at first two, then three. Then they had a piece of luck. They fell in with a well-equipped company of men led by William Sublette, an old mountain fur trader, just setting out to do business with the local inhabitants. Now they had knowledgeable people to accompany them. Marching to Oregon soon turned out to be not quite the afternoon picnic they had envisioned Saturday evenings back at Wyeth's warm house in civilized Cambridge.

Months later, they reached the Teton Basin, where Sublette met with representatives from several Native American tribes. Here he began his trading activities and so the party parted ways. Wyeth's brother Jacob was too ill with dysentery to go on, and his young cousin John had had his fill of adventure. Seven returned, leaving an expedition of only twelve to continue the journey. It was October 14 before the intrepid dozen reached their destination, Fort Walla Walla on the upper Columbia River. Back in Boston that October, Frederic had spent a few glorious Indian summer days sailing his boat, the *Ohio*, round Boston Harbor and preparing his garden in Nahant for the winter. He noticed a touch of frost. Winter was coming.

"New and untried paths" Wyeth had called his Oregon expedition, and new and untried paths also constituted Frederic's current interest.[7] He had discovered speculation. Frederic's cousin William Savage had suggested this new game to him early in 1831, and by the first of July he was ready to begin: "I am proposing to make a speculation in coffee & shall if at all purchase next week in a considerable extent."[8] It promised to make one enormously rich and it required no cash to play.

Frederic speculated in coffee futures. He did not grow, harvest, roast, pack, or ship it. He did not market coffee. He never even saw the stuff. What made the speculation especially interesting to cash-poor Frederic was that he did not even have to pay for it. Since the speculation worked all on credit, Frederic was responsible only for the interest on the money involved. He could easily do this, and the value of his ice business was all the collateral that the banks required. At the end of the day all one did to become enormously rich was sell the futures for more than they had cost. Nor was Frederic foolish enough to become interested in coffee. In those years 16 million Americans consumed 80 million pounds of coffee annually. The American population grew by 750,000 persons a year. At that rate, there was bound to be a rising market for coffee. So into speculation Frederic Tudor jumped.

He intended the fling to be short and onetime only. He would purchase coffee for one week, so he wrote in his diary on July 1, 1831. On June 28 he wrote again in his diary, "I have nearly completed my speculation in coffee." But then he got hooked. "Coffee rising fast in Europe. . . . Coffee since my purchases has risen 20 to 25%. . . . Prices now getting a little too forward." Sandwiched in between comments on the market in his diary are notations of continued purchases: "bought 17 to 1800 bags of St. Domingo coffee. . . . 1102 bags Rio Coffee. . . . 800 bags of Rio Coffee of an inferior quality. . . . 1102 bags at 10 3/4 & 11 C." Frederic was in the grip of an uncontrollable demon. "This," he told his diary on October 20, "will be my last purchase in my coffee speculation." But it was not. Once bitten by the gambling bug, he became addicted: "wagered a suit of clothes with R. C. Cabot today on $50 that St. Domingo coffee (on the 22d Oct. 1831 58% in London) would in the course of 12 months in that place reach 118 [bet lost & paid]."[9]

He was to pay far more than he had bargained for before his speculation was over. Meanwhile, he kept buying and buying. The first indication of the size of his investment came in his diary entry for April 30, 1832: "Coffee, after a period of dullness in Europe, is beginning to advance again. Have arranged my principal money matters & the coffee in which I have about $250,000 invested is again in a state of good advance and my calculations are in train for being proved." But it did not stop there. After a year of coffee speculation his investment had grown to $300,000. Gaily he wrote, "credit does everything now-a days."[10] That was the seducing beauty of the speculation. It all seemed only numbers on a piece of paper.

August 1832 brought him one of his first reported sales, and this was gratifying, for he sold the coffee for three cents more per pound than the price at which he had bought it. This gave him a false sense of success, so he continued to buy. On the other hand, the need for cash in the ice business continued to exceed the supply.

> Altogether things look pretty bad & I fear I must have recourse to my coffee for supplies to meet my engagements in my other business. Having to pay before the end of the year $20m with not more than $3m coming in I have a pretty good loss of obligation upon me & have to cast about speedily for resources. My coffee in Boston upwards of a million of pounds is about $15m richer than it was & what I have in Europe as much more a good advance in the value of this article in the course of this month which may be expected will make all things easy: but without it I shall have need of strength & ability.[11]

So far, Frederic's speculation in coffee seemed to be a great success.

Throughout the fall and winter, sluggish coffee sales caused a decline in price, alarming some of Frederic's "backers," as he termed them. By the start of 1833, Frederic "owned" five to six million pounds of coffee: one-sixth of all the coffee consumed in America, or enough to supply a million Americans with their favorite beverage for a year.

> The New Year begins with many discouraging circumstances & more particularly in matters relating to my extensive speculation in coffee. . . . My confidence is hardly shaken although the opinion is almost universal against it & I was told by C. I. Carenove I should lose $200m before the business was wound up. I think I may make as much.[12]

He would have had less confidence had he known that in Boston Thomas Wrenn Ward, the American agent for the English banking firm of Baring Brothers, with whom he was dealing in the coffee speculation, was writing anxious letters back to London predicting that the fall in coffee prices would bankrupt Frederic. Later in March he wrote London, "I wish you'd settle up Tudor & coffee & let me know what the balance is at once that I may collect it and have no more to do with him. He will probably fail some time or other."[13] By mid April 1833, even Frederic was beginning to have doubts. He decided to suspend coffee sales in Boston until the fall, hoping the autumn demand would increase prices. However, even on the falling market he kept purchasing more coffee. Throughout the summer, the news was alternately good then bad. When the autumn arrived, the market did not improve. Still Frederic remained hopeful.

Then, on November 8, 1833, Nathaniel Wyeth appeared at his door, back from what Frederic termed "his wild goose chase."[14] Wyeth, who was fit and healthy, claimed that his journey to the Pacific had been more routine than romantic. He had never gone without food for more than two days, and they had never suffered from cold weather. He figured that, while the trip had not been a great financial success, it was not a complete financial disaster for he had collected enough furs to pay all his expenses. Unfortunately for his plans, however, the vessel he had sent round Cape Horn had been wrecked in the South Pacific. That meant that the supplies it had been bringing were lost and so he did not have the goods he needed to set up his trading post. He had spent the winter exploring, and the more he saw the more he became confident that he should make a second expedition.

The very day Wyeth visited Frederic, Wyeth wrote a long letter to Henry Hall, an agent for the Lowell textile mills and the firm of Tucker and Williams, outlining a new scheme. The principal trader in the Rocky Mountain area was the Rocky Mountain Fur Company. Among its partners were Milton Sublette and Thomas Fitzpatrick. The firm was three years old and in that time had gathered eighty thousand dollars worth of furs. The problem with the business was the cost of getting supplies to the mountains. Wyeth had devised a scheme that would overcome the difficulties of the fur trade and earn him a good profit. He would send them each year by ship the supplies they needed. On the vessel's return trip it would carry a cargo of salmon. The value of the salmon would pay the transport charges both ways. Supplies could be delivered from the Columbia River to the site where the fur trappers held their annual rendezvous for a fraction of the cost of delivering them overland from St. Louis. He had already a signed contract with the Rocky Mountain Fur Company to deliver to them three thousand dollars worth of supplies for the 1834 rendezvous. He would be paid in furs, which he would send to Boston on the same vessel that took the salmon. If timed correctly, the scheme could be repeated each season and so make everyone rich.

Not aware of what Wyeth had planned, Frederic hoped to persuade him to rejoin him in the ice business. As an inducement, he boasted that he had made forty thousand dollars during the two years Wyeth was away, all from selling ice. The offer he made was, in Wyeth's words, "more than equal anything I left," but it paled against the prospect of his own new scheme—if he could pull that off. On Wednesday, November

20, 1833, Wyeth wrote to his brother Charles that "It is now a matter settled that I go again to the Pacific. A concern is made up here to invest $20,000. I have for my services one quarter of all profits and no risk."[15] Hall, Tucker, and Williams's gain was Frederic Tudor's loss. Wyeth lost no time in authorizing his agent in Liberty, Missouri, to buy supplies. He wrote to Milton Sublette, urging him to come and help him select the goods he was to buy for the Rocky Mountain Fur Company. Sublette did come to Boston to be displayed to the Boston business community.

Frederic Tudor was not the only one in Boston who wanted to see Wyeth on his return from his first western expedition. Harvard professor Thomas Nuttall had instructed Wyeth on techniques for collecting and preserving herbarium specimens before the first trip. Nuttall hoped Wyeth would return with a collection of new and interesting plants from the Rocky Mountains. Wyeth did not disappoint him. The specimens he brought back were well preserved and yielded 112 new species of flowering plants. Fifty-one of these Nuttall had never seen before. One of them he named after Wyeth.

Nuttall was invited to join the second western expedition; traveling to western America was a dream he had had for some years. Nuttall was to meet Wyeth in St. Louis. A man in his fifties, Nuttall brought with him a young colleague, twenty-four-year-old John Kirk Townsend, a budding ornithologist from Philadelphia. Townsend was also invited to come along. Along with the plants, Wyeth brought back two young Native Americans, a twenty-year-old member of the Nez Perce tribe and a thirteen-year-old Flathead. He exhibited them at fundraising meetings held by the Methodist Mission to the Flathead Indians, a group that planned to send missionaries with Wyeth on his second trip.

As Wyeth went on to the second phase of his "new and untried paths" that fall of 1833, the fifty-year-old Ice King proposed to embark on the most untried path of his career. A certain nineteen-year-old country girl from upstate New York was continuously on his mind, and the untried path he hoped to tread was not that to Oregon but that to matrimony.

CHAPTER 23

Love Loving, Kiss Kissing

FREDERIC SPENT HIS BACHELOR DAYS in what was one of Boston's exclusive residential areas, the Pearl Street section, near Post Office Square. In 1822 it still was a good address, but as commerce slowly encroached upon it some of the "top drawer people" began moving to the less-settled areas around Boston Common. After he lived for some years at Betsey Lekain's boardinghouse at 3 Pearl Street, Frederic moved next door to 4 Pearl Street and took his meals at Miss Lekain's. The Ice King even had a door cut between the two buildings so that he would not get wet in inclement weather.

When he lived at the boardinghouse, Frederic shared company with a number of other bachelors. A Mr. R. Fisher boarded with Betsy Lekain for ten days in March 1830 and left a jingle describing "the bachelor club."

If you're going to Boston that beautiful city,
It's well worth your while to give ear to my ditty;
For as comfort's the thing you would wish to obtain,
You should go to the house of one Miss Lekain,
She lives in Pearl Street, go there if you're wise,
The street is called Pearl, but the house is the prize,
There's everything there that the heart can desire,
If you wish anything pray only enquire,
For whatever you want you're sure to obtain

The thing in demand from Miss Betsey Lekain.
She's a true lady bountiful always at hand.
And her servants the best you've had at command.

Fisher ended his jingle with some words about Frederic Tudor.

But what shall I say of this Frederic Tudor,
This Frederic the great who has hit on a device
To produce in the tropic abundance of ice
Who is warm and is cold at the very same time
Possessing the virtues of every clime;
Whose compound of essences curiously mixed,
So strangely indeed that they cannot be fixed.
You think he is mad and would kick up a rumpus.
His heart's at the opposite point of the compass,
He makes a great noise about temper and passion,
But scolding with him is only a fashion;
A sort of way he has to be queer,
They say he will show it to friends that are dear;
But those who best know him always have said,
That the warmth's at his heart,
 while the frost's on his head.[1]

Capt. Basil Hall, another traveling diarist, noted that many Bostonians lived in boardinghouses, and so it was not unusual to find important people staying with Miss Lekain. For instance, John James Audubon and his family arrived there to spend the autumn of 1832 and the winter of 1833. He had come under the patronage of Thomas H. Perkins, a well-known Boston merchant, to work on the second volume of his *Birds of America* and to sign up purchasers for the first volume. In his diary, Frederic noted that "Audubon works the whole day not allowing himself more than 10 minutes at his meals. . . . As he spares nothing his work must be one which can never be surpassed or equalled."[2]

On February 24, 1833, Audubon visited the Boston Museum. The proprietor had just purchased a male golden eagle, which he sold to Audubon for $14.74. Audubon immediately returned to Miss Lekain's with the bird and spent the rest of the day studying him. The next day he came to a determination as to the position in which he might best represent him, and on the third day he consulted Dr. George Parkman about the least painful way to kill the bird. According to the instructions which he had received, Audubon put the bird and his cage covered with blankets into a small room. Then he placed a can of lighted charcoal in the cage.

> I waited, expecting every moment to hear him fall down from his perch; but after I listening for *hours*, I opened the door, raised the blankets and peeped under them amidst a mass of suffocating fumes. There stood the Eagle on his perch. . . . Instantly re-closing every aperture, I resumed my station at the door and toward midnight, not having heard the least noise, I again took a peek at my victim. He was still uninjured, although the air of the closet was insupportable to my son and myself, and that of the adjoining apartment began to feel unpleasant. I persevered, however, for ten hours in all, when finding that the charcoal fumes would not produced the desired effect, I retired to rest wearied and disappointed. Early next morning I tried the charcoal anew, adding to it a quantity of sulphur, but we were nearly driven from our home in a few hours by the stifling vapours, while the noble bird continued to stand erect, and to look defiance at us whenever we approached his post of martyrdom.[3]

In the end, Audubon had to kill the bird with a knife. He sat up all the next night outlining him.

Someone far more important than Audubon, as far as Frederic Tudor was concerned, arrived at Betsy Lekain's on Tuesday, June 11, 1833. The newcomer was Euphemia Fenno. She came with her great-aunt, sixty-year-old Miss Euphemia Johnston. Frederic's heart began to dance at the sight of the younger Euphemia.

That Tuesday he was, by the calendar, forty-nine years, nine months, and seven days old. By that same calendar, Miss Euphemia Fenno, of Mt. Upton, in Otsego County, New York, was nineteen years, two months, and nine days old, the difference in age between them being thirty years, six months, and twenty-eight days. But age is in the heart as well as on the calendar, for when he first saw Euphemia Fenno at the dining-room table Frederic suddenly discovered that his heart was fifty years young. His white hair and weathered face could not suppress that heart, which was as romantic and as susceptible as any youth's. He had not grown heavy with age but maintained a trim 137 pounds. Miss Fenno, while a bit plain, was full-bosomed and, as was fashionable in that era, pleasingly plump at 124 pounds.

On the Monday following her arrival, Dr. Edward Robbins, the proprietor of the Nahant Hotel, invited Euphemia and her aunt to dinner there. Frederic was also present, along with another of her admirers, for Miss Fenno had caused other hearts to dance as well. Euphemia described the occasion:

> He gave us a splendid dinner & as my two *beaus* followed me I felt like a belle & enjoyed myself very much. My two *devotees* are an officer of the navy who offers me *presents* and says he will come to Otsego if I will give him the least encouragement. The other I was consigned to by Mrs. Davis. You

> would be amused at his devotion & as he is worth some hundreds his devotion is worthy of attention from others. I was asked yesterday if I was *engaged* to him. . . . Aunt looks upon the affair in a very favorable light. She has grown ambitious all at once and you would too if you could see his beautiful *cottage* at Nahant.[4]

That delightful dinner engagement was but the first of many for Euphemia. She had old friends to visit, new friends to meet, and evening balls and parties to attend. She may have been only a country girl, but those who entertained her were some of Boston's social elite.

The beau she called her "old bachelor" was not negligent. On the Friday after her first visit to Nahant he walked her over to South Boston, where he undoubtedly pointed out the property that the Tudors still owned there. It was two weeks before Frederic's diary noted any other activity with the two charming ladies from Otsego County, New York. On that occasion they drove to Nahant in his barouche, ate a dinner by the sea, and rode back in the evening. Then, the ladies were gone.

Who was this young country girl who had so suddenly become "quite agreeable"? She was distantly connected to English nobility. Her great-grandfather was the Earl of Pemberton, whose rightful name was Clotworthy Upton. For his gallant services in the Royal Navy, King George III had rewarded him with twenty thousand acres of land in central New York in 1770. The Revolution interrupted the development of the earl's land, but in 1787, after the war was over, the earl's son, Capt. Francis Upton, came to New York to exploit this large grant in the Butternut Valley. He married Joanna Johnston of Hyde Park, New York, and brought her to the valley to live. These were Euphemia's grandparents.

The captain and Joanna had two daughters: Elizabeth, the elder, and Mary Frances. The latter married Richard Morris, whose family had received a land grant of thirty thousand acres the year before the earl had been given his. Conveniently, the Morris land adjoined the Upton grant. When Mary Frances married, the captain built the newlyweds a large frame house, elaborate for the region, and ostentatiously called it "Upton Park." He had it modeled after his wife's parental home in Hyde Park.

The elder daughter did not seem to do as well as her sister. Elizabeth married an English immigrant, George Fenno, who had come to settle in Mt. Upton via New York City. The captain was not so generous to his elder daughter. Soon after her marriage, her husband opened a country store in a log cabin on the main road from Utica to Binghamton. A crossroads and George Fenno's store comprised pretty much all of Mt. Upton. A few houses were strung out along the main road on either side of the store. Down the crossing road and across the narrow Unadilla River, which ran parallel to the main road, stood the small farmhouse on a hill in which the Fennos lived. A half mile further down the road was Upton Park, where Aunt Morris lived.

The Fennos had three children. Euphemia was born in 1814, making her five years older than Frederic's niece Delia. John came in 1817 and Francis Upton Fenno in 1819. Euphemia's parents probably were surprised when she returned from Boston and declared that fifty-year-old Frederic Tudor, Boston's Ice King, was smitten with her. On the other hand, since there were few, if any, suitable marital prospects for their only daughter in isolated, distant Butternut Valley, they may have been relieved.

Even though Euphemia had left Boston, Frederic's passion for her remained red hot. Indeed, the separation only fanned its flames. So he began showering her with a torrent of letters and on July 13 he noted in his diary that "I wandered again over grounds made interesting as the scenes of the highest of human affections."[5] By the end of July he was reduced to writing mushy nonsense in his diary: "Love Loving—Kiss Kissing and then the lover, sighing like a furnace with woeful ballad made to his mistress' eyebrow."[6]

In September, Frederic decided on a trip to upstate New York with his brother Harry, so Harry could examine the saltworks at Salina. Perhaps he would learn some useful ideas for his own saltworks at Hull. Frederic, who was feeling poorly, hoped the journey would improve his health. And the seven-hundred-mile trip did seem to do just that. Indeed, Frederic felt that he was in excellent physical shape as he set out to woo the woman of his dreams.

Icehouse at Madras, India
Tudor Ice Co. Collection. Baker Library, Harvard Business School, Boston, Mass.

CHAPTER 24

The Jewel in His Crown

HAVING ALMOST REACHED THE HALF-CENTURY MARK, Frederic was now about to embark on two risky adventures. In his business life, he would try to expand his ice shipments around Africa to far-distant India. In his personal life, he seriously contemplated marriage and even becoming a parent.

If Frederic could not become an instant millionaire from speculation in coffee, his only hope of financial survival was to return to his basic commodity—ice. Even before he knew how bad the disaster of his 1834 coffee venture would be, he began to redouble his efforts in the ice business.

The older operations in Havana, Charleston, and New Orleans were now routinely successful. Others had pioneered in shipping ice from Wenham Pond, north of Boston, to England. But the great chance would be to open a market in a large tropical country such as India, which teemed with people who surely would appreciate his product. Such a venture would be a speculation with great risks, however, as India lay on the other side of the world, many sailing months away. Could ice last that long? Moreover, the attempt to sell there would tie up capital, something Frederic always found in short supply. When Samuel Austin approached him in April 1833 on the subject of a joint venture shipping ice to Calcutta, Frederic fairly leaped at the opportunity—he could make a trial with a partner to share the risk. In the end, they also shared the risk with a third businessman, W. C. Rogers.

Within a week of Austin's proposal, Frederic engaged the brig *Tuscany*. It would be a journey of some four months and would require the ice to withstand the heat of crossing the equator twice. To preserve the cargo required more than the usual insulation. First, Frederic sheathed the holds with boards one inch away from the interior planking of the ship. Next came six inches of tanbark (shredded bark without the tannin) and then six inches of hay covered by one-foot boards. The ice was further packed round with dry straw and hay that connected with the straw of the bulkheads. Loading commenced on Sunday, May 5—a day when the overcast sky favored their work.

Each day Frederic went to Charlestown to watch the progress. He was proud of the effort he had made—even though it was costly—to insure that the ship and its cargo would reach Calcutta safely. On May 12, the *Tuscany* sailed out of the port of Boston for India with 180 tons of ice. Frederic wrote in his diary that day that the venture was "an experiment" he had been wanting to undertake for twenty years.

Frederic estimated that 50 pounds of ice per hour might melt away during the passage of 120 days. That meant that at best about 110 tons would arrive at Calcutta. However, that fact was not as important as was the question of whether the inhabitants would be willing to buy his product. He knew that the British, who were his potential customers, already cooled their drinks with a slush (ice skimmed from the surface of

View of Calcutta
Ballou's Illustrated Drawing-Room Companion, *June 2, 1855.*
Collection of the Massachusetts Historical Society.

clay pots immersed in a mixture of water and saltpeter) that was produced at Hooghly, forty miles upriver from Calcutta.

He need not have been concerned, however, for when the *Tuscany* arrived with its cargo of large blocks of ice on September 10, the British were astonished. And elated. The prospect of having real ice year-round rather than slush for six weeks was irresistible. Furthermore, as he had done before in other areas, Frederic sold his product below the current price of the slush. As a result, it was an instant hit. "How many Calcutta tables," remembered a resident, "glittered that morning with lumps of ice! The butter dishes were filled; the goblets of water were converted into miniature Arctic seas with icebergs. . . . Everybody invited everybody to dinner, to taste of claret and beer cooled by the American importation."[1] The lure of ice proved so irresistible that the money needed to build an icehouse was subscribed in three days.

Frederic heard that the *Tuscany* had arrived safely in Calcutta in January 1834. In March, he learned that the governor-general of India, William Bentinck, had presented a silver-gilt cup in recognition of this great achievement to Rogers, the only one of the partners who had gone to India with the ice.[2] The voyage of the *Tuscany* resulted in a profit of $3,300—the real silver cup—for the three partners.

Besides selling ice in India in 1834, Frederic also contemplated sending ice to Brazil. If he could furnish ice to the southern states, to the Caribbean islands, even to the East Indies, why should he ignore South America? So the brig *Madagascar* was loaded and dispatched to Rio on June 1, 1834. By October 15 he received the welcome news of the sale of the cargo for a profit of $1,500 to $2,000. Frederic was delighted that he had opened another new market but, unfortunately, he realized that he was not going to be able to develop it now—once again he was short of cash. So Brazil had to wait for a better day. But not India.

Even before Frederic and Samuel Austin knew the outcome of their Calcutta investment they began to discuss their next moves. Frederic suggested three ice cargoes be sent, one early in April 1834 and others in August and November. As usual, Frederic had trouble with his partners; his plans were much too ambitious for Austin, who was not the business gambler that Frederic was. Accordingly, Frederic withdrew from the concern, and Austin continued on his own, sending further cargoes of ice to Calcutta that year. He also sent another kind of cargo—missionaries. After severing all connections with Austin, Frederic proceeded with his own plans, which were on a grand scale.

He arranged for a ton of butter, six hundred barrels of grafted apples of various kinds, and about three-quarters of a ton of cheese to be sent—as an experiment—to Calcutta, Havana, and New Orleans. Since William Rogers, who had stayed on in Calcutta as a boardinghouse operator with a dental practice on the side, had left the ice business, it became necessary for Frederic to send his own man there. So he arranged for Marcus D. Bacon to go. Bacon had worked for Frederic at his Nahant estate doing odd jobs, such as purchasing and fetching supplies, and had helped out from time to time in the ice business. Bacon agreed to go to Calcutta as Frederic's icehouse keeper. Armed with thirty pages of instruction, he boarded the brig *Apthorp* along with four hundred barrels of apples, other fruit, butter, and cheese packed in 150 tons of ice. He also carried copies of a letter from Frederic to the governor-general of India, which he was to circulate once he reached Calcutta. Frederic composed the letter in an effort to set the record straight: it pointed out that he should receive the credit for sending the first ice to India and that only he could provide a regular supply. The *Apthorp* sailed on December 24.

A month later Frederic learned—with pleasure—that Austin's second attempt to send ice to Calcutta had not been very successful. With that good business news ringing in his ears, he awaited the fate of his own second venture. He heard nothing for nine months and then learned that the *Apthorp* had had a problem with its wheel (it had been "spoken") just east of Cape Horn. So instead of being in Calcutta as Frederic had planned, it was still on the high seas. Undaunted, the Ice King continued the project.

He engaged the *Concord* at the end of September 1835 to carry apples and other produce as well as ice. When the *Apthorp* was loaded back in December 1834, Frederic had put samples of the cargo into his icehouse packed as they were in that shipment. On October 1, 1835, as the *Concord* was being loaded, he opened the samples. The apples and cheese had kept well; indeed, all the items had survived perfectly for nine months, which was four months longer than should be required for a trip to Calcutta. The *Concord* set sail on October 18 loaded with 162 tons of ice and 200 barrels of Baldwin apples. Two days later the first news came from Bacon—and it was bad—for most of the *Apthorp*'s cargo had been lost during transit. Then a second letter arrived, declaring that due to the long 163-day passage the entire shipment had been destroyed.

At the end of December 1835, Samuel Austin proudly showed Frederic a letter he had received. His ice on the *Mary & Susan*, which sailed the previous April, had arrived in good condition. Frederic figured it would produce when sold about five thousand dollars. Although Austin had broken his partnership with Frederic, he had consigned the ice on the *Mary & Susan* to Frederic's agent Marcus Bacon. This made Frederic anxious, as he feared that Bacon would price it too low—contrary to Frederic's orders regarding the price of any ice sold by his agent. While he waited to learn how the ice sold, Frederic was in the midst of loading the ship *Warsaw*. This was his fifth shipment of ice to Calcutta.

No news reached Boston until early in March 1836. Then Frederic got a letter from Bacon that had been written the previous October. It told him that only sixty tons of ice had arrived on the *Mary & Susan* and that it lasted in the icehouse but thirty days due, Frederic thought, to poor construction. Although the ice sold well there just was not enough of it to produce a handsome profit. Indeed, its costs exceeded its return. Bacon also informed his boss that his health was poor and that he wanted to come home.

In his search for a replacement, Frederic thought of thirty-one-year-old Caleb Ladd, who collected the tolls on the dam that connected Boston and Brighton. Caleb had once suggested to Frederic that he might like to work in the ice business. The dam manager recommended Caleb, who had worked for the company for ten years. So Frederic hired him, gave him a copy of the thirty-page letter of instructions he had previously given to Bacon, and sent him off to India on April 6 on the *Ruthelia*. Along with his agent, the ship carried 212 tons of ice and 100 cases of cider. When the *Ruthelia* sailed out of Boston Harbor it did so accompanied by a little fleet of Frederic's other ice ships bound for other destinations.

Frederic turned his attention to his Nahant estate, but while he entertained himself and his family in the balmy breezes of Nahant during the spring and summer of 1836, Caleb Ladd was not a happy traveler aboard the *Ruthelia*. He had paid for a single stateroom but instead found himself in a rough berth in steerage. He shared his space with three sailors, the cook, and the steward. For 132 days he had to put up with the terrible heat, the impossible odors of the crowded space, and the constant smells of putrid vegetables. He could not have endured it, he wrote Frederic, if he had not had the constitution of a horse. He never complained to the captain for fear that that gentleman might retaliate by mishandling the discharge of the ice. But Ladd definitely felt he deserved a refund for the price of a stateroom.

When the *Ruthelia* dropped anchor in the Hooghly River at Calcutta on August 15, Caleb was the first to check the condition of the cargo. He found the ice very cold in spite of the long voyage and the intense sunshine that had persisted for much of the trip. "The cakes of ice," he wrote Frederic, "came out as frosty as if they had been packed in a snow bank in our own country."[3] Once ashore he found that Bacon had already departed for Boston back in March and had left another man in charge of the local business. The *Warsaw* was still in port when the *Ruthelia* arrived. The two cargoes would fill the icehouse. A local broker, Charles Huffnagel, gave Caleb good reports of successful sales. People said good things about Bacon's work, although it was clear to Caleb that the icehouse needed to be expanded. The first task, however, was to unload the *Ruthelia*.

The transfer from the vessel to icehouse fell to unskilled laborers, who carried the ice on their heads. They ran ninety feet from ship to shore over a walkway made up of boats and then another three hundred feet (at high water) to the icehouse. Each trip took about two minutes. In other words, they had to run the length of a football field plus a third in 99-degree heat. Caleb estimated that the workers unloaded 186 tons of ice in four days. Their labor served Mr. Tudor well: almost all of the ice made it to the icehouse intact.

Caleb soon found the produce chosen for his cargo had been a good selection. The apples sold well and frozen butter was in demand—as Calcutta had nothing to offer of such high quality. In the next shipment, Caleb hoped Frederic might send him a few "oisters" for himself. While Caleb reported back to Frederic in a letter that would arrive in perhaps four or five months, Frederic got his first report of the situation in Calcutta on September 6 from Bacon, who had arrived home on the ship *Concord* after a passage of 144 days. He told Frederic that, after all the initial trouble and difficulty, the business was now on a firm footing; he also brought Frederic his first bonus from the venture—an East Indian servant called Buxoo. Frederic, obviously pleased with Bacon's performance, gave him a present of $450 plus $52 worth of silverware for his wife.

While Caleb sent frequent reports to Boston about conditions in Calcutta, Frederic was always five months behind what was happening and at least ten months away from responding to developments there. Caleb told him that the ice sales were holding up and they were getting three annah per pound. He would hold to that price, he told Frederic, until the demand began dropping. In a later letter, he told the boss he was thinking of fitting a small room in which to sell the apples. The present accommodations, he felt, were appropriate for the natives but not good enough for the gentry. This elitist attitude pervaded all of his reports. He told Frederic, for example, that the servants who came to the shop were such chronic liars that if he sold them six apples they told their master he only gave them five.

Eventually, Caleb asked Frederic for an assistant from the United States. He did not trust any of the candidates in Calcutta, including the man Bacon had left to run the icehouse. Not only did Caleb sometimes find that individual drunk while on duty, he also suspected that the man was cheating the concern. When Caleb administered the sales himself, using the scales to weigh up the ice, the daily income was higher than on the days he was absent. So Caleb stayed in the shop the whole day himself and found that the firm's profits increased very fast. Indeed, sales had risen to almost a ton a day.

Caleb was full of merchandising ideas. He urged Frederic to expand the icehouse so it could contain two cargoes at once and also have room to sell fruit and ice cream. He was sure that he could make ice cream from the broken ice that the customers did not bother to take with them. He told Frederic that the cost of enlarging the icehouse would run to four or five thousand dollars. If Frederic was not interested, Caleb would like permission to try himself. Caleb was cunning, too. He intended to store the local fruit he had purchased for sale—like oranges and mangoes—out of sight in the cold icehouse until they were out of season, when he would bring them out for sale at a higher price.

On the Boston end, Frederic was pleased with his Calcutta experiment, especially when he learned in November 1836 that there was a draft of £1,100 in London to his account as a result of his sales in India. This was, as Frederic called it, "first fruits." Further fruits ripened the following summer when an addition to the icehouse was made and entirely paid for by the local Calcutta ice committee. In April, Caleb was sent the assistant he had requested earlier and several ships arrived filled with excellent ice. By the end of 1838, the original icehouse had tripled in size and remittances amounted to $20,000. With the success of the Indian experiment, Frederic finally understood that his future lay not in coffee but in ice, where he had begun. The same revelation lay in store for his friend Nathaniel Wyeth, who had left Frederic thinking *his* fortune lay in the Western trade. He too would soon be coming back to ice and to Frederic.

But what of Euphemia?

CHAPTER 25

Happy to Be a Married Man

WHY FREDERIC DID NOT VISIT MT. UPTON on his September 1833 trip west with Harry he never explained. Possibly he had been waiting for an invitation that never came. However, the second day after his arrival home from that trip a letter did come from Mt. Upton. He replied to it on October 5 and two days later he left Boston on the afternoon stage. This time there was no looking at saltworks or examining the falls of the Trenton or walking around Albany. His goal was Euphemia and to her he pressed with all the deliberate speed that traveling in those days permitted.

The fast coach to Worcester took six hours, and the mail coach from there took another twelve hours to Northampton. Here he boarded the 2:30 A.M. coach for Pittsfield. He arrived at 8 P.M. after having been overturned in the stage and crossing the Westfield River on a raft made for the occasion because a freshet of extraordinary height had carried away nearly all the bridges. The rain had gullied the road dangerously, and so he had made the last leg of the trip to Pittsfield by wagon. The next morning he was off to Albany. From there it was a comfort to take the railroad to Schenectady. Then he took the stage to Utica. Here he discovered that he had missed the Saturday stage to Mt. Upton and that the next one did not leave until Tuesday. This was, in fact, a relief. "I shall have," he wrote in his diary, "3 days repose in this place which is desirable as I have pressed forward rather too fast since Monday for my present state of health."[1] Clearly it would not do for the "old bachelor" to greet his love bearing the weight of his full fifty years.

Frederic passed the three days impatiently. Finally on October 15 he took passage in the mail coach for Mt. Upton. Part of the road was almost impassable, but they jogged along and when he arrived he was welcomed by Richard Morris, Euphemia's uncle, who took him to stay at his home. The next day Frederic and his lady took a walk. This was Wednesday. His diary contains no further references to their affair of the heart until Sunday, October 20: "The day of the proposal."[2] In those five succinct words, Frederic recorded what might be the biggest change in his life.

Having done the deed, he planned his return to Boston. Rain and the erratic stagecoach schedule, however, delayed his departure. This gave him three more days of bliss with Euphemia. As she had not said yes or no to his proposal, Frederic was not sure where he stood. To press too hard, he thought, was dangerous. This was probably the most difficult negotiation he had undertaken in a long life of negotiations. Finally, Thursday, October 24, dawned and it was a beautiful day. Richard Morris agreed to drive him to the banks of the Susquehanna River, less than ten miles distant, where he could catch the stage for Pennsylvania. Happily for Frederic, Euphemia came too as did Mrs. Morris. On the way Euphemia gave Frederic her answer to his proposal. In his diary he wrote: "The day of acceptance."[3]

His journey homeward was slow and full of annoyances. He went by way of stagecoach to Mount Pleasant, Pennsylvania, and then to Newburgh, New York. There he took the steamer *Novelty* down the Hudson River to New York City. He stayed just one night in the city and then returned to Boston on the steamboat *Providence*. Frederic ended his diary for the month of October with "Love rules the camp, the Court, the Grove."[4]

Now it was love letter time. Frederic's love letters to Euphemia sounded more like business correspondence, but perhaps a recitation of the assets of a man of fifty wooing a girl of nineteen was appropriate. He told her that business had been his adult life, that the annual profits from his ice business had risen to $20,000 a year, that the real estate connected with the ice business was worth, by his reckoning, at least $60,000, and that the value of the Court Street property, the Nahant property, and the black lead mine doubled that sum. With his other activities he thought his income to be in excess of $30,000 a year. This was a substantial fortune to a young woman who came from the farming country along the Unadilla and whose father ran a store in a log cabin.

Frederic worried about potential impediments to their marriage. He admitted to her his persistent health problems, which might prove a plus to her if she anticipated that she would not have long to put up with her "old bachelor" after their wedding. Much could be said for being a young widow with $30,000 a year. One wonders how the themes of these love letters played to her back in Mt. Upton. If Euphemia's motivation was money, Frederic's was loneliness.

During the turbulent early days of his career, Frederic told her, he thought that when things got bad he always had his family. They were his happiness, and he felt that he had supported them generously and fairly. That was how he interpreted his feelings toward his family. It is obvious, however, that they did not view him with the same rosy perspective. And he was aware of that. So he had removed them from his heart. Thus, after half a century of living, he was by himself, and he found that he was lonely. All he asked of Euphemia was that she give him—in return for love and support—some kind of proper response.

Although Frederic wanted to keep his plans a complete secret, and the Gardiners in Maine only learned of them when their son read about his marriage in a Boston paper, this proved impossible. On Monday, December 2, Frederic noted in his diary that it had been "Reported in town today F. Tudor is engaged to be married." The news came from New York. "Whereupon it was denied by said Tudor, he choosing to keep his own counsel in all matters relative to any subject of this kind." The rumor of course was true, and the time for the wedding was set for the beginning of the new year. While all the letter writing was going on Frederic continued to feel his fifty years. On Christmas day he was due to go to Mt. Upton, and in spite of his health problems—lumbago and a bad back—he went. Accompanied by his servant, John, he took passage on the one o'clock stage to Worcester. Wyeth was put in charge of the ice business while Frederic was away.

The day before he left he wrote in his diary:

> I go to be married to a woman who has excited a higher interest than ever woman did before & who with a generosity of her own is willing to forget that I am 30 years older than herself. I have studied to find excuses for myself to make good the differences & I have found some. One is the remarkable precociousness of mind & the other that we seem able to be companions—in feeling & inclination so much so that the differences of age seem perpetually to be forgotten when in company of each other.

He ended his reflections this way: "life is so full of uncertainties."[5]

Frederic arrived at Mt. Upton on the last day of 1833, and the wedding occurred on the second day of the new year. It took place in the evening at the home of Richard Morris. Mr. Morris's house, known locally as Upton Park Castle, was said to have been designed by a European architect. It sat in a park of some nine hundred acres and had fifteen rooms, all of which measured seventeen by nineteen feet. It boasted an ornate tower, several rounded chimneys, and ten lavishly decorated fireplaces. The ceremony was quiet, as Frederic had wished, performed by a local minister in the presence of about forty friends. On Sunday, January 5, 1834, Frederic and his bride went to church at Gilbertville, three miles from Upton Park, and walked home together. On January 16, in mild, beautiful weather, Mr. and Mrs. Frederic Tudor left Mt. Upton for Boston.

They were accompanied by one of her cousins and a waiting woman. Frederic's servant had been sent before with ten trunks of baggage. The new Mrs. Tudor did not intend to arrive in Boston without a stitch to wear. They traveled from Utica to Schenectady by sleigh. On the way the sleigh overturned in Herkimer but no one was hurt. The sleigh overturned again as they went through the mountains of Vermont, and they endured cold weather until they arrived in Boston on Thursday, January 23. The first Sunday home Frederic went "to church a married man—it is happy to be a married man."[6]

CHAPTER 26

I Was a Bachelor Too Long

THE NEWLY MARRIED COUPLE SETTLED DOWN in Frederic's lodgings at 4 Pearl Street for the rest of the winter. Before his marriage, Frederic had informed no one in Boston of his intentions, but once his bride was signed, sealed, and delivered he was bursting to tell the world of his great accomplishment.

So one Tuesday afternoon in January he held a grand gathering at the boardinghouse on Pearl Street to introduce the new Mrs. Tudor to everyone in Boston. Francis Russell, a friend of Harry's, attended and sent an account of the event to him in far-off New Orleans.[1] Russell, who arrived between one and two o'clock, found the reception was in a room hung with mirrors, which made it seem much larger and gave many pleasing reflections. Russell, Harry, and Frederic had spent many cheerful evenings in this same room. As they entered, guests were received and presented to Euphemia, who was sitting on a sofa. Russell thought she was very attractively dressed and that she had a certain graceful elegance.

Frederic meanwhile occupied himself in conversation with the guests. When Russell talked with him he sensed that Tudor was happy and pleased to be Effie's husband. Others, however, suspected Frederic of showing Effie off as if she were a newly purchased prize filly. Certainly some of the gentlemen must have gossiped about the prospects of the elderly bridegroom and the bride who was young enough to be his daughter. Others undoubtedly speculated, probably not too kindly, on her motives for marrying him. Surely some felt that it must have been for mercenary reasons. And so did Boston society become acquainted with Mrs. Frederic Tudor.

For the newlyweds, their first winter together was one of walks. These began a few days after they had settled in. They made a regular destination of Fresh Pond, for Frederic wanted Effie to see the ice operations. They also walked to Mr. Sparks's on the west side of Cambridge common, to Wyeth's, and around the mill dam. They took short walks at first, then longer and longer: five miles, then seven, later even nine. On one occasion, she preferred to go to church. Frederic told her that while church attendance was a duty, there was an even higher duty—exercise, for that helped to keep one healthy. Body before soul was the Tudor gospel. So after she had gone to church he marched her out and over to the Great Spring in Chelsea.

Sometimes, other than the usual hearty walk, they took exciting rides on the newly opened Worcester and Boston Railroad, the first railroad in the area. Indeed, Frederic and Effie were among the special one hundred passengers on the train that officially opened the line. The trip started at 4:20 P.M. when the locomotive, the *Meteor,* which had been built in England, and its eight passenger cars left Boston for Newton. It should have taken them thirty-nine minutes to go the nine miles, but frequent breaking of the connecting rods between some of the cars made it a much longer journey. Indeed, it was 8:20 before the Tudors arrived back in Boston. On another day they walked the railroad tracks for a while and then watched the cars go by.

Frederic proposed to spend that summer at his cottage in Nahant. At Miss Lekain's, the Tudors had relied upon her staff to take care of all the housekeeping. At Nahant it would be a different story—the old rough and ready of Frederic's bachelor days would not do. A proper staff had to be assembled and an inexperienced nineteen-year-old taught to run an extensive household. The first and most important member of that staff was the cook—at least so thought Frederic, who promptly hired one. Real housekeeping, however, did not begin until June 24—the day they left Pearl Street and moved to the cottage.

Nahant had been a summer resort for a bit over a decade by the 1834 season. The hotel that Col. Thomas Handasyd Perkins erected eleven years earlier on the eastern point of the peninsula proved not so great a commercial success as a social one. The improved transportation that the hotel provided with a regular boat from Boston encouraged many of the city's fashionable families to build their own cottages near the hotel. In 1825 Cornelius Coolidge, a Boston land developer and sometime architect, started a small speculative development outside the hotel grounds. The cottages he built had piazzas supported by red cedar posts surrounding the ground floor. Each cottage had a privy and a woodshed. In all, Coolidge erected thirteen of these rough stone-and-wood cottages before he went bankrupt in the depression of 1829. Frederic thought little of Coolidge's efforts, calling them "miserable houses," an interesting observation as his own cottage closely resembled Coolidge's designs.

Apparently others did not share Frederic's opinion, for the cottages sold, and to such important Bostonians as David Sears, reputed to be one of Boston's first millionaires. He had come by his money through inheritance, while another buyer, William Appleton, came by his wealth through trade. Nearby, Judge William Prescott built a cottage inhabited by his nearly blind and eventually famous literary son, William Hickling Prescott. A former secretary of the navy, Benjamin Crowninshield, also built a cottage here.

Two other Nahant neighbors, the Eliot brothers, Samuel and William, owed their social prominence to their merchant father, from whom they had inherited just

View of Nahant showing the steamboat landing
Gleason's Pictorial Drawing-Room Companion, *Aug. 30, 1851.*
Collection of the Massachusetts Historical Society.

enough money to support themselves without the bother of a vocation. When they came to Nahant in 1830 they attempted to purchase Frederic's estate, which was perennially for sale. Once they learned that they could buy a lot of land on the top of the cliff at east point with a magnificent view of the sea and build a satisfactory cottage on it for $3,000, the $10,000 for Frederic's estate ceased to interest them. The following year Frederic turned down several offers for his cottage, the largest being $6,000.

By the time Frederic brought Effie for her first summer in Nahant, at least twenty Boston families were summering there. While Frederic considered himself the equal of these grand Boston families, his association with them remained limited and formal. His years as a bachelor were probably responsible for this, and undoubtedly his young wife from the country did not improve his outreach in a time when snobbishness ruled the day.

One community project at Nahant that did interest Frederic was the establishment of a church for, as he expressed it in his diary, "christian worship of some kind."[2] He contributed fifty dollars toward the project. At the time no one realized that they were erecting what was to be the first nondenominational church in the country—and that during a time of strict religious sectarianism. Frederic sat on the committee to select the ministers who were to preach the first season. Samuel A. Eliot, who proposed the list, had arranged for a Unitarian preacher on alternate Sundays. He thought this proper since half the congregation were Unitarians and they had been the ones who had given most of the money to build the church. The committee took care to get good men, as they feared that otherwise attendance would be small. But gaining hearers never turned out to be a problem.

Like many of the other summer residents, Frederic continued his business in Boston, which meant he became a frequent commuter to and from the city. He found that this practice often did not give him enough time to conduct his business properly, and so on July 15 he decided to stay overnight in his lodgings at 4 Pearl Street. But he did not like the reminder of his bachelorhood. "I was too long one," he grumbled. "Why E. were you born so late?"[3]

By 1834, Frederic had been coming to Nahant for eight seasons. All these years he kept a garden. Although it flourished and grew, his little Eden was in the midst of a barren, rocky waste. The first settlers had deforested the peninsula in the seventeenth century so that they could pasture their cattle, which made the place almost devoid of vegetation. Frederic's success with his own garden convinced him that he could extended his Eden over the whole peninsula. The scoffers who claimed that the salt air and the winds would kill all vegetation, including trees, only spurred him on.

He started with Balm of Gilead trees, planting some 150 of them. They grew quickly and offered protection to slower-growing trees. By the time of his first summer in Nahant as a married man he had some 4,000 trees in his nursery. On August 2 he ordered them extensively trimmed. Further, he cut an average of 15 shoots of one foot in length from each tree, and these he used to reforest Nahant, which was now one of his goals. Many he gave away to his neighbors *if* they agreed to plant them.

On October 13, Frederic's workmen started planting the Balm of Gilead trees wherever they could. He wished to have 4,000 trees planted by the next spring. As with all of his enterprises, he went into this project in a massive way. To accomplish this he asked his neighbors for subscriptions. His friend Colonel Perkins agreed to give thirty dollars. A week later he had enough pledges to plant an additional 300 trees. By winter, Frederic's great program had planted 1,226 trees in various parts of Nahant, including 426 trees along public roads.

As summer ended, Effie and Frederic had to plan for their return to Boston. But where in Boston would they go? During the summer, Frederic had quarreled with Betsy Lekain because she had let a boarder use one of the rooms in his apartment while still charging him for it. On October 27, in the midst of a storm, he went to Boston in his chaise to order the intruder out. Back in town a week later, and clearly fed up with the inconvenience of married life in a boardinghouse, he decided to make a change.

It soon became clear that it was not so easy to change a residence. Tudor turned to Effie's great aunt, Miss Johnston, for help. They visited ten different boardinghouses, finding nearly all of them full and the others not worth bothering about. In the end, he selected Boston's newest and best hotel, the Tremont House. There he rented for fifty-five dollars a week a suite of four rooms. Frederic obviously desired to impress his new wife by this selection. The Tremont House was the country's first modern hotel, and the largest, with 170 rooms. It was also the most expensive. In an era when one could get a room in an inn for fifty cents a night, the Tremont House charged transient guests two dollars.

The hotel filled most of the block on Tremont Street where it meets Beacon Street. A massive four-story granite building with a classical porch, it became the textbook for future hotel design, particularly as to the interior arrangement of the rooms. The ten public rooms were decorated in the latest French style. The halls and guest rooms had carpets, and there were curtains on the windows. The south wing, where Frederic stayed, contained ten suites with private parlors, most elegantly furnished. A lock on each apartment insured privacy—another first for the Tremont House. The plumbing at the time of Frederic's residence was as up-to-date as possible. It consisted of a group of eight water closets in the basement for use of all the guests. These were the first water closets to be built in a public building in Boston. Also in the basement were eight bathing rooms, but permanent guests could bathe in portable tubs in their apartments if they chose.

On November 22, 1834, the Tudors moved from the Nahant cottage to their new

View of the Tremont House, Boston
Engraving [1834], by James Archer.
Samuel Walker, Publisher: Boston.
A/B64B6/Hot.t.1834
Boston Athenæum.

quarters in Boston. The next day, they ate their first dinner at the Tremont, renowned for its excellent French cuisine. The Tudor dinner consisted of "Pease soup, Roast Partridge, Sweet Breast of Veal, Boiled Cod, Oyster patties, Turnips, potatoes, cranberry, Sour apple pie & sago pudding, Cheese, butter, apples, raisins, almonds."[4] Frederic weighed himself a week later and found that he had gained three and a half pounds since the summer. Apparently marriage agreed with him.

CHAPTER 27

Very Delicate Situations

Frederic Tudor did not find coffee as agreeable as marriage. During the first year of his marriage, Frederic made a show of his wealth, spending his summers on his estate in Nahant, wintering in Boston's best and most expensive hotel, attending parties and the theater with his beautiful young wife, and generally living comfortably and genteelly, attended by a bevy of servants. The economic truth was far different from this display.

The great bubble of the coffee speculation that hovered over his head during his courtship of Euphemia burst in the second month of his marriage. He was—in the words of Thomas Wren Ward, the Boston agent for the great London banking house Baring Brothers—thrown "back to nothing." The disaster began in early February 1834. By mid March his creditors called for a settlement of what he owed them, but Frederic asked for a delay. By the end of the month they proposed to sue him. All that summer, while Frederic planted trees in Nahant, coffee prices in Europe plunged and he continued to absorb the losses as his agents sold his holdings. Autumn brought no better news. In December 1834 his cousin William Savage failed as a result of his own coffee speculation. He told Frederic that he had lost $200,000.

How much did Frederic lose? He guessed that he must have bought and sold seven million pounds of coffee and in doing so had lost upwards of $175,000. What saved his goose was ice. He estimated that five or six years with ordinary prosperity in the ice business would enable him to get back on his feet. Characteristically, he saw a silver lining in even these dark clouds, for he felt that the failure of his coffee undertaking further invigorated him in his ice endeavors. What concerned him most about the coffee speculation was the possible censure others might pass upon his business judgment. On the whole, he believed he had planned his coffee investment correctly; the adversities arose from circumstances beyond his control. He consoled himself with the thought that in six years he would turn the whole situation around and have a yearly income larger than the whole fortune of his grandfather. All of this he would owe only to his own efforts.

Meanwhile, there were pressing day-to-day demands, which included the living arrangements at the Tremont House. Soon after they had settled in, Frederic began having trouble with its manager, Mr. Boyden. For example, Frederic discovered charges he had not agreed to on his bill, such as five dollars a week for the room of a female servant. Moreover, the hotel kept their suite too warm for Effie, who by now—May 1834—was pregnant. She lost the baby in July. If Effie had thought that her old husband would be moderate in his sexual demands, she was mistaken. Frederic at fifty was as randy as a goat in springtime, and as soon as nature allowed Effie was again pregnant. This time Frederic was determined it would succeed, but by the end of August he was complaining that Effie did not feel well. He wrote in his diary that "Her situation is very delicate."[1]

Effie's health continued to be troubling. On September 22, when Frederic was in Boston on business, he had to rush back to Nahant because of her condition. He found the local physician in attendance and that she was somewhat better. But the next day saw little improvement and the doctor spent the night. In the morning Frederic arranged for a Dr. Hale from Boston and a nurse to come to Nahant to care for her. For the next two weeks Effie soldiered on, but on October 7 Frederic again summoned the local physician. His wife later claimed that her "troubles" were largely due to Frederic's apparently insatiable sexual appetite. By the end of the month it appeared to one of the doctors that she had lost her baby while the other maintained that she was still pregnant. Such was the state of medicine in 1834. She had indeed had a miscarriage. By now the Tudors had moved from Nahant to their apartment in the Tremont House.

Effie's health remained uncertain in the opening months of 1835. She decided that she needed a trip to Mt. Upton and that it would be made back on horseback. To prepare for it, Effie rode daily for a month in a riding school and Frederic began searching for horses to buy. At the last minute it seemed that the trip might have to be postponed as Effie was again pregnant. Frederic, who had had enough of doctors, decided to become his wife's physician. His course of treatment: avoidance of all animal food and eggs. Unfortunately for the doctor, her indisposition continued. Now Effie went her husband one better and became her own physician. Her course of treatment: avoidance of all food and nourishment. She starved herself for four days, and on the fifth she was back in the riding school. She miscarried again.

Early in May, Effie was well enough to undertake the trip. Frederic by then had purchased horses and sidesaddles for the ladies—for Effie, making the journey without him, was riding with her friend Harriet Inglis. On May 8 the Mt. Upton expedition got underway at quarter to eight in the morning. Harriet's sister Fanny Appleton, young Thomas Gold Appleton—the son of Boston's foremost textile millionaire—as well as three other members of the Inglis family came to see them off. The visitors led on horseback; next came Harriet riding on "Silver Tail," followed by the Effie on "Betsy Baker," attended by the Ice King on a black mare. Also in the party were Frederic's new footman, William Tobin, and a carriage with Miss Johnston, Tina the waiting maid, Jacob Sanborn the driver, and a pile of baggage. They proceeded down Beacon Street, crossed the mill dam that separated the Back Bay from the Charles River, and headed for West Newton, nine miles away. Here they spent the night at the popular Davis Tavern.

At Davis's, Frederic took leave of his wife of sixteen months. He claimed they were greatly affected by the parting. Four days later, however, Frederic complained that he had not yet received a letter from her. The next day one arrived. Then he had to wait nineteen anxious days before another came saying that the party had arrived safely at Mr. Morris's house a week before. Now a continuous stream of mushy letters flowed from Boston to Mt. Upton. Far fewer letters came from Effie.

In spite of the temporary absence of his wife, Frederic's life continued. He went on walks with his brother Harry, and with a crowd of four thousand attended the annual gathering of the Ancient and Honorable Artillery Company of Boston. That day opened with rain, which Frederic remarked would be awkward since "the ancient & honorable company of holiday soldiers . . . are good for no field but one of sunshine & no enemy."[2]

As the days wore on, Frederic became anxious for Effie to return. In his June 3 letter to her he suggested that he would go to Mt. Upton and escort her home. Then he waited for a reply. The only response was silence. Frederic became annoyed, for patience was hardly one of his virtues. Finally Harriet Inglis replied saying that he was expected.

Frederic immediately set off by rail for Worcester, where he stayed the night and booked the Albany coach for the next morning. After being thrown about in the stage for two days, he finally reached Albany on Saturday night. There he was delayed because the next day was Sunday and there was no coach service on the Sabbath. He took lodging in the Congress Hall Hotel and asked if there was a letter for him. There was none. Now he became disturbed that Effie might have already started for home and they would miss each other.

Bright and early Monday morning, Frederic climbed into his stagecoach for the thirteen-hour trip to Cooperstown. On Tuesday the man he had hired to take him on the last leg of his journey picked him up after breakfast; they reach the Morris house at two in the afternoon. To Frederic's extreme disappointment he found no one home but Miss Johnston. The others had gone off on a visit and would not be back until the next afternoon. Exhausted from the journey, Frederic went to bed before nine o'clock, in what was his "matrimonial couch & chamber without the tenant that should have been there."[3] The next afternoon, unable to contain his anticipation any longer, he rode out hoping to intercept the returning party. Alas, he did not. When he finally met Effie again they spent three days riding and walking in the countryside. However, Frederic had not come to dally in Mt. Upton but to escort his Effie home. And that he did.

The travelers left Mt. Upton on June 22, and after a stopover at the Shaker village in Lebanon Springs, New York, they arrived back in Boston on July 2. Soon afterward, they gave up their rented rooms at the Tremont House and moved to Nahant for the summer. One of the first things Frederic did there was to inspect the trees he had planted by the roadside over the last few years. To his disappointment none had survived; he blamed their destruction on the wild animals who also inhabited the peninsula. Fortunately he had in his nursery another 1,291 trees, many of which he proposed to give to his neighbors for planting. Indeed, by the time the Tudors returned in October to Boston for the winter his own men had planted, staked, stoned, and tarred on his own lot 432 of them.

Now that Frederic had a wife, he started to host dinner parties and make afternoon visits to the other summering Bostonians. For example, he and Effie went to the Nahant Hotel to see a tableau vivant and to a subscription ball. Effie even gave a tea and supper party for about sixty of their neighbors. But mostly Frederic and Effie lived a quiet life while in Nahant. He described their days this way in a letter to Miss Johnston: "Effie wished me to say she had become a mere wife & is now at the moment I am writing roasting chestnuts & opening them for her despot to devour—who very thanklessly gulps them down."[4]

The great accomplishment of the summer—Frederic's reconciliation with his mother, whom he had not seen for eight years—came at the urging of his young wife. "She is now in her 82nd year," Frederic wrote in his diary, "but is well & cheerful. We invited her to come & spend a week with us. The unfortunate circumstances of her adhering to the desperate course of Mrs. Stewart & her bad counselling has been the cause of the separation. She is now too old for any other feeling than forgiveness & oblivion for her past mistakes & errors."[5] Although there was clearly a surface reconciliation between Frederic and his mother, the son never allowed it to go any further than that.

In September, Frederic and Effie made an excursion to New York City. The high point of this visit was Niblo's Garden, a popular place of entertainment—with its own theater, saloon, and hotel—on Broadway at Prince Street. It also had landscaped grounds known for their rare native and exotic plants. Since Niblo's had been open for only six years, visiting it may have given Frederic ideas for his own garden at Nahant.

Before they went to New York, Frederic bought his first spectacles. Not only had age whitened his hair, but now it was also blurring his vision. For some months he had been having trouble reading in the evening, but his vanity had compelled him to put off getting glasses. Finally he had given in, although he still waited for three weeks after their arrival before he started to use them.

The time came at last to make a decision on their winter residence. Frederic had started to long for a house of his own, a place "where we can keep a cat & have a place that we can harbor a mouse or two to steal cheese which is our own."[6] Nothing came of that longing in the fall of 1835, however, and they returned to the Tremont House. Their winter life here continued the pattern of their summer life—hosting dinner parties, going for walks and rides, and attending the theater and even the Lion Circus. But there was a major complication to their swirl of social activity: Effie's health. Once again she had become pregnant and once again she lost the child. And until the miscarriage she was often violently ill. It began to seem that no matter how much Frederic wanted to be a father, he never would become one. Frederic also continued to find fault with the manager of the Tremont House. In the end, on March 25, 1836, the Tudor family abruptly left the Tremont House and took lodging at Mrs. Putnam's in Pearl Street. Frederic never gave a reason for this sudden move, which he made when his wife was very ill and in pain.

This winter was so disagreeable that Frederic looked forward to another summer on Nahant. When Effie fell ill once again, however, and could not run the Nahant household, they stayed in Boston. All in all, Effie was housebound until September. She continued to lay her health problems at her husband's doorstep, especially to his inability to abstain temporarily from sexual intercourse. As proof of the charge, she found herself pregnant once again, for the fifth time. Frederic substituted frequent trips to Nahant for the rest of the summer. His project for the season was the addition of a library, which he had designed, to the cottage.

Frederic and Effie had lived the first two years of their married life in a boardinghouse and a hotel, and they were fed up with both. So Frederic went house-hunting and eventually located a suitable one on West Street, which he leased for three years. He also purchased most of the contents of the house from the owner and engaged a staff, with which he perennially had trouble. On October 19 the family and their staff moved in. The Tudors were generally pleased with their new home, although Frederic did wish it were a bit larger. The first visitor was Frederic's mother, who stayed several days.

By this time Effie was about six months along in her pregnancy and was feeling quite well. She was able to host a tea party for Frederic's mother, and she enjoyed walks and riding in the carriage her husband had purchased for her. In November her brother John arrived. She hoped that her husband would give him a job, but that Frederic did not do. Effie did show John the sights of the city and they took frequent walks. Evenings were passed in entertainment, such as a visit to "Mr. Maelzel's original, splendid Mechanical Panorama of the Conflagration of Moscow." By February 16 her time was near, so Frederic sent for Mrs. Wood, Effie's old nurse. Two days later at two o'clock in the morning Effie woke Frederic with the news that the baby was about to come. "At 35 minutes past 8 o'clock a little (or rather a large) Euphemia came into the world."[7] So Frederic Tudor, the Ice King, was now a father.

CHAPTER 28

Back to the Ice Business

NATHANIEL WYETH HAD LEFT BOSTON SEPTEMBER 7, 1834, on his second trek west, convinced that this time he would make a success. But everything went wrong. He encountered too much competition; the Native Americans, alarmed at so many expeditions crossing their lands, became hostile; and others beat him to the most lucrative trading areas. Furthermore, the weather proved disappointing, men deserted, and illness disabled his company. On the West Coast the salmon season proved unfavorable and he could only obtain half a cargo for the ship he planned to send back to Boston. Wyeth concluded that he had to give up any hope of establishing a salmon business. The fur trade was no better. He found it was impossible to compete with the Hudson Bay Company. The Native Americans refused to trade with him, and his own efforts at trapping beaver were inadequate. The supply end of the business turned out to be impractical, as the mountain men who were to buy the goods proved to be treacherous and easily upset.

On September 6, 1835, Wyeth wrote Frederic about the failure of his business plans and about his impending return to Boston. When the letter arrived in Boston the following June it told Frederic exactly what he wanted to hear: Wyeth wanted to come back and work for him if those who backed his western business venture would not continue to do so. Frederic's judgment was terse. "They will not." He was correct. When Wyeth had conceived his grand scheme he had not known that the fur trade was in decline. Trappers and Native Americans had all but destroyed the beaver population and no other fur was in demand. In the end, the Hudson Bay Company purchased all his goods and his forts, which allowed him to pay off his men and return to Boston.

In September 1836 Wyeth made his way back to St. Louis, where he wrote a sad and humble letter to Frederic saying that he intended to reach Boston about October 25. This, a Friday, was the very day Frederic received his letter. The next Monday morning, Frederic walked to Wyeth's house in Cambridge for a visit, but Wyeth did not ask him for a job until the following Wednesday. Frederic did not wish to appear too anxious, since he wanted to make the best possible deal. So he took Wyeth to Nahant to discuss their future together. On Thursday afternoon they dined at the Rice Tavern on the typical business luncheon of the era: broiled chicken, beef steak, and partridge. They did not, however, finalize any business deal. The next morning Frederic took the train to Worcester. His ultimate destination was Sturbridge, where Effie and her aunt were vacationing for a fortnight. On the four-hour carriage ride from Sturbridge back to Worcester on Saturday, Frederic considered the prospect of having Wyeth back in his employ.

At this point in his business career, Frederic was fifty-three years old and had worked hard at the ice trade for nearly thirty years. He had tried to lighten his load before but had failed. Hoping to do better this time, he wondered what he would need to offer Wyeth to gain his exclusive services. What other employment options did Wyeth have? Anxious to follow up the Nahant meeting, Frederic wrote Wyeth from the hotel in Worcester. With his pregnant wife and elderly aunt for companions, he found the trip back to Boston anything but swift. He did not arrive home until noon on Thursday, October 11.

The very next day he conversed again with Wyeth and also with James W. Fenno about joining his business. Fenno (no relation to Frederic's wife), thirty-four years old, was an attorney with an office in the building Frederic owned in Boston. He had formerly been a dealer in English goods and had helped Frederic in the Ixion venture. Unknown to Frederic, Wyeth had already corresponded with Fenno regarding their participation in the ice business together.

Back in late September, before Wyeth returned from the West, Frederic learned from his agent in New Orleans that all of his icehouse keepers wanted to come home. As alarming as this news was, it paled in comparison to the disturbing report that a plot had been uncovered involving one of the ice keepers and a Boston businessman who was proposing to establish his own icehouse in New Orleans. This development made a successful negotiation with Wyeth doubly important, yet discussions between Frederic and Wyeth dragged on for another ten days.

Finally Wyeth agreed, as a first step back into Frederic's business, to take charge of all ice operations. Four days later Frederic engaged the brigs *Harriet* and *Grand Turk* and gave Wyeth the responsibility for fitting them out. As for the New Orleans plot, which grew to include all three of his icehouse keepers, he vowed to get rid of them and so he sent his brother Harry to clear up the problem. Also hoping to use this opportunity to expand his business there, Frederic gave Harry instructions to build a new icehouse and in other ways to improve sales.

Frederic offered to pay Wyeth and Fenno $3,400 per year in a complicated arrangement based on profits. At this time factory managers in the textile industry around Boston earned from $5,000 to $6,000. Nonetheless, Frederic thought that his offer held more incentives and the potential for a high annual return. He also remembered that he had hired Wyeth years before at $500 a year. The offer seemed good enough for Wyeth, who reentered the business with a great burst of activity. A study of Frederic's diary shows that he consulted with Wyeth on everything:

Nov. 2: Talked to Wyeth upon the conspirators in N.O.

Nov. 26: Talked to Wyeth upon the erection of a house to contain 1500 tons to be kept over summer for autumn shipments.

Nov. 28: Debated with W about building a new larger house at Charlestown to hold 500 cords.

Dec. 6: Went in chaise with W to the "Virgin of the woods" of 1828 when the ice trade was so much distressed with a warm winter. We found the ice 5 ½ & 6 inches thick at the same time that Fresh Pond was barely skimmed over. Wyeth is to examine another pond at West Cambridge to see which has the preference in thickness.

Dec 8: Talked with W & Barker upon doubling ice. The latter is against the process as expensive & uncertain. Urged the necessity of it & W is to give it a good trial on Saturday if possible.

By 1836 the railroad system between Boston and her industrial suburbs was established. Since transport from the ponds to the Boston wharfs was one of Frederic's largest costs, he was keen to try the rail lines. On December 20 he went to the terminal of the Boston and Lowell Railroad in Cambridge to receive a shipment of ice he had purchased in Lowell. Later he wrote in his diary that "This rail road mode of transportation is good: but not yet in sufficient training to work well."[1]

Meanwhile, the ice business flourished. Increased sales meant more ice and more ice storage, which required the acquisition of more property. So Tudor had Wyeth purchase some land at Spot Pond in Stoneham. By now others were aggressively active in the ice business, both at the retail level—in Mobile and New Orleans—and at the supply end at Fresh Pond. To address the latter problem, Frederic directed Wyeth to do something about it—which he did. He advertised Tudor ice at a price lower than that offered by their chief competitor at the pond. He also arranged to have a five-hundred-cord icehouse built there and a three-hundred-cord one at Deven's Wharf in Boston. On January 19 Frederick wrote in his diary that "Wyeth has 60 men at work loading wagons, filling houses & building new houses. . . . There is now daily employed in the ice business an average of 127 men, 105 horses & one bull."

Throughout these two months of winter activity Frederic had been discussing possible terms for permanent employment with Wyeth and Fenno. Fenno balked at Frederic's insistence that he go to New Orleans to take charge of that part of the business. By this time Frederic was having second thoughts about Fenno anyway. Finally, Frederic dismissed him. "He has too much the regular citizen principle in him to be a good soldier who must sometimes go without his mutton at the exact feeding time. Habits of life too much in rule do injury & interfere with good action in a business like mine."[2]

At the end of February, Frederic sent Wyeth to Mobile, Alabama, to regain his lost business. Wyeth started to build an icehouse that would serve as an outpost for future sales in New Orleans. Even before it was finished the first shipment of ice arrived from Boston. Frederic's opposition in New Orleans—those he called "snakes in the grass"—were angry that he was selling his ice at one cent per pound. This competition, although it upset Frederic, actually heralded the expansion of the ice trade. Frederic had originally approached the market challenges by trying to monopolize the business. He later discovered that competition greatly expanded the market—and that volume was the key to success.

Strong remittances in 1837 from his retail outlets gave him for the first time in his career twenty thousand dollars in surplus. So on June 1 he ordered Wyeth, who was still in Mobile, to go to Brazil and see about once again opening up that market for ice sales. Instead of doing so, however, Wyeth notified Frederic that he was returning to Boston because of the financial panic now sweeping the Northeast.

For years previous, Frederic had often complained that credit was tight. In 1834 the shortage of credit caused a panic along the eastern seaboard—but not in the West, which was booming. This lack of credit proved short-lived, and as a result, speculation in western lands became rampant with demand for government land far exceeding the supply, and the same plots were often sold and resold several times, whence came the term "doing a land-office business." With the Treasury of the United States in the black and the national debt paid off, Congress voted to return the surplus to the states. This windfall spurred the building of roads, canals, and railroads, a process that had already begun on credit. Construction in Boston boomed as well. By 1837, the total indebtedness of the states reached $170 million, a tremendous sum for the time.

All this speculation took place with paper money, as American banks were unaccustomed to doing business in gold and silver specie. In fact, most of their specie had gone to Europe to cover the country's unfavorable trade balance. When American bills of exchange began to sell at a discount in England, English merchants became frightened and called for immediate settlement of their American accounts—and the fatal chain began. Soon there were reports from New Orleans of proliferating business failures. The financial panic had started.

Throughout April 1837, Frederic peppered his diary with reports of panic and failures. He wrote Phineas Pierce, his agent in Charleston, to send him as much money in specie and bank checks as possible. As he feared, many southern states suspended specie payments, and soon New York banks did the same. During a large meeting in Fanueil Hall the same measure was recommended for Boston banks. More merchants failed as they were required to repay their debts in nonexistent specie and none was to be had. Even Frederic was worried. "I live in hope of relief from East India & Charleston, S. C. remittance & from Havana."[3]

Against this economic background, an old controversy between Frederic and his business partner in Havana, John Wade Damon, came to a head. It had been simmering since 1823, and it would only reach a final solution in 1849. "Who to trust or who is trustworthy seems to be the question amongst business men."[4]

CHAPTER 29

The Great Fallings Out

PERSONAL RELATIONS WERE ALWAYS DIFFICULT for Frederic Tudor. Sooner or later he managed to alienate nearly everyone. He could go the short distance, but he was not fitted for the long haul. Men who worked for Frederic did not seem to last; their leave-taking required continual replacements. Personal servants in his household came and went with amazing regularity. They all found the old man difficult to serve.

Brother-in-law Robert Hallowell Gardiner had stuck with Frederic through all his troubles. Was Frederic prepared to be there for Gardiner when hard times came that gentleman's way? On November 11, 1834, a fire destroyed Gardiner's mansion on the Kennebec. The flames consumed many of his books and papers. A beautiful stone house, designed by the famous architect Richard M. Upjohn, replaced it. The new home was much more expensive than Gardiner anticipated, and he suffered financial losses in 1834, just as Frederic had in his coffee speculation that year. From 1834 on, a theme of economic distress echoed in the letters Frederic received from Gardiner. Repeated destruction of his mills and their machinery by fires further diminished his fortune.

Through the years, Frederic had been materially helped by his ability to have money advanced to him on the strength of Gardiner's signature. Gardiner began to draw on Frederic for assistance when the Panic of 1837 put him in a tight spot. Since his estate consisted mainly of land, it was not easy to turn it into cash when needed. By

February 1838, instead of returning money he had borrowed from Frederic, he borrowed more. Sometimes, however, Frederic found it difficult to make the loan. "I can not refuse to do every*thing in my power* to relieve him but I do it at great expense & wear & tear of anxieties for my own most pressing wants."[1]

Gardiner had borrowed $1,050 from Frederic that February, expecting and promising to return it in a few days. When he was unable to do this, Frederic had to scratch his plan to send Harry to Jamaica and Wyeth to Brazil. By May, Gardiner's situation had worsened. He hurried to Boston to see what could be done to ease his plight. With the help of Frederic and William H. Gardiner, a rich lawyer friend who had married Thomas Handasyd Perkins's daughter, he was able to borrow $2,700 for four months at the City Bank. Into this difficult situation, however, Frederic's sister Emma threw a match—a match Frederic was ready and willing to use. That she meant no harm by her letter, that she only answered a friend's query, that she only stated what she thought everybody knew to be the truth, all these had little bearing on her brother's reaction.

In 1839, in a letter to her friend Mrs. George Lee, Emma Jane mentioned that the idea of shipping ice to the Caribbean had originated not with Frederic but with brother William. Frederic, of course, had long since suppressed any role that William might have had in originating the idea of sending ice to the tropics and had given himself alone full credit for the plan. So when Mrs. Lee showed the letter to Frederic, he shot off an indignant letter to Robert Gardiner "demanding in the most peremptory manner if [Gardiner] was concerned in the attempt to deprive him of the honor due to him."[2] Gardiner made the mistake of replying that he had always understood that William had first had the idea, but that William lacked the ability to carry such a scheme to a successful conclusion; that Frederic, having taken up the scheme and brought it off so handsomely, might just as well take the full credit for the idea. Besides, Frederic still smarted from what he conceived was a slight to his wife by the folks in Gardiner five years earlier. He wrote a most insulting reply to Gardiner, stating that in the future he would have nothing more to do with any member of the Gardiner family. To this letter, Gardiner had the good sense not to reply.

If Frederic no longer wanted his society, Gardiner would not force the situation. Nor would he reject any attempt to renew their intercourse. "We have occasionally met since, and common civilities have passed between us."[3] But the only long friendship Frederic ever had was now irretrievably broken. One benefit of the breech was that Frederic would not have to lend Gardiner any more money. Perhaps this idea figured in Frederic's sudden umbrage.

One of Frederic's most intransigent relationships was with John Wade Damon, whom he had hired as a carpenter to go to Havana in 1819. Two years later, Damon was elevated to icehouse keeper and continued in charge of the business in Havana when Frederic left there in the spring of 1823. To assure that Damon would stay on in Havana, Frederic offered to sell him a 10 percent interest in the business for three thousand dollars. When Damon returned to Boston late in 1823 for a visit, Frederic increased his interest in the Havana icehouse to a one-fifth share for six thousand dollars. At the time, however, their personalities started to clash—they did not have compatible temperaments. Indeed, it was amazing that their relationship managed to survive for as long as it did in what came to be an exceedingly awkward harness.

One of their earliest clashes concerned the Havana icehouse, which was old and in need of repair. When Damon filled it with ice he had brought with him on his return from Boston in March 1824, the sides of the house simply gave way. In addition, its capacity could not match the fourteen-months supply that Frederic deemed necessary to have on hand. A new site had to be found, but Damon was unable to locate one for several years. Frederic shared his displeasure about that inadequacy with Damon.

As time went on their misunderstandings grew. For example, Frederic wrote Damon on December 1, 1824, that he was going to charge the concern five hundred dollars for his own annual commission for the Havana business. This meant that Damon, with his one-fifth interest, owed Frederic one hundred dollars. Damon, claiming that he had not been informed about any commissions before now, protested the practice. Indeed, he went further. Unless Frederic withdrew his commission, Damon warned, he would charge the concern an additional three dollars per day for the extra work he had been doing. On his side, Frederic learned that Damon had some private speculations in lard and molasses outside the ice business. Frederic remonstrated with Damon, saying that the ice business required his full attention. The last straw came when Damon ceased to send remittances. "I have written today in the strongest possible terms that they must come or J. W. Damon will cease to be Ice House keeper."[4]

A remittance finally came two months later. Frederic fumed: "The neglect of J. W. Damon of his instructions causes me great inconvenience. He must either be displaced or return to his duty upon reduced allowance." What was to be done? Frederic decided to send brother Harry to Havana to straighten out the problem. Harry, however, demanded a stiff price for his services. The final agreement cost Frederic one thousand dollars, the cancellation of all Harry's debts to him, and the compensation of all Harry's expenses to Havana and back. Yet Harry had no better luck on the scene than Frederic had had with letters. Left with no other recourse, Harry discharged Damon on the pretext of his refusal to accept Frederic's efforts to reduce his pay by half. After appointing a new icehouse keeper, Harry left Havana for Boston. That was in April 1830. By the following August, Damon had made up with Frederic and was once again icehouse keeper. Problems persisted, however, and by November Frederic was again grumbling in his diary about Damon's "ingratitude & bad faith."[5]

Damon appeared in Boston on January 11, 1831, and by February 8 Frederic noted in his diary that he had settled accounts with Damon, who returned to Havana to put up a new icehouse. He had to cover the building costs with receipts of sales in Havana, as Frederic could not afford to send cash. Frederic's money was entangled in Boston building costs: he had unanticipated expenses in reconstructing his Court Street property, which had been destroyed by fire. What he had thought would cost sixteen thousand dollars turned out to cost twice that.

Meanwhile, Damon dealt with the persistent cholera, malaria, and other tropical disease that made Havana a summer death trap. His own health had suffered considerably. Indeed, Damon became so ill that his only solution was to return to Boston. Medical advice availed him nothing. A diet of bread and water proved ineffectual. Nonetheless, he stuck it out until the end of the summer of 1833, weathering the cholera and fever season. In fact the cholera brought increased business, as people thought ice helped either to cure or to ameliorate the disease. Finally, in July 1833, leaving a nephew in charge of the business, Damon embarked for Boston. Being nearer to Frederic gave the two men more occasion for misunderstanding. One such incident arose over money Damon wanted to borrow in order to help a relative purchase land. Frederic agreed to the loan, but when Damon came around to get the money Frederic reneged on his promise, thus planting another seed of bad feeling between them.

By winter, Damon was well enough to return to Havana. He had not been there long before another dispute arose. Frederic wanted to increase the price of ice, but Damon resisted, convinced that both previous increases had hurt business. Then, once again, continued ill health required Damon to return to Boston. When Damon arrived in Boston that fall of 1834, he and Frederic settled their accounts up to the moment without any difficulty. Then trouble began. Frederic proposed that Damon should return to Havana on a fixed salary as soon as he felt well enough. Damon refused, saying that if Frederic thought he could get somebody else to do a better job there, he needed only to refund him the amount he paid Frederic for his interest. What interest? Frederic asked, stating that he was unaware that Damon held a share of the business. Damon replied that he did indeed have an interest.

The point of the dispute was yet another misunderstanding. Frederic held that his agent's one-fifth interest was contingent upon Damon staying in Havana and running the business under Frederic's direction. In Frederic's eyes, this was not a true partnership but only an inducement for Damon to stay in Havana. Frederic felt that he had supplied the money with which Damon bought his interest. Of course, Damon insisted that he had indeed earned that money with his hard work. Finally Damon decided to return to Havana in the hope that this might change Frederic's view. When Damon reached Havana in March 1835, the substitute icehouse keeper Frederic had chosen, Samuel Davenport of Charleston, South Carolina, refused to relinquish his position. So Damon sailed back to Boston to try one last time to resolve their differences in a friendly way. Frederic's answer was simple. "You have no interest in the ice-business. I have taken my stand, and you may take yours."[6]

Damon felt that he had now no recourse but to bring suit in the Tribunal of Commerce at Havana to oust Davenport. After much legal maneuvering, the court decided to reinstate Damon. Davenport would be associated with him to represent Frederic's interest. Damon was back in control by October 29, 1836. It turned out that, while in control, Davenport had converted the icehouse into a cigar factory. The place was stacked high with cigar boxes and the tables and benches of the cigar makers, leaving little room for the ice business. Further disputes with Boston ensued as Davenport had let the ice stocks fall dangerously low. Finally, on February 4, 1837, the brig *Criterion* arrived with a load of ice.

It also brought Marcus Bacon, who had done such a good job for Frederic at Calcutta, as the new agent for Havana. Bacon commenced negotiations with Damon, which dragged on throughout the winter, spring, and summer. Then, on July 26, Bacon was relieved of his commission by dying of "the black vomit" (yellow fever). Now Davenport, who was put back in charge, twice tried to seize control of the money drawer that Damon held. As all this went on, Davenport was still making cigars in the icehouse. His workmen wanted to open the windows so they could have the amusement of watching vessels going in and out of the harbor, but this would allow heat to enter the room and melt the ice. When Damon needed additional work space, Davenport refused to give him any, and in the end the police had to be called to quiet them just before they came to blows. Frederic was disgusted when he heard of the goings on in Havana.

Then, in 1838, Frederic learned that when Damon had renewed their Havana ice license he did so in his own name and not in Frederic's name. Consequently, for ten years, from January 1839 until January 1849, Frederic did not receive a penny from the sale of ice in Havana. In an effort to win his business back, Frederic brought suit against Damon in the courts of Massachusetts, which led Damon in 1846 to publish a 270-page book entitled *The Havana Ice-House Controversy: or Facts versus Falsehood in Regard to Transactions between Frederic Tudor and John W. Damon.*

Frederic's brother Harry urged him to reply to it. So Frederic decided to publish a short circular, which was printed on January 15, 1847. "With great reluctance," he offered a few pages of the principal points of the case. Frederic saw it all as an attempt by Damon to steal the Havana ice monopoly from him. His loss by Damon's conduct was "a sum in gold and silver not less than two hundred thousand dollars." Damon replied with *Damon's Vindication*, which refuted all of Frederic's allegations, and he termed Frederic's claim of damage "the merest fragment of a heated imagination."[7] The courts ground on for another year and a half before making a decision. While Frederic collected no such sum as he had adduced in his circular, his share of the proceeds were paid, and on January 22, 1849, twenty-six years after the dispute started, Frederic Tudor was once again fully in charge of his Havana ice business.

Nathaniel Wyeth, inventor of the ice cutter, also quarreled with Frederic. In November 1837 Frederic made another new agreement with Wyeth and sent him on an inspection tour of the southern cities in which he did business. But Frederic also had his eye on the coming winter, and he wanted Wyeth back in Boston as soon as possible to take charge of ice harvesting operations in Maine. He wrote Wyeth to this effect, but six weeks went by and Wyeth had not returned. When he had not returned by the end of March 1838, Frederic wrote him condemning his independent spirit and ordering his immediate return if he wanted to continue in his employment. Wyeth, who was now in New Orleans, finally responded, but Frederic was not pleased with the tone of his letter. Wyeth did not come to Boston until the end of June; on July 5 he went to Nahant to see his boss and explain his actions. His explanation proved satisfactory and it seemed that good feelings between the two men were mutually restored.

During the 1830s, Leonard Stone had been using a version of Wyeth's ice-cutting machine on Fresh Pond in violation of Wyeth's 1829 patent, or so Frederic believed. Frederic had made a failed attempt to buy out Stone. Now he decided to sue Stone for patent infringement. The patent application claimed to cover any machine that harvested ice "by any other power than human." This claim was so broad that undoubtedly the court would have not supported it, so Wyeth recorded a disclaimer in the Patent Office on October 24, 1840. When Wyeth went to Oregon he had raised the necessary money by assigning his 1829 patent to Frederic. Accordingly, it was necessary for Frederic to sign the disclaimer. He refused, and in doing so he lost the patent case. The failure of the lawsuit due to Frederic's stubbornness greatly strained Frederic's relationship with Wyeth.

In the meanwhile, Wyeth had received the proceeds of the sale of Fort Hall from the Hudson Bay Company, which brought him a tidy sum of ready money. He had planted fruit trees in Cambridge before leaving for Oregon. They had now matured and were bearing nicely. He sold his fruit in Calcutta, South America, and the southern ports. At last in a financial position to strike out on his own, he parted company with Frederic. As an independent operator, Wyeth continued to make contributions to the ice trade. For example, he invented a second horse-drawn cutter that worked like a farm plow, marking the ice into squares for efficient harvesting.

Collecting ice on Fresh Pond had been a free-for-all for some time. To establish his right to harvest ice, Frederic purchased a farm of 120 acres on the end of Fresh Pond. Wyeth, as the largest landowner on the edge of the pond—he had inherited his father's hotel property—called a meeting of the abutters of the pond. They agreed to appoint Prof. Simon Greenleaf, of Harvard Law School, to allocate the ice-harvesting rights among the property owners. This precedent established ice right as an asset that could be used, leased, or sold. Now Wyeth and the landowners obtained a charter from the Massachusetts legislature for a railway from the pond to the docks in Charlestown—the Charlestown Branch Railroad. Wyeth designed the insulated cars and the device to load them.

To take advantage of the potential increase of ice harvesting on Fresh Pond, now that it was connected to the wharf by the railroad, Wyeth decided to build a monster icehouse of thirty-six thousand square feet; it would hold forty thousand tons of ice. The new railroad did have one problem, however: the fire under the engine threw sparks, sparks could cause fires, and wooden icehouses could catch fire. Consequently, Wyeth decided to build his new icehouse of brick. A deposit of clay existed not far from the pond, so he entered the brick-making business to supply his needs and others as well. The first ice was transported from Fresh Pond to the wharfs at Charlestown by train in December 1841. Wyeth's plan was to supply ice to the Boston ice dealers. His storage area was so great that he would be able to reap the profits during warm winters, when the only other supply came from Maine.

In the year after Wyeth completed his icehouse, a railroad was chartered to connect Fitchburg to Boston. It soon absorbed the Charlestown Branch Railroad. Wyeth had depended upon his fellow directors on the board of the Charlestown Railroad to keep his freight charges from Fresh Pond low. However, Wyeth and his friends were not elected to the board of the new railroad, and the new directors increased the rate. In addition, the route of the new railroad went past Walden Pond in Concord, another fine place to cut ice. So Frederic purchased ice harvesting rights to that pond. It cost no more to ship ice to Boston from there than from Fresh Pond.

Besides Wyeth, someone else was unhappy to see Walden Pond added to the sources of ice. It was Henry Thoreau, living in a small cabin on the edge of the pond and carrying out his famous experiment. Thoreau's friend Ralph Waldo Emerson was also worried. On March 7, 1847, he wrote that "Mr Tudor has invaded us with a gang of Irishmen & taken 10,000 tons of ice from the Pond in the last weeks."[8] Emerson was concerned that Frederic's crew, as many as fifty or sixty men, would spoil the value of his woodlot and force him to sell it. While Emerson thought about economic losses, Thoreau mused instead about the water from the pond where he bathed being shipped around the world to be sipped by Indian sages. Would drinking his bath water, he wondered, make them wiser?

At Walden, Frederic had no need for an icehouse. His men simply stacked the ice on the edge of the pond and covered it with hay. After it had been there for eighteen months, Thoreau observed that the ice was still good. Rather than buy from Wyeth, Frederic preferred to continue to seek his own supply elsewhere, as he had always done. Wyeth, a consummate technician, was not a businessman. He bore no grudge against his former employer, however, and they remained on cordial terms until Wyeth's death in 1856.

While Frederic had fallen out with many people over the years, his brother Harry was not among them. Because of Harry's success in New Orleans in the 1820s, Frederic frequently employed him. In 1844, when he was fifty-three, Harry got married; like Frederic he chose a much younger woman: Fanny Hortense Foster, who was twenty-eight when they married. They had three children, two of whom died quite young. When not absent on a project for Frederic, Harry spent much of his time in Hull at his saltworks.

Frederic never returned to cordial relations with Gardiner. The breach with his mother was only cosmetically healed by Effie. But with sister Delia, Mrs. Commodore Stewart, the breach was permanent.

CHAPTER 30

A Trio of Oddities

In the summer of 1834 a twenty-three-year-old Irish gentleman visited West Point, New York, with his young cousin, Lord Powerscourt. They were both touring North America for their enlightenment and education, but above all for their pleasure. Earlier in the year, in Washington, D.C., they visited a family they had met on the way over. Elsewhere in the same house Delia Stewart and her daughter Delia, now eighteen, were visiting the same family. Soon the young Delia met the two young gentlemen and found them both very attractive—especially the shy one, John Henry Parnell.

Later that summer, the three Delias and young Charles Stewart moved from Washington to West Point to escape the heat, which was particularly oppressive to Mrs. Tudor. Anna Quincy, daughter of the mayor of Boston, was there. In her journal she referred to the three Delias as "the trio of oddities." Indeed, she thought that all three of them lacked "one grain of common sense."[1]

During the summer the two Irish lads showed up again at West Point and stayed at the same hotel as the Delias. They all went to a ball for the West Point cadets. During the evening the two Irish boys monopolized young Delia's dance card. The next day Parnell took her to Kosciusko's Retreat and proposed. Young Delia did not answer him immediately, and Parnell and his cousin were soon gone on their travels. They next met Delia in December at a Christmas dance in New York City and then, briefly, back in Washington. But the randy roving Irishmen were soon off to Cuba and Mexico, not returning to New York until April. Then, almost out of the blue it seemed,

John Henry Parnell and Delia Stewart were married in Grace Church on May 31, 1835. He was twenty-four and she nineteen. It was clear that the new bride thought that her husband was rich. The couple left immediately for the Parnell home in Rathdrum, County Wicklow, Ireland.

Her new home, Avondale, was a smallish, sixty-year-old Palladian house set in a beautiful park overlooking a deep river gorge. The structure was plain, bleak, and isolated. To make matters worse, Avondale was a farm and John Henry Parnell spent much of his day managing it. When the farm did not occupy him fox hunting did. Since young Delia detested anything done out-of-doors, she spent a great deal of time alone. As to society, the local gentry were in her eyes rude farmers—a far cry from the "greats" who had entertained her in Washington and New York. She enjoyed an immediate visit from her mother, who then went on to Paris to live with her son Charles. Young Delia soon found herself pregnant.

Her first child, named after her uncle William Tudor, was born in 1837. Her husband proved lusty, for Delia was regularly pregnant during the next sixteen years. In all, she bore John Henry twelve children, the last in 1853 when she was thirty-six. By then, she had had enough of Avondale and of her husband. She moved permanently to Paris, where her mother and brother Charles were living. Only after John Henry's death in 1859 did Delia return to Avondale and then only to settle his estate. There she discovered that he was not as rich as she had imagined. In any event, he left all his property to their children and provided only a small annuity for her. Now in her early forties, she finally escaped a marriage that had bored her. Deciding to return to such "civilization" as Ireland offered, she moved her family to a house near Dublin and launched herself as a widow into society.

As for her mother, Delia Stewart, she lived as best she could. In 1849, when she was sixty-three, her son Charles approached the family with a plan to assist his mother financially in exchange for her interest in the South Boston shares. Frederic, still holding the same old grudge that he had for twenty years, was not interested in the son's "hocus pocus." Delia Stewart continued to live primarily with her son for the next eleven years. She died on September 7, 1860, in the middle of lunch while on a visit to her daughter. She was seventy-four. She had expressed her wish to be buried next to her mother, who after her death at eighty-nine in 1843 had been interred in a cemetery in Washington, D.C. Ultimately, the family brought both bodies to Boston and on December 7, 1861, placed them together in the Tudor family vault in the King's Chapel burial ground.

As for Commodore Stewart, he never went to sea again after he was exonerated of any wrongdoing at his court martial hearing. In 1830 Pres. Andrew Jackson made him one of the three Navy Commissioners. He received an appointment in 1837 to oversee the construction of the largest warship in the world, the USS *Pennsylvania*, at the Philadelphia Navy Yard. In between commissions and after the completion of the *Pennsylvania*, he spent much of his time at Montpelier. In 1844 the Democratic Party briefly considered him as a possible presidential candidate, but he took no interest in that honor. When the Civil War opened, Stewart, now eighty-three, offered his services to the North. When Congress voted in 1862 to create the rank of admiral for the U.S. Navy—there had been no admirals before due to the government's avoidance of monarchic terms—Stewart was one of the nine individuals given this honor. He died in 1869, aged ninety-one. For the last forty years of his life, he had had no contact with any of the Delias or their families, but on his death he left a substantial fortune to his daughter, Delia Parnell, which allowed her to leave Ireland for good.

The widow Parnell's interest in Dublin society had already begun to wane. She made a habit of visiting her brother in Paris for long periods. Charles Stewart, who had been brought up by the Commodore and trained as both a lawyer and engineer, lived a bachelor's life in Paris, supported by the fortune he had made in the development of the Reading Railroad in Pennsylvania. Since Delia and Charles had always been very close, life in Paris suited her well. By 1870, with the inheritance from her father, she gave up Ireland altogether. When her brother died two years later he left her even more money. Since her money was largely in America, she moved to her father's estate, Montpelier, in late 1873. Now that she had a regular and substantial income, contacts in Paris, a fortune in America, and a family in Ireland, she divided her time among the three places.

By 1880, her son Charles Stewart Parnell had become the leading figure in Irish nationalist politics with his Land League organization and its fight for land reform and Irish Home Rule. Charles, thirty-four and still unmarried, was called the "uncrowned King of Ireland." In the late 1880s, however, Charles's political career came to an abrupt end. Some years before, he had fallen in love with the wife of one of his subordinates. He succeeded in keeping the affair quiet until 1889, when the husband filed for divorce. Then followed in quick succession his marriage to the lady, his precipitous fall from power, and his death on October 6, 1890.

His mother's last years were tragic too. She tried investing in the stock market but suffered significant losses in the 1873 panic. It was only a matter of time before she bled away most of her fortune—much as had her mother and grandmother. She died in March 1898 while she was visiting Avondale. One evening, her daughter Emily organized a dinner party at which Delia held forth, as usual, in support of the Irish Cause and Irish nationalism. The next morning, while sitting near the fire in her room, a spark set her ablaze and burned her so severely she died. She was in her eighty-fourth year. Parnell's political party made a great occasion of her funeral. Delegates came from all over Ireland, and the procession through the streets of Dublin would have thrilled the three Delias if they could have been there to see it.

What Frederic might have said can only be imagined.

Frederic Tudor's cottage in Nahant
Unidentified photographer.
Courtesy of the Nahant Historical Society and the Friends of the Nahant Public Library.

CHAPTER 31

Squire of Nahant

WHILE THE LAST TWENTY-FIVE YEARS OF FREDERIC'S LIFE continued to be busy ones, they were also lived with a sense of serenity and happiness often missing in the earlier decades, which had been so marked with anxiety, fierce struggles, and desperate problems. In his business affairs, by hard work and diligence, he fully repaid the debts brought on by his reckless speculation in the coffee market. In his marriage, he found pleasure in his wife and children. And, finally, at Nahant, he discovered the meaning of place. It truly became year after year his community, and he is rightly termed the Squire of Nahant.

Clearly one of Frederic's deepest joys was his own family. For Effie, after so many miscarriages, had finally had a child. And once she started bearing she produced six children for the patriarch over seventeen years. The first, Euphemia, was born on February 18, 1837. She weighed just a little more than nine pounds. Her father, now fifty-four years of age, marveled that his child yawned and cried and slept in the most natural manner. This first offspring was the subject of many notes in her father's diary reporting her behavior and progress. He quickly named her "Effita" to distinguish her from his "Effie." She was christened at Trinity Church after the evening services on April 16 with Miss Johnston joining in the responses. By the time Effita was three months old, she was an amusement to the household and the doting father thought her "one of the finest little infants that is to be seen."[1]

When Frederic's coffee speculation had failed in December 1834, his creditors could find few assets upon which to levy their claims other than his ice business. They had proposed that Frederic should carry on the business as their agent and that he limit his personal expenses. They criticized, too, the money he spent on his Nahant estate. He explained that his two dwelling houses and nearby one hundred acres of land there were part of their security and that they had an interest in its improvements. "Allow me to proceed," he told his creditors, "and I will work for you better than I can under any restriction. Give me the largest liberty, and I will pay the whole, in time, with interest."[2] With his usual tenacity Frederic persuaded his creditors to agree to this plan, and he set out to pay off the whole sum plus interest.

He had hardly started when he began the altercation with Damon that interrupted his revenue from Havana. "This loss was grievous."[3] On one hand, his creditors were urging him to repay them faster, and on the other, his revenue source was shrinking. Then the winter of 1842–1843 failed to produce ice. Frederic spent the thirty thousand dollars intended to pay his creditors to secure poor and partial supplies of ice from Maine. That year the creditors only got their interest and were lucky to get that.

Another diversion of Frederic's capital in those years was the necessary purchase of property. With the development of the ice business, it became important to buy harvesting rights on the ponds where his ice was cut and to build additional icehouses to expand his retail market. Finally, near the end of January 1849, he was able to write to his creditors that his debt had at last been paid. It had taken him fourteen years. In addition to the principal, he had paid an additional $70,000 in interest for a grand total of over $280,000, a great sum for that period.

Once he was on his own again, the improvements at Nahant continued. Some were ordinary fruits and vegetables. Some were unusual crops, such as cotton and tobacco. Even though he tried over several summers to make the latter grow, in the end it was impossible to do so in this northern climate. He had more success with his apple, plum, and pear orchards. To protect them he did what he had seen his father do at Rockwood and constructed high fences around them. While the fences proved effective they did not add to the beauty of his garden. Henry David Thoreau, sailing by Nahant on his way to Maine in 1853, complained that these fences, "a rod high, designed to protect a few pear-shrubs," were very ugly.[4] Frederic continued to be busy at his garden until his death, but both the house and the gardens had now reached their fullest development.

One of the delightful events he sponsored for several Octobers was a festival for Nahant's schoolchildren. He invited them, and usually they were joined by the whole town, to come to his estate, taste his home-made apple cider and "perry" (made from his pears), collect berries in their baskets, sing, and generally have fun. In addition, he gave each guest a bottle of cider or perry and conducted everyone on a tour of the South Garden. "As God gave to me, so I give to you," he told them.[5]

Frederic was interested in building a road over the main beach. Convenient access to Nahant was only available at low tide over the hard beach. When the tide was in, the traveler had to struggle through the rocks and sands of the neck of land connecting it to the mainland. Frederic led the fundraising to provide such a road. The outcome was just another of the good things he did for this community.

Robert C. Winthrop, a direct descendant of the founder of Boston, accepted Frederic's invitation to hold the August 1858 meeting of the Massachusetts Historical Society in Nahant. Frederic had just been elected a member of the Society, the first historical society in the United States, to which many of the most important men in Boston belonged. It was appropriate that Frederic's cottage should host the Society's third meeting outside of Boston, as its very first meeting in 1791 had been held in the Boston home of his father. The meeting, on Wednesday, August 11, began with the bang of the president's gravel at 11 A.M. After the business session Frederic spoke on his attempts to reforest Nahant as well as about his own garden with its various unusual vegetables and flowers. Then he toured the members of the Society around his estate. Before they left, a stereograph view of the group was taken in front of his coarse, dark, granite cottage with its hemlock bark roof.

Frederic's final enterprise on Nahant was the Maolis Gardens. The gardens started out behind his house on ten acres of pasture bordering the north shore of the peninsula, looking towards Swampscott and Marblehead. On the ocean side of this parcel bubbled up a font of cold fresh water called North Spring. Since the end of the eighteenth century local neighborhood families had used it as a place to hold their summer picnics. Now that the area belonged to him, Frederic reasoned in one of his inventive moods, why not develop it, add various desirable attractions such as pavilions, flowering gardens, games for children and adults, as well as food and ice cream stands, and open it to the general public? And so he did.

Construction started early in 1859. He called his new recreation center Maolis Gardens, taking the name from "Siloam," a famous pool mentioned in the Bible. It was also, as someone pointed out to him, the name of a Greek patriot who fought for the freedom of his homeland at the battle of Navarino. Soon there was a crew busy moving trees; planting flowers; building one of his high fences around the property (except seaward); erecting pavilions, swings, and tilts; and preparing a croquet court.

Maolis Gardens was not free to the public. Adults paid five cents and children three. Later that price was increased. Those who lived on Nahant were admitted without charge except on Sundays. Of course, Frederic's own family and their friends, as well as a few others, were always admitted free. Like modern amusement parks, the admission charge was only the beginning. Inside there were plenty of other ways to spend money. Visitors would soon run into the balloon man or the candy man or the tintype artist whose wares cost a few more pennies. An ice cream pavilion and a dining hall lured more cash out of one's pocket. Frederic had generously provided free eating pavilions with stoves, but users had to buy the wood stacked in them. For the more athletically inclined there were bowling alleys, but the rock shore did not allow for swimming.

The entrance house had a narrow gate for foot passengers and a wide gate for those arriving by carriage. To the right of the entrance stood a series of horse sheds. Frederic claimed the manure that accumulated here as his. Below the sheds, near the ocean, was Maolis Spring, which had been widened into a circular pool about eight feet across. Winding steps curved around the pool down to the shore. On the wall above the pool was a marble slab inscribed "Pool of Maolis 1859." The dining hall was built close to the shore. At first there was a dance hall in the back part of it, but it was soon moved into the upper corner of the lot near the road. The Tea House was a small marble structure that looked like a temple with its colored tiles and its frieze of varied seashells. Inside there was a small house made entirely of seashells, a great attraction for children. Near the Tea House was a rock rigged to spout water when struck. In the Biblical spirit of the times it was named the Moses Rock. On it were inscriptions in both Greek and Hebrew of the Biblical verse: "He smote the rock and the waters gushed out and they drank from the rock."[6]

There was also at Maolis Gardens a great swing. It was held to the ground by poles fifty feet high. Its seat could hold several individuals, but it only needed one to get it going. It proved to be a daring ride for the adventuresome. For those who preferred their swinging to be more decorous and gentle, Frederic provided smaller ones.

Near the North Spring was an octagonal pavilion. It had clam shells on its side and a great shell for its roof. Inside was a pool and a boy covered by seashells and holding a horn. From that came water, for, of course, the boy was no boy but a fountain. But the most exciting object at Maolis Gardens was the "Witch House," or the Rock Temple, which was located at the entrance to the Gardens. Frederic wanted something strange and amazing in his Garden and this proved to be it. Octagonal, with eight gables and a hemlock bark roof, it had on top of all this a huge seashell with scalloped edges. Two satyrs held the shell high. Below, there was a natural cave in which, behind bars, stood a fierce granite lion. Its twin stood at the main entryway to Maolis Gardens.

Frederic did not want people to make only one visit to his Garden, so next to the Rock Temple he built a small boardinghouse that he named, naturally enough, Maolis House. A hundred-foot-long, slatted wooden fence ran alongside the hotel; on it was painted the sea serpent to end all sea serpents. Depending on where one stood, the result would turn into a mass of colored paint or suddenly appear to be a serpent again. Children found this very amusing.

Ultimately, as if all this was not sufficient, flying horses, wheels of fortune, a rifle range, tilting boards, a Punch and Judy show, and a bear den with two real bears in it were added. During the Civil War the two resident bears were cheerfully named "Jeff Davis" and "Ben Butler."

Certainly this was the strangest of all the undertakings of the Ice King. It showed that he was a child at heart. Perhaps it gave him more fun, though certainly not nearly as much money, as all his labors in developing the ice trade. Not all his rich and powerful Nahant summer neighbors liked Maolis Gardens. They saw it as a nuisance and a place that attracted ordinary folk to their small bit of earthly paradise. But as for Frederic—he reveled in his bears and flying horses and sea serpents on fences and stone lions. As he had loved living. But his ending was approaching, and—as people often do—he knew it.

Entrance Gate of the Maolis Gardens, c. 1870
Unidentified photographer.
Courtesy of Lynn Museum.

Tudor Wharves, Charlestown, about 1870
Joseph G. Minot, photographer, Neg. #17454.
Photograph courtesy of Peabody Essex Museum.

CHAPTER 32

What Shadows We Pursue

THE TROUBLE WITH A MAY-DECEMBER MARRIAGE is that both age at the same rate, but December has not as far to go. Frederic began to realize this early on. He was not immortal. What would happen to his enterprises when he was gone? What provisions should he make for his wife and his family? In 1847, he wrote to his wife about some of his concerns:

> On the subject of educating you to be able to understand some business affairs it was my duty to do so. I am 64 years old & you are not yet 34. . . . It was necessary to harden you a little in the affairs of life, in case my vigor & spirit should leave me too soon. . . . On the whole, as man & wife, Father and mother, I think I see, we have been happier than many of our acquaintance. . . . The difference of our age, has so far not made any great discrepancies between us. . . . I am happier every day & better willing to meet many of the troubles of life which are to be avoided.[1]

Would his wife's opinion of the marriage have been the same as Frederic's?

There is no reply to this letter, and one can only guess. But it cannot have been easy for a young woman to be married to a much older man, especially of Frederic's temperament. One story early in the marriage tells of their coming to Nahant on the steamboat and Frederic, in a fit of anger, throwing books Effie had with her into the ocean. Henry Wadsworth Longfellow reports in his diary that at a dinner party in 1857 in Nahant, Tudor "flamed like a comet from the top of the table," insisting that "the

Frederic Tudor, about 1860
Frederic Tudor (1783–1864), engraving [ca. 1860], by George Edward Perine.
Portrait file.
Boston Athenæum.

wife is the natural enemy of the husband."[2] What did his "natural enemy" truly think of Frederic? One indication may be what happened to Tudor's diaries. The volumes, which he had begun in 1805 and continued faithfully up to the year 1838, suddenly stop. One consequence of the absence of diaries after 1838 is that many of the personal details of Tudor's life are not available. We know how delightedly he reacted to his first child, but the birth of five more children and his response to them is left in limbo.

His first son, Frederic, was not born until 1845, when little Euphemia was eight years old. The third child, named Delia Jarvis for Frederic's mother, was born two years later. His second son, William, was born the next year. A third daughter, Eleanora Elizabeth, arrived in 1850. And in 1854, when Frederic was seventy-one years old and Effie was forty-one, she bore their last son, Henry. It would be particularly interesting to know Frederic's response to this child, who was described as "non compos mentis," or mentally deficient.

When Frederic died in 1864, in the eightieth year of his age, none of his children had married. Euphemia was twenty-seven and would not marry until 1872. Young Frederic would marry in 1867 when he was twenty-two, not emulating his father or his uncle's example of a late marriage. Frederic, Sr., had no grandchildren to enjoy before he died.

In these last years of his life, Frederic set about putting his affairs in order. He tried to find someone who would manage the ice business for him, taking on a burden that he had been carrying since 1805. He had hoped to have the assistance of James Fenno after Wyeth went his own way, but by 1843 Fenno was gone, to be replaced by another candidate from the large Cabot family. This time, it was Stephen Cabot's brother Richard, who was forty-eight and had been a commission dry goods merchant. Frederic thought Richard's twenty years in foreign trade would be useful, but Cabot stayed only until 1851, when Frederic had a falling out and fired him. Cabot was replaced with John B. Minot, who had long experience as a ship broker, but Minot only lasted one year.

Frederic now decided to incorporate. So in the fall of 1860 he petitioned the legislature to charter the Tudor Ice Company, with a net worth of one and one-third million dollars, the value of his operations in India, Singapore, Jamaica, and Brazil. Only Havana and New Orleans were left from the old days. Henry Saltonstall was a stockholder in Frederic's new company, but not for long. During the stockholders meeting in 1861 Saltonstall claimed that he was the head of the Tudor Ice Company and acted as if he were. This was all Frederic needed. He bought Saltonstall out.

On his seventy-ninth birthday, September 4, 1862, Frederic wanted to sign a new will. Effie was staying with her Morris relations in Mt. Upton. The issue revolved around Frederic's plan to leave Effie a lump sum if she would release her dower interest in his extensive property holdings. A series of letters went between Effie and Frederic, not directly but through their lawyers. But Effie insisted on being able to choose which bequests she wanted, so in the end nothing was settled.

Frederic had not been well in his last years. For a long time he had suffered from what the imprecise medicine of the day called lumbago—lower back pain, possibly from a slipped disk. His first attack had occurred back in 1837. Effie felt that it was the beginning of a malady from which her husband suffered for the rest of his life and was an annual visitor until his death.

The summer of his eightieth year he was still active at business. Minot wrote to him daily at Nahant. The year 1864 was a crucial one, however. It was almost as if it had been planned by a very neat playwright who wanted things to end tidily. Brother-in-law Robert Hallowell Gardiner died that year in March. Brother Harry, that companion of so many occasions, died in November. But none of this mattered to Frederic. Just as he had moved faster in life than either of them, so he was ahead of them in death.

Frederic Tudor died in Boston at his house on the northwest corner of Beacon and Joy Streets on Saturday, February 6, 1864. The next issue of *The Boston Transcript*, that for Monday, February 8, carried an announcement of his death as well as a short, respectful obituary. It first mentioned his horticultural activities at Nahant and then included a long quotation about his ice business taken from his 1849 letter in the *Proceedings of the Massachusetts Historical Society*. On February 9, at 11 A.M., the Rt. Reverend Manton Eastburn, D.D., bishop of the diocese and rector of the parish, conducted the funeral service at Trinity Church in Boston. It was the same church where the beloved friend and relative by marriage of the Tudor family the Reverend John Sylvester John Gardiner had served for a quarter of a century, where Frederic's brother William had been a pewholder and vestryman, and where Tudor had been a warden from 1834 to 1851. After the service, his body was laid to rest in the King's Chapel cemetery on Tremont Street in the family tomb (number thirteen), which he had cleared out some years before to make ready for its new tenants. The Massachusetts Historical Society, at its February meeting a few days later, paid its own tribute to him. After the regular business meeting, Society president Robert C. Winthrop briefly eulogized the Ice King, praising both his business activities and his work beautifying Nahant.

His widow, that young girl he had married when she was nineteen and he was fifty, was now just two months short of fifty herself. By his will, allowed the next month, one-third of his estate went directly to her and the rest to her in trust for the children. Now she was in her own right "inevitably and unavoidably rich." Years before Frederic had written a haunting line, "What shadows we pursue."[3] The "shadows" listed in the appraisers' account were quite substantial, but now were nothing but "shadows" to him.

After his death Effie did several odd things. For one, she changed her name. In 1867 she went to court and petitioned that her first name, Euphemia, be changed to Fenno. Since she continued to run the business of the Tudor Ice Company, it may have been because she felt that the name Fenno Tudor sounded masculine.

The second odd thing she did in 1879. On December 20 she drew up a long, complicated will. She made scant provision for her children but generous provisions for her

Fenno relatives. She protected them by disinheriting any legatee who attempted to challenge her will. What had been her relations with her children? Was this an effort to disassociate herself from anything connected with Frederic? Was she losing her mind? After Euphemia died on March 9, 1884, while visiting in Newbury, Vermont, her son Frederic Tudor challenged the will on the grounds that his mother was of unsound mind. The matter was settled outside court as an appeal was pending in the Massachusetts Supreme Court.

The third odd thing was done some months after Frederic's death. In November of that year she read through his diaries about the early years of their marriage and annotated it with at least twenty-four marginal notes, frequently contradicting Frederic's version of events. The most startling comment that Effie made about her husband was her annotation at the end of February 1834.

> It could hardly be expected that a honeymoon would last after the wife had discovered that the marriage privileges were shared with a woman who had lived with him with occasional interruptions since 1824. That in my youth and helplessness I should have felt compelled to a complicity in what the laws recognize as crimes my children must excuse as best they may.

"Truth," Effie wrote in one of the marginal notes, "is a strong antagonist!" This truth also helps us understand more fully Frederic's life.

What neither Effie nor time itself can change is the enormous contribution that Frederic made to the everyday society of his time. By showing that it was possible to transport ice great distances, by educating people to its value in the preservation of food, by introducing them to foods from other climate zones, he spawned a whole new source of revenue for himself and others. He wanted to monopolize the whole system, but that proved impossible. After all, he did not invent ice. He only took it out of ponds and transported it to where it did not occur naturally. Nature itself and the passage of time have also edited his life into a stranger shape than the owner of it saw it to be. It was as if history had been carved in some cold ice sculpture. Then, when the rays of the spring sun had touched it and caused it gradually to melt away, all his substantial accomplishments disappeared in the heat of the day. But they are not gone. We still enjoy them.

What shadows we are! What shadows we pursue!

NOTES

CHAPTER 1

1. *Deacon Tudor's Diary, or Memorandoms from 1709, &C.*, ed. William Tudor (Boston, 1896), 1.
2. Ibid., 1.
3. Ibid., 7.
4. For other biographical accounts of Col. William Tudor in addition to the memoir cited above, see *Collections of the Massachusetts Historical Society*, 2d ser., 8:285–325; *American National Biography* (New York, 1999), 21:919–920; Robert Hallowell Gardiner, *Early Recollections of Robert Hallowell Gardiner, 1782–1864* (Hallowell, Me., 1936), 156–161; and *Sibley's Harvard Graduates* (Boston, 1873–), 17:252–265.
5. Sheldon S. Cohen, "The Turkish Tyranny," *New England Quarterly* 47(1947):564–583.
6. *Papers of John Adams*, ed. Robert J. Taylor et al. (Cambridge, Mass., 1977–), 2:112.
7. John Adams to William Tudor, July 26, 1775, Tudor-Adams Papers, Massachusetts Historical Society.
8. *The Writings of George Washington*, ed. John C. Fitzpatrick (Washington, D.C., 1931–), 4:54.
9. See the Tudor Family Papers, Massachusetts Historical Society. There are 36 letters in the correspondence running from Jan. 23, 1773, to Jan. 10, 1778.
10. William H. Sumner, *A History of East Boston* (Boston, 1858), 354.
11. *Deacon Tudor's Diary*, 68.
12. Ibid., 75–76.
13. Ibid., 93–94.

CHAPTER 2

1. *Deacon Tudor's Diary, or Memorandoms from 1709, &C.*, ed. William Tudor (Boston, 1896), 102–103.
2. Ibid., 107.
3. Ibid., 108–110.
4. In 1801 the Judge added 101 acres to the Rockwood estate, bringing it to a total of over 200 acres.
5. Frederic Tudor to William Tudor, Nov. 10, 1796, Tudor Papers, bMS Am 1197 and bMS Am 2027, Houghton Library, Harvard University.
6. Ibid. We wonder if "Laidain" could be a childish misspelling of "Lekain," with whom he boarded much later. There is no "Laidain" in the *Boston Directory* of this period.
7. Frederic Tudor to William Tudor, Jr., June 15, 1799, Tudor Papers, bMS Am 1197 and bMS Am 2027, Houghton Library, Harvard University.
8. Rockwood Agriculture Records, Feb. 12, 1814, Tudor Ice Company Collection, Baker Library, Harvard Business School, Boston, Massachusetts.
9. John Tudor to Moody Noyes, Nov. 7, 1800, Tudor Ice Company Collection, Baker Library, Harvard Business School, Boston, Massachusetts.
10. Ibid.
11. John Tudor, "Journal of a Tour in Search of Health," Feb. 26, 1801, Tudor Papers, bMS Am 1197 and bMS Am 2027, Houghton Library, Harvard University.
12. Ibid., Mar. 28, 1801.
13. Ibid., Apr. 10, 1801.
14. Ibid., Apr. 30, 1801.
15. Frederic Tudor to the Gentlemen of the Royal Society of London, May 26, 1801, Miscellaneous Bound Collection, Massachusetts Historical Society.
16. John Tudor, "Journal of a Tour in Search of Health," May 16, 1801, Tudor Papers, bMS Am 1197 and bMS Am 2027, Houghton Library, Harvard University
17. Ibid., June 4, 1801.
18. Ibid.
19. Ibid., June 16, 1801.
20. Ibid.
21. Ibid., June 24, 1801.
22. Ibid., Aug. 16, 1801.
23. Ibid., Sept. 13, 1801.
24. Delia Tudor to Susan Lee, May 1, 1802, Palfrey-Lee Papers, Library of Congress, Washington, D.C.
25. Delia Tudor to Susan Lee, Mar. 16, 1802, Palfrey-Lee Papers, Library of Congress, Washington, D.C.

26. William Sullivan to William Tudor, June 9, 1802, Tudor Ice Company Collection, Baker Library, Harvard Business School, Boston, Massachusetts.
27. Frederic Tudor to William Sullivan, Aug. 6, 1804, Tudor Ice Company Collection, Baker Library, Harvard Business School, Boston, Massachusetts.

Chapter 3

1. Frederic Tudor to James Savage, Jan. 18, 1804, Ms. N-230, James Savage Papers, Massachusetts Historical Society.
2. Ibid.
3. Ibid.
4. Robert Hallowell Gardiner, *Early Recollections of Robert Hallowell Gardiner, 1782–1864* (Hallowell, Me., 1936), 92.
5. Ibid., 98–101.
6. Frederic Tudor to William Tudor, Jr., Aug. 23, 1805, Tudor Papers, bMS Am 1197 and bMS Am 2027, Houghton Library, Harvard University.

Chapter 4

1. Frederic Tudor, diary, 1805, front cover, Tudor Ice Company Collection, Baker Library, Harvard Business School, Boston, Massachusetts.
2. Ibid., Aug. 1, 1805.
3. Ibid.
4. Ibid.
5. Ibid.
6. Ibid., front cover.
7. Theodore Chase and Celeste Walker, "The Journal of James Savage and the Beginning of Frederic Tudor's Career in the Ice Trade," *Proceedings of the Massachusetts Historical Society* 97 (1985):103–134.
8. Ibid., 120.
9. Ibid., 124.
10. Ibid., 124.
11. Ibid., 125.
12. Ibid., 128.
13. James Savage to Elizabeth (Tudor) Savage, June 1, 1806, Ms. N-231, James Savage II Papers, Massachusetts Historical Society.
14. Frederic Tudor to William Tudor, Jr., Nov. 26, 1805, Tudor Ice Company Collection, Baker Library, Harvard Business School, Boston, Massachusetts.
15. Frederic Tudor, diary, Jan. 10, 1806, Tudor Ice Company Collection, Baker Library, Harvard Business School, Boston, Massachusetts.

16. Ibid., Jan. 20, 1806.
17. Ibid.
18. *Boston Gazette*, Feb. 10, 1806.
19. Frederic Tudor to Robert Hallowell Gardiner, Mar. 10, 1806, Tudor Ice Company Collection, Baker Library, Harvard Business School, Boston, Massachusetts.

Chapter 5

1. *Letters of James Savage to His Family,* ed. Emma Rogers (Boston, 1906), 3–4.
2. *Robert Hallowell Gardiner, Early Recollections of Robert Hallowell Gardiner, 1782–1864* (Hallowell, Me., 1936), 159.
3. Frederic Tudor, diary, fall 1807, Tudor Ice Company Collection, Baker Library, Harvard Business School, Boston, Massachusetts.

Chapter 6

1. Delia Tudor to William Tudor, Sr., July 5, 1801, Tudor Ice Company Collection, Baker Library, Harvard Business School, Boston, Massachusetts.
2. Frederic Tudor to William Hallowell Gardiner, Sept. 23, 1811, Tudor Ice Company Collection, Baker Library, Harvard Business School, Boston, Massachusetts.
3. Frederic Tudor to Robert Hallowell Gardiner, Jan. 11, 1810, Tudor Ice Company Collection, Baker Library, Harvard Business School, Boston, Massachusetts.
4. Frederic Tudor, diary, Aug. 1810, Tudor Ice Company Collection, Baker Library, Harvard Business School, Boston, Massachusetts.
5. Ibid.
6. For the full description, see "The New-Modelled Vessel," *Boston Daily Advertiser*, Apr. 27, 1813.
7. Frederic Tudor to Euphemia Fenno, Nov. 22, 1833, Tudor Ice Company Collection, Baker Library, Harvard Business School, Boston, Massachusetts.
8. William Tudor, Jr., to Frederic Tudor, Apr. 29, 1813, Tudor Ice Company Collection, Baker Library, Harvard Business School, Boston, Massachusetts.
9. William Tudor, Jr., to Frederic Tudor, June 30, 1814, Tudor Ice Company Collection, Baker Library, Harvard Business School, Boston, Massachusetts.
10. Ibid.
11. Robert Hallowell Gardiner, *Early Recollections of Robert Hallowell Gardiner, 1782–1864* (Hallowell, Me., 1936), 168.

Chapter 7

1. *American National Biography* (New York, 1991), 20:745–746.

2. Robert Hallowell Gardiner, *Early Recollections of Robert Hallowell Gardiner, 1782–1864* (Hallowell, Me., 1936), 169.
3. There is no record of the birth dates of Delia's children. The authors have worked out approximate dates from other sources. It is possible that Delia was pregnant before the wedding, which could account for its precipitous timing.

Chapter 8

1. Frederic Tudor to Harry Tudor, Apr. 20, 1817, Tudor Ice Company Collection, Baker Library, Harvard Business School, Boston, Massachusetts.
2. William Tudor, Jr., to Frederic Tudor, Apr. 12, 1816, Tudor Ice Company Collection, Baker Library, Harvard Business School, Boston, Massachusetts. Goberto was, said William, a "downright adventurer." He had been a merchant in New York, failed there and went to Florida. During the War of 1812 he came to Washington and tried to persuade the government without success to let him lead an expedition to take Florida from Spain.
3. Frederic Tudor, diary, Feb. 6, 1816, Tudor Ice Company Collection, Baker Library, Harvard Business School, Boston, Massachusetts.
4. Ibid.
5. Ibid.
6. Carlos Goberto de Ceta to John Russell, Jan. 27, 1816, Tudor Ice Company Collection, Baker Library, Harvard Business School, Boston, Massachusetts.
7. William Tudor, Jr., to Frederic Tudor, Jan. 28, 1816, Tudor Ice Company Collection, Baker Library, Harvard Business School, Boston, Massachusetts.
8. "It consists of a jar of about 14 gallons suspended by ropes & surrounded with one thickness of dry sawdust two inches thick & another of dry moss of the same thickness with two covers one below the other with blanket & a crane with a cock to it to draw off the water. By an experiment I made today I find that it will answer the purpose perfectly." Frederic Tudor, diary, Mar. 24, 1816, Tudor Ice Company Collection, Baker Library, Harvard Business School, Boston, Massachusetts.
9. Frederic Tudor, diary, Apr. 15, 1816, Tudor Ice Company Collection, Baker Library, Harvard Business School, Boston, Massachusetts.
10. Ibid.
11. Ibid., May 23, 1816.
12. Ibid.
13. Ibid., Nov. 15, 1816.
14. Frederick Tudor to Harry Tudor, Apr. 20, 1817, Tudor Ice Company Collection, Baker Library, Harvard Business School, Boston, Massachusetts.

Chapter 9

1. Frederic Tudor to Harry Tudor, Apr. 20, 1817, Tudor Ice Company Collection, Baker Library, Harvard Business School, Boston, Massachusetts.
2. Frederic Tudor to William Tudor, Sr., June 2, 1817, Tudor Ice Company Collection, Baker Library, Harvard Business School, Boston, Massachusetts.
3. Frederic Tudor to Nathaniel Fellows, Aug. 11, 1817, Tudor Ice Company Collection, Baker Library, Harvard Business School, Boston, Massachusetts.

Chapter 10

1. Frederic Tudor to Harry Tudor, June 5, 1810, Tudor Ice Company Collection, Baker Library, Harvard Business School, Boston, Massachusetts.
2. Frederic Tudor, diary, Oct. 15, 1811, Tudor Ice Company Collection, Baker Library, Harvard Business School, Boston, Massachusetts.
3. William Tudor, Jr., to Frederic Tudor, Mar. 4, 1816, Tudor Ice Company Collection, Baker Library, Harvard Business School, Boston, Massachusetts.
4. Ibid.
5. Frederic Tudor to Harry Tudor, Apr. 20, 1817, Tudor Ice Company Collection, Baker Library, Harvard Business School, Boston, Massachusetts.
6. Ibid.
7. William Tudor, Jr., to Delia J. Tudor, Mar. 2, 1817, Tudor Papers, bMS Am 1197 and bMS Am 2027, Houghton Library, Harvard University.
8. Harry Tudor, diary, Nov. 20, 1817, Tudor Papers, bMS Am 1197 and bMS Am 2027, Houghton Library, Harvard University.
9. Ibid., Nov. 25, 1817.
10. Harry Tudor to Delia J. Tudor, Dec. 31, 1819, Henry James Tudor Papers (Mss 29), R. Stanton Avery Special Collections Department, New England Historic Genealogical Society, Boston, Massachusetts.
11. Frederic Tudor to William Tudor, Sr., Dec. 17, 1818, Tudor Ice Company Collection, Baker Library, Harvard Business School, Boston, Massachusetts.
12. Frederic Tudor to Delia J. Tudor, July 3, 1820, Tudor Ice Company Collection, Baker Library, Harvard Business School, Boston, Massachusetts.
13. Ibid.

Chapter 11

1. Frederic Tudor, diary, Oct. 26, 1817, Tudor Ice Company Collection, Baker Library, Harvard Business School, Boston, Massachusetts.
2. Frederic Tudor to John Hunter, Sept. 24, 1817, Tudor Ice Company Collection, Baker Library, Harvard Business School, Boston, Massachusetts.

3. Frederic Tudor to William Tudor, Sr., Nov. 22, 1817, Tudor Ice Company Collection, Baker Library, Harvard Business School, Boston, Massachusetts.
4. Frederic Tudor, diary, Dec. 7, 1817, Tudor Ice Company Collection, Baker Library, Harvard Business School, Boston, Massachusetts.
5. Ibid.
6. Ibid., Dec. 14, 1817.
7. Ibid., Jan. 1, 1818.
8. Frederic Tudor to Robert Hallowell Gardiner, Apr. 4, 1818, Tudor Ice Company Collection, Baker Library, Harvard Business School, Boston, Massachusetts.
9. Ibid.
10. Ibid.
11. Frederic Tudor, diary, Apr. 10, 1819, Tudor Ice Company Collection, Baker Library, Harvard Business School, Boston, Massachusetts.
12. Frederic Tudor to Delia J. Tudor, Jan. 16, 1819, Tudor Ice Company Collection, Baker Library, Harvard Business School, Boston, Massachusetts.
13. Frederic Tudor to Delia J. Tudor, Jan. 23, 1819, Tudor Ice Company Collection, Baker Library, Harvard Business School, Boston, Massachusetts.
14. Ibid.
15. Frederic Tudor, diary, May 15, 1819, Tudor Ice Company Collection, Baker Library, Harvard Business School, Boston, Massachusetts.
16. Frederic Tudor to William Tudor, Sr., Apr. 12, 1819, Tudor Ice Company Collection, Baker Library, Harvard Business School, Boston, Massachusetts.
17. Frederic Tudor, diary, July 4, 1819, Tudor Ice Company Collection, Baker Library, Harvard Business School, Boston, Massachusetts.
18. Ibid., Nov. 21, 1819.
19. Ibid.

Chapter 12

1. Kenneth Wiggins Porter, *The Jacksons and the Lees: Two Generations of Massachusetts Merchants, 1765–1844* (Cambridge, Mass., 1937), 2:1128.
2. Frederic Tudor to William Tudor, Jr., Apr. 25, 1817, Tudor Ice Company Collection, Baker Library, Harvard Business School, Boston, Massachusetts.
3. Ibid.
4. Ibid.
5. Frederic Tudor, diary, Dec. 2, 1818, Tudor Ice Company Collection, Baker Library, Harvard Business School, Boston, Massachusetts.
6. Ibid.
7. Frederic Tudor to Stephen Cabot, Dec. 15, 1820, Tudor Ice Company Collection, Baker

Library, Harvard Business School, Boston, Massachusetts.

8. Frederic Tudor to Stephen Cabot, Oct. 26, 1820, Tudor Ice Company Collection, Baker Library, Harvard Business School, Boston, Massachusetts.
9. Frederic Tudor to Stephen Cabot, Feb. 5, 1821, Tudor Ice Company Collection, Baker Library, Harvard Business School, Boston, Massachusetts.

CHAPTER 13

1. Frederic Tudor, diary, Dec. 2, 1818, Tudor Ice Company Collection, Baker Library, Harvard Business School, Boston, Massachusetts.
2. Frederic Tudor to Lucius Woodbury, Sept. 19, 1817, Tudor Ice Company Collection, Baker Library, Harvard Business School, Boston, Massachusetts.
3. Frederic Tudor, diary, Aug. 5, 1820, Tudor Ice Company Collection, Baker Library, Harvard Business School, Boston, Massachusetts.
4. Ibid., Sept. 25, 1820.
5. Ibid., Oct. 26, 1820.
6. Ibid., Nov. 8, 1820.
7. Ibid., Feb. 1, 1821.
8. Ibid., July 12, 1821.
9. Henry C. Pearson, "Frederic Tudor, Ice King," *Proceedings of the Massachusetts Historical Society* 65(1932–1936):213.

CHAPTER 14

1. Robert Hallowell Gardiner, *Early Recollections of Robert Hallowell Gardiner, 1782–1864* (Hallowell, Me., 1936), 165.
2. Ibid., 166.
3. Frederic Tudor to Delia J. Tudor, Jan. 23, 1822, Tudor Ice Company Collection, Baker Library, Harvard Business School, Boston, Massachusetts.
4. Frederic Tudor to William Carlisle, Nov. 22, 1821, Tudor Ice Company Collection, Baker Library, Harvard Business School, Boston, Massachusetts.
5. Shredded bark used as a source of tannin.
6. Frederic Tudor to John W. Damon, Dec. 14, 1821, Tudor Ice Company Collection, Baker Library, Harvard Business School, Boston, Massachusetts.

CHAPTER 15

1. Frederic Tudor to Robert Hallowell Gardiner, Mar. 23, 1821, Tudor Ice Company Collection, Baker Library, Harvard Business School, Boston, Massachusetts.
2. William Tudor, Jr., to John Quincy Adams, June 30, 1823, Tudor Ice Company Collection, Baker Library, Harvard Business School, Boston, Massachusetts.

3. Delia T. Stewart to William Tudor, Jr., Aug. 9, 1822, Tudor Ice Company Collection, Baker Library, Harvard Business School, Boston, Massachusetts.
4. William Lee to William Tudor, Jr., May 8, 1823, Tudor Papers, bMS Am 1197 and bMS Am 2027, Houghton Library, Harvard University.
5. Ibid.
6. William Lee to William Tudor, Jr., May 24, 1823, Tudor Papers, bMS Am 1197 and bMS Am 2027, Houghton Library, Harvard University.
7. Ibid.
8. Ibid.
9. William Lee to William Tudor, Jr., May 28, 1823, Tudor Papers, bMS Am 1197 and bMS Am 2027, Houghton Library, Harvard University.
10. William Lee to William Tudor, Jr., Oct. 15, 1823, Tudor Papers, bMS Am 1197 and bMS Am 2027, Houghton Library, Harvard University.
11. Delia Stewart to William Tudor, Jr., Aug. 29, 1822, Tudor Ice Company Collection, Baker Library, Harvard Business School, Boston, Massachusetts.

Chapter 16

1. Linda M. Maloney, *The Captain from Connecticut: The Life and Naval Times of Isaac Hull* (Boston, 1986), 374. For some comments on Delia and family during the return passage, see Charles Tyng, *Before the Wind: The Memoir of an American Sea Captain*, ed. Susan Fels (New York, 1999), 113–117.
2. Delia T. Stewart to William Tudor, Jr., Apr. 21, [1825], Tudor Ice Company Collection, Baker Library, Harvard Business School, Boston, Massachusetts.
3. Delia T. Stewart to John Quincy Adams, Nov. 10, 1824, Adams Papers, Massachusetts Historical Society.
4. Ibid.
5. Robert Hallowell Gardiner, *Early Recollections of Robert Hallowell Gardiner, 1782–1864* (Hallowell, Me., 1936), 172.
6. William Tudor, Jr., to Delia J. Tudor, Feb. 21, 1826, Adams Papers, Massachusetts Historical Society.
7. Delia J. Tudor to William Tudor, Jr., Mar. 1, 1826, Tudor Papers, bMS Am 1197 and bMS Am 2027, Houghton Library, Harvard University.
8. Gardiner, *Early Recollections*, 172.
9. Delia T. Stewart to Charles Stewart, Dec. 8, [1825], Tudor Papers, bMS Am 1197 and bMS Am 2027, Houghton Library, Harvard University.
10. Ibid.
11. Delia J. Tudor to William Tudor, Jr., Mar. 1, 1826, Tudor Papers, bMS Am 1197 and bMS Am 2027, Houghton Library, Harvard University.

12. Delia T. Stewart to Charles Stewart, Dec. 8, [1825], Tudor Papers, bMS Am 1197 and bMS Am 2027, Houghton Library, Harvard University.

Chapter 17

1. Delia J. Tudor to William Tudor, Jr., Mar. 1, 1826, Tudor Papers, bMS Am 1197 and bMS Am 2027, Houghton Library, Harvard University.
2. Robert Hallowell Gardiner, *Early Recollections of Robert Hallowell Gardiner, 1782–1864* (Hallowell, Me., 1936), 177.
3. Ibid., 175–176.
4. The Historical Society of Pennsylvania (HSP), Meredith Family Papers, Mrs. William Meredith to William Meredith (her son), Feb. 2, 1826, 1509.
5. Delia Stewart to John Quincy Adams, Oct. 31, 1826, Adams Papers, Massachusetts Historical Society.
6. Delia J. Tudor to William Tudor, Jr., Sept. 23, 1828, Tudor Papers, bMS Am 1197 and bMS Am 2027, Houghton Library, Harvard University.
7. John Quincy Adams, diary, May 8, 1827, Adams Papers, Massachusetts Historical Society.
8. Ibid.
9. Frederic Tudor to Harry J. Tudor, July 5, 1828, Henry James Tudor Papers (Mss 29), R. Stanton Avery Special Collections Department, New England Historic Genealogical Society, Boston, Massachusetts.

Chapter 18

1. See Carl G. Seaburg and Stanley C. Paterson, *Nahant on the Rocks* (Nahant, Mass., 1991).
2. Frederic Tudor, diary, Oct. 5, 1828, Tudor Ice Company Collection, Baker Library, Harvard Business School, Boston, Massachusetts.
3. Robert Hallowell Gardiner, *Early Recollections of Robert Hallowell Gardiner, 1782–1864* (Hallowell, Me., 1936), 167–179.
4. William Tudor, Jr., to John Quincy Adams, Sept. 1, 1824, Adams Papers, Massachusetts Historical Society.
5. *Memoirs of John Quincy Adams*, ed. Charles Francis Adams (Philadelphia, 1874–1877), 8:135–136.
6. Frederic Tudor, diary, Mar. 9, 1830, Tudor Ice Company Collection, Baker Library, Harvard Business School, Boston, Massachusetts.
7. John Quincy Adams, diary, May 3, 1830, Adams Papers, Massachusetts Historical Society. See also entries for May 5, 6, 24, 26, June 22, 1830; Feb. 5, Mar. 7, 23, 1831.

CHAPTER 19

1. Frederic Tudor, diary, Oct. 15, 1825, Tudor Ice Company Collection, Baker Library, Harvard Business School, Boston, Massachusetts.
2. Ibid., Oct. 26, 1825.
3. Ibid., May 5, 1826.
4. Ibid., May 20, 1826.
5. Ibid., June 2, 1826.
6. Frederic Tudor to Harry J. Tudor, Dec. 31, 1827, Tudor Ice Company Collection, Baker Library, Harvard Business School, Boston, Massachusetts.
7. Frederic Tudor to Harry J. Tudor, Feb. 12, 1828, Tudor Papers, bMS Am 1197 and bMS Am 2027, Houghton Library, Harvard University.
8. Ibid.
9. Ibid.
10. Frederic Tudor to Harry J. Tudor, June 1830, Tudor Papers, bMS Am 1197 and bMS Am 2027, Houghton Library, Harvard University.
11. Frederic Tudor, diary, Aug. 7, 1830, Tudor Ice Company Collection, Baker Library, Harvard Business School, Boston, Massachusetts.
12. The Historical Society of Pennsylvania (HSP), Frederic Tudor to W. D. Lewis, Dec. 9, 1830.
13. James L. Homer, *Notes on the Sea-Shore; or Random Sketches* (Boston, 1848), 37.

CHAPTER 20

1. Frederic Tudor, diary, Nov. 1827, Tudor Ice Company Collection, Baker Library, Harvard Business School, Boston, Massachusetts.
2. Ibid., Jan. 13, 1828.
3. Ibid.
4. Ibid.
5. Henry G. Pearson, "Frederic Tudor, Ice King," *Proceedings of the Massachusetts Historical Society*, 65(1932–1936):196.
6. Frederic Tudor, diary, Jan. 22, 1828, Tudor Ice Company Collection, Baker Library, Harvard Business School, Boston, Massachusetts.
7. Ibid., Jan. 27, 1828.
8. Ibid., Feb. 21, 1828.
9. Ibid.
10. Ibid., Jan. 25, 1830.

CHAPTER 21

1. Charles Palache, "The Sturbridge Graphite Mine," *Rocks and Minerals* 22(1947):503.

2. Ibid., 503.
3. Frederic Tudor, diary, Dec. 18, 1828, Tudor Ice Company Collection, Baker Library, Harvard Business School, Boston, Massachusetts.

Chapter 22

1. Nathaniel J. Wyeth to Charles Wyeth, Oct. 5, 1831, "The Correspondence and Journals of Captain Nathaniel J. Wyeth, 1831–1836," ed. F. G. Young, in *Sources of the History of Oregon* (Eugene, Ore., 1899), v. 1, part 3–6:2.
2. Frederic Tudor, diary, Jan. 6, 1832, Tudor Ice Company Collection, Baker Library, Harvard Business School, Boston, Massachusetts.
3. Ibid., Jan. 8, 1832.
4. John B. Wyeth, *Oregon; or a Short History of a Long Journey* (Cambridge, Mass., 1833), 31. This edition is included in Rueben Gold Thwaites, *Early Western Travels,* 1748–1846 (Cleveland, 1905), vol. 21.
5. Ibid., 31–32.
6. Ibid., 31.
7. Samuel Atkins Eliot, "All Aboard the 'Natwyethum'!" *Proceedings of the Cambridge Historical Society* 28(1942):40.
8. Frederic Tudor, diary, July 1, 1831, Tudor Ice Company Collection, Baker Library, Harvard Business School, Boston, Massachusetts.
9. Ibid., Dec. 8, 1831.
10. Ibid., July 3, 1832.
11. Ibid., Sept. 10, 1832.
12. Ibid., Jan. 1, 1833.
13. Thomas Wren Ward to Baring Brothers, London, Mar. 8, 1833, Baring Brothers Canada Papers, Library of Congress. Permission to quote courtesy of ING Barings, London.
14. Frederic Tudor, diary, Nov. 8, 1833, Tudor Ice Company Collection, Baker Library, Harvard Business School, Boston, Massachusetts.
15. Nathaniel J. Wyeth to Charles Wyeth, Nov. 20, 1833, "The Correspondence and Journals of Captain Nathaniel J. Wyeth, 1831–1836," 85.

Chapter 23

1. R. Fisher to W. Foster, Mar. 20, 1830, Henry James Tudor Papers (Mss 29), R. Stanton Avery Special Collections Department, New England Historic Genealogical Society, Boston, Massachusetts.
2. Frederic Tudor, diary, Mar. 3, 1833, Tudor Ice Company Collection, Baker Library, Harvard Business School, Boston, Massachusetts.

3. John James Audubon, *Writings and Drawings* (New York, 1999), 355–356.
4. Euphemia Fenno to Mrs. Richard Morris, June 23, 1833, Tudor Papers, bMS Am 1197 and bMS Am 2027, Houghton Library, Harvard University.
5. Euphemia Fenno to Mrs. Richard Morris, July 13, 1833, Tudor Papers, bMS Am 1197 and bMS Am 2027, Houghton Library, Harvard University.
6. Euphemia Fenno to Mrs. Richard Morris, July 30, 1833, Tudor Papers, bMS Am 1197 and bMS Am 2027, Houghton Library, Harvard University.

Chapter 24

1. Susan S. Bean, "Cold Mine," *American Heritage* 42(1991):74.
2. The cup is now a part of the collections of the Peabody Essex Museum of Salem, Massachusetts.
3. Caleb Ladd to Frederic Tudor, Aug. 17, 1836, Tudor Ice Company Collection, Baker Library, Harvard Business School, Boston, Massachusetts.

Chapter 25

1. Frederic Tudor, diary, Oct. 13, 1833, Tudor Ice Company Collection, Baker Library, Harvard Business School, Boston, Massachusetts.
2. Ibid., Oct. 20, 1833.
3. Ibid., Oct. 24, 1833.
4. Ibid., Oct. 30, 1833.
5. Ibid., Dec. 24, 1833.
6. Ibid., Jan. 26, 1834.

Chapter 26

1. Francis Russell to Harry J. Tudor, Jan. 29, 1834, Henry James Tudor Papers (Mss 29), R. Stanton Avery Special Collection Department, New England Historic Genealogical Society, Boston, Massachusetts.
2. Frederic Tudor, diary, Apr. 15, 1831, Tudor Ice Company Collection, Baker Library, Harvard Business School, Boston, Massachusetts.
3. Frederic Tudor, diary, July 15, 1834, Tudor Ice Company Collection, Baker Library, Harvard Business School, Boston, Massachusetts.
4. Frederic Tudor, diary, Nov. 23, 1834, Tudor Ice Company Collection, Baker Library, Harvard Business School, Boston, Massachusetts.

Chapter 27

1. Frederic Tudor, diary, Aug. 30, 1834, Tudor Ice Company Collection, Baker Library, Harvard Business School, Boston, Massachusetts.

2. Ibid., June 1, 1835.
3. Ibid., June 17, 1835.
4. Frederic Tudor to E. Johnston, Oct. 20, 1835, Tudor Papers, bMS Am 1197 and bMS Am 2027, Houghton Library, Harvard University.
5. Frederic Tudor, diary, July 29, 1835, Tudor Ice Company Collection, Baker Library, Harvard Business School, Boston, Massachusetts.
6. Ibid., July 15, 1835.
7. Ibid., Feb. 18, 1837.

CHAPTER 28

1. Frederic Tudor, diary, Dec. 20, 1836, Tudor Ice Company Collection, Baker Library, Harvard Business School, Boston, Massachusetts.
2. Ibid., Jan. 31, 1837.
3. Ibid., May 17, 1837.
4. Ibid.

CHAPTER 29

1. Frederic Tudor, diary, Feb. 13, 1838, Tudor Ice Company Collection, Baker Library, Harvard Business School, Boston, Massachusetts.
2. Robert Hallowell Gardiner, *Early Recollections of Robert Hallowell Gardiner, 1782–1864* (Hallowell, Me., 1936), 224.
3. Ibid., 225.
4. Frederic Tudor, diary, Oct. 27, 1829, Tudor Ice Company Collection, Baker Library, Harvard Business School, Boston, Massachusetts.
5. Ibid., Nov. 6, 1830.
6. John Wade Damon, *The Havana Ice House Controversy* (Boston, 1846), 121.
7. See John Wade Damon, *Tudor's Circular and Damon's Vindication. Additional Chapter of the Havana Ice House Controversy* (Boston, 1847).
8. *The Letters of Ralph Waldo Emerson*, ed. Ralph L. Rusk (New York, 1939), 3:383.

CHAPTER 30

1. Anna C. Quincy, journal, Aug. 4, 1834, Quincy Family Papers, Massachusetts Historical Society.

CHAPTER 31

1. Frederic Tudor, diary, May 14, 1837, Tudor Ice Company Collection, Baker Library, Harvard Business School, Boston, Massachusetts.

2. Frederic Tudor, "Tudor's Letter on the Ice Trade and Payment of Great Losses," *Proceedings of the Massachusetts Historical Society*, 1st ser., 3(1855–1858):53.
3. Ibid.
4. Henry David Thoreau, *The Maine Woods*, arr. Dudley C. Lunt (New York, 1950), 319.
5. Carl G. Seaburg and Stanley C. Paterson, *Nahant on the Rocks* (Nahant, 1991), 133.
6. Ibid., 137.

CHAPTER 32

1. Frederic Tudor to Euphemia F. Tudor, Dec. 7, 1847, Tudor Ice Company Collection, Baker Library, Harvard Business School, Boston, Massachusetts.
2. Carl G. Seaburg and Stanley C. Paterson, *Nahant on the Rocks* (Nahant, 1991), 136.
3. Frederic Tudor, diary, Oct. 28, 1834, Tudor Ice Company Collection, Baker Library, Harvard Business School, Boston, Massachusetts.

Sources Not Identified in the Notes

CHAPTER 1 Deacon John Tudor's diary, as well as his letters, are at Baker Library, Harvard Business School, Boston, Massachusetts. There are William Tudor letters at the Massachusetts Historical Society, Baker Library, and Houghton Library. A superb account of William Tudor's life appears in Clifford K. Shipton, *Biographical Sketches of Those Who Attended Harvard College in the Classes 1768–1771* (Boston, 1975), 17:252–265. As a founding member of the Massachusetts Historical Society, there are many references to William Tudor's activities in connection with that Society in the *Index to the First Twenty Volumes of the Proceedings of the Massachusetts Historical Society, 1791–1883* (Boston, 1887), 459–460. The story of the Judge swimming to East Boston is told in William H. Sumner, *A History of East Boston* (Boston, 1858), 354, where the author says it was told him by Frederic Tudor. Tudor and Austin's orations can be found in James S. Loring, *The Hundred Boston Orations* (Boston, 1852), 135–139 and 133.

CHAPTER 2 There are no book-length biographies of Frederic Tudor. The most complete account of his life is in Henry G. Pearson, "Frederic Tudor, Ice King," *Proceedings of the Massachusetts Historical Society* 65(1940):169–215. This is good, clear, and mainly accurate. Lewis P. Simpson worked extensively from this account in his chapter on the Tudor brothers in *The Man of Letters in New England and the South* (Baton Rouge, 1973). See "The Tudor Brothers: Boston Ice and Boston Letters," 32–61. Other accounts of Tudor and his ice business appear in Philip C. F. Smith, "Crystal Blocks of Yankee Coldness: The Development of the Massachusetts Ice Trade from Frederic Tudor to Wenham Lake," *Essex Institute*

Historical Collections 97(1961):197–232; and "Frederic Tudor—Ice King," *Bulletin of the Business Historical Society* 6:1–8 and 9:1–6. See also Daniel J. Boorstin, *The Americans: The National Experience* (New York, 1965), 10–16; Stewart H. Holbrook, *Lost Men of American History* (New York, 1946), 114–123; and Samuel Eliot Morison, *The Maritime History of Massachusetts, 1783–1860* (Boston, 1921), 282–283. See, too, Frederic's entry in *American National Biography* 21:918–919. Regarding his brother John, there is a long obituary notice in the *Columbian Centinel*, Feb. 6, 1802.

Chapter 3 For information on Joseph Woodward and land speculation in Boston at this period, see Thomas C. Simonds, *History of South Boston* (Boston, 1857), 244–250. In addition to Robert Hallowell Gardiner's autobiography, *Early Recolletions of Robert Hallowell Gardiner, 1792–1864* (Hallowell, Me., 1936), see George Burgess, "Notice of Robert Hallowell Gardiner," *Collections of the Maine Historical Society* 7:403–428. Concerning James Savage, see George S. Hilliard, "Memoir of the Hon. James Savage," *Proceedings of the Massachusetts Historical Society* 12(1873):433–442.

Chapter 4 The definitive account of the natural ice business in America is Richard O. Cummings, *The American Ice Harvests* (Berkeley and Los Angeles, 1949). We have found this fundamental to our work, although we have some different interpretations of material pertaining to Tudor. A more recent treatment is Gavin Weightman, *The Frozen Water Trade* (London, 2001). See also Joseph C. Jones, *America's Icemen: An Illustrative History of the United States Natural Ice Industry, 1660–1925* (Humble, Tex., 1984).

Chapter 5 Interesting glimpses of the Judge and his family abroad can be found in the letters of William Lee in the Library of Congress, particularly Dec. 13, 1806, and for 1807: Jan. 11, "Thurs. 19," and Mar. 30. See also the printed edition of some of these letters in Mary Lee Mann, ed., *A Yankee Jeffersonian* (Cambridge, Mass., 1958), 54, 61–66. Regarding Tudor's coal mines on Cape Cod and Martha's Vineyard, there are two folders of papers at Baker Library.

Chapter 6 Material on the ship model in Baker Library includes the correspondence with Washington, D.C., as well as Tudor's patent application, which was issued Dec. 17, 1812. See "No. 225. In building or modelling ships or vessels," in *A List of Patents . . . April 10, 1790 to Dec. 31, 1836* (Washington, D.C., 1872), 216.

Chapter 7 For Charles Stewart, see *Biographical Sketch and Services of Commodore Charles Stewart of the Navy of the United States* (Philadelphia, 1838). For a short popular account, see chapter 13 in Fletcher Pratt, *Preble's Boys: Commodore Preble and the Birth of American Sea Power* (New York, 1950).

Chapter 8 For information about General Pinckney, see Charles Cotesworth Pinckney, *Life of General Thomas Pinckney* (Boston and New York, 1895). A description of his house on Sullivan's Island is on pp. 221–222.

Chapter 10 A picture of Stewart's estate, Montpelier, and a description of it can be found in the *Proceedings of the New Jersey Historical Society* 69(1951):85–88. For information on Joseph Bonaparte, see C. E. Macartney and G. Dorrance, *The Bonapartes in America* (Philadelphia, 1939), and Mary Bartlett Cowdrey, "Charlotte Bonaparte, Draftsman," also in the *Proceedings of the New Jersey Historical Society* 81(1963):47–49. For an impression of the Bonaparte estate, see Charles B. Bradley, "Point Breeze and the Mailliards," *Proceedings of the New Jersey Historical Society* 78(1960):75–81.

Chapter 12 See L. Vernon Briggs, *History and Genealogy of the Cabot Family, 1475–1927* (Boston, 1927), for information on the Cabots.

Chapter 13 For the story of the Anthology Society, see the *Journal of the Proceedings of the Society, Which Conducts the Monthly Anthology and Boston Review, October 3, 1805 to July 2, 1811* (Boston, 1910). For a short modern account of William Tudor's life, see his entry in *American National Biography*, 21:919–920.

Chapter 15 The full bibliographical citation for William's life of Otis is *The Life of James Otis, of Massachusetts* (Boston, 1823). Further details on the Bunker Hill monument are in *Act of Incorporation, By-Laws, and a List of the Original Members* (Boston, 1830) and George Washington Warren, *The History of the Bunker Hill Monument Association* (Boston, 1877). For the life of Commodore Hull, consult Linda M. Maloney, *The Captain from Connecticut: The Life and Naval Times of Isaac Hull* (Boston, 1996).

Chapter 16 For the full account of Stewart's trial, see Records of the Court Martial of Charles Stewart, Record Group 125, Navy Records, U.S. National Archives. The *Columbian Centinel,* on Sept. 4, 1824, reported the arrival in New York of the *Franklin* on the previous Sunday. The ship was ninety-five days from Valparaiso via Rio and thirty-nine days from Rio. For an eyewitness account of this voyage, see Charles Tyng, *Before the Wind: The Memoir of an American Sea Captain, 1808–1833,* ed. Susan Fels (New York, 1999), 113–117.

Chapter 19 There are many entries in Frederic's diary about Harry's saltworks covering the years 1825–1827, 1829–1831, and 1836–1837. The Cambridge Historical Society has published in its *Proceedings* two articles dealing with the life of Wyeth: see Stephen P. Sharples, "Nathaniel Jarvis Wyeth," 2(1906–1907):33–38, and Roger Gilman, "The Wyeth Background," 28(1942):29–40. There are brief references to Elizabeth Hopkinson in Burton A. Konkle, *Joseph Hopkinson* (Philadelphia, 1931). We noted her blue eyes and brown hair in a small miniature possessed by the Historical Society of Pennsylvania. The love letters from Frederic which she returned apparently have not survived. At least they are not in the Tudor papers in public repositories.

Chapter 20 See these entries in Tudor's diaries referring to the artificial pond idea: July 22, 1828, and Mar. 31, Apr. 14, 16, 21, 28, May 25, Sept. 30, and Oct. 30, 1829. For entries about the doubling of the ice, see for 1830: Jan. 17, 19, 22, 25; for 1831: Jan. 1, 3, Feb. 26; and for 1833: Feb. 10. For entries for the new icehouse, see Mar. 7, 1830, and for 1831: Jan. 1, 3, 6, 11, Feb. 27, Mar. 2, Apr. 3, 24, Aug. 22, and Sept. 19.

Chapter 21 For information on the graphite mine at Sturbridge, see George Davis, *A Historical Sketch of Sturbridge and Southbridge* (West Brookfield, Mass., 1856), 138–141; Edward Hitchcock, *Report on the Geology, Mineralogy, Botany, and Zoology of Massachusetts* (Amherst, 1833), 47–48.

Chapter 22 For an interesting account of Thomas Nuttall's expedition with Wyeth, consult Jeannette E. Graustein, *Thomas Nuttall: Naturalist Explorations in America, 1808–1841* (Cambridge, Mass., 1967), 277–312.

Chapter 23 Basil Hall's American observations and his data on the ice trade, provided by Tudor, are in his *Travels in North America in the Years, 1827 and 1828* (Edinburgh, 1830), 2:127–129. For information on Mt. Upton and the Fenno roots there, see James H. Smith, *History of Chenango County* (Syracuse, N.Y., 1880), 241–243. There is an account of the Morris family in D. Hamilton Hurd, *History of Otsego County* (Philadelphia, 1878). We also consulted the *Chenango County Cemetery Records*, vol. 1, and several other mimeographed materials in the Guernsey Memorial Library of Norwich, N.Y., when we visited Mt. Upton.

Chapter 24 For an excellent review of the nineteenth-century ice trade in India, with illustrations and charts, see David G. Dickason, "The Nineteenth-Century Indo-American Ice Trade: An Hyperborean Epic," *Modern Asian Studies* 25(1991):53–70. For the story of the brig *Tuscany*, see Harry L. Foster, "History of the Ship *Tuscany* and One of Her Masters, Capt. Clement Littlefield" (typescript ca. 1958), at the Boston Athenæum. The *Tuscany* carried the first ice across the equator from Boston to Calcutta in 1833. Tudor had been thinking about extending the ice trade to India since 1816. See his diary entry for Sept. 23, 1816.

CHAPTER 26 Further material on Tudor, his Nahant cottage, and his varied activities there—especially those concerned with his Maolis Gardens—can be found in greater detail in Carl Seaburg and Stanley Paterson's recent history of that community, *Nahant on the Rocks* (Nahant, 1991), 13–16, 71–75, 130–165. Information about Tudor's forestry efforts at Nahant has been culled from his diaries. For the story of the Tremont House, see William H. Eliot, *A Description of Tremont House, with Architectural Illustration* (Boston, 1830).

CHAPTER 29 The United States Patent Office records list many Wyeth patents. For examples, Letters Patent No. 1,877, dated Dec. 1, 1840, was for "Improvement in Machines for Cutting Ice"; No. 1,878, also dated Dec. 1, 1840, was for a "Machine for Raising Blocks of Ice"; No. 1,879 with the same date was for "Ice Implement." On Oct. 25, 1843, he registered Patent No. 3,317 for "Improvement in Ice Cutters and Markers" and three days later he was given Patent No. 3,323 for his "Ice Elevator." The material on Damon comes from his *The Havana Ice House Controversy* (Boston, 1846). This book is hopelessly organized. We collated it in chronological sequence and contrasted it with entries for the same period in Tudor's diary and letterbook.

CHAPTER 30 The literature on Charles Stewart Parnell is extensive; two of the more recent titles are R. F. Foster, *Charles Stewart Parnell: The Man and His Family* (Atlantic Highlands, N.J., 1976), and F. S. L. Lyons, *Charles Stewart Parnell* (New York, 1977). Lyons's information on the Tudor background, however, is secondary and not always to be relied upon. For a more reliable account, see Jane Cote, "The Tudors and the Stewarts: American Ancestors of Charles Stewart Parnell," *Eire-Ireland* 27(1993):7–19.

CHAPTER 31 For further details on life at Nahant, see Fred A. Wilson, *Some Annals of Nahant* (1928; Nahant, 1977). For another account of Maolis Gardens, see the unpublished typescript at the Nahant Public Library by Mrs. Caroline M. Foye, "The Maolis Gardens."

CHAPTER 32 There is an obituary for Tudor in *The Boston Transcript*, Feb. 8, 1864. His will was proved Mar. 7, 1864. It is docket #45225, Registry Office, Suffolk County Court House, Boston. Euphemia's will (or Fenno's will) is docket #60763, Essex County Registry, Salem. Her son's petition to disallow his mother's will is dated May 17, 1884, and is also in the Salem Registry, as is the printed "Agreement of Compromise," Jan. 1, 1886.

Note on Manuscript Sources

FREDERIC TUDOR WAS A PACK RAT and saved everything that related to his life. At his death this collection of material seems to have been relatively intact. Fortunately for the student of the Tudors most of this has entered public repositories and is accessible. Even more fortunate, the large bulk of this material is available at Harvard University in Cambridge and at the Massachusetts Historical Society in Boston.

The largest portion of the Tudor material went to the Baker Library of the Harvard Business School. There it has been divided into three major categories. The first is devoted to the financial records (1860–1903) of the Tudor Ice Company, the second consists of family records (1753–1868), and the third concerns papers (1806–1814) relating to "Rockwood" and agricultural matters. The family section includes the journal (1752–1774) of Deacon John Tudor, his letterbook (1760–1787), Frederic's diary (1805–1838), most of which is now also available on microfilm, his letterbook (1803–1830), and various family letters (1801–1855). The remainder of this category is made up of business correspondence, ledgers, and cash books.

The second largest portion of Tudor materials went to the Houghton Library of Harvard University. It includes additional Frederic Tudor letters (1783–1864) to various correspondents as well as twenty-six letters to his father and fifteen to his brother Henry. Of special value, this collection possesses Henry's journal (1817–1823) and his correspondence with his brother William during his years of diplomatic service at Lima and Rio de Janeiro.

Finally, the Massachusetts Historical Society holds a small Tudor collection that includes correspondence between William Tudor and Delia Jarvis before her marriage to Stewart.

Index